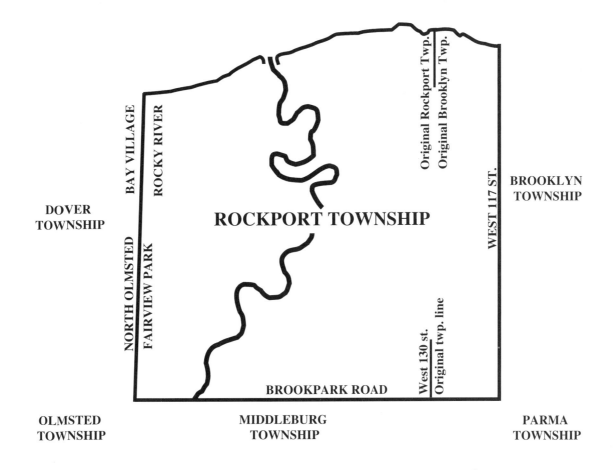

DOVER
TOWNSHIP

BAY VILLAGE

ROCKY RIVER

NORTH OLMSTED

FAIRVIEW PARK

ROCKPORT TOWNSHIP

Original Rockport Twp.

Original Brooklyn Twp.

WEST 117 ST.

BROOKLYN
TOWNSHIP

West 130 st.

Original twp. line

BROOKPARK ROAD

OLMSTED
TOWNSHIP

MIDDLEBURG
TOWNSHIP

PARMA
TOWNSHIP

From Rockport To West Park by Ralph A. Pfingsten 2004.

ISBN 0-9759618-0-2

Printed in Canada.

FROM ROCKPORT TO WEST PARK
Table of Contents

ACKNOWLEDGEMENTS

I wish to thank the following individuals and institutions for use of their photographs in this publication. Lou Abraham, Bill Barrow Special Collections Cleveland State University Library, Ross Bassett, Laverne Lanphair Buch, the late William Chambers, Cleveland Metroparks, Cleveland Public Library Plain Dealer and Zoning Board Collections, Cleveland Yachting Club, John Eles, Fairview Park Historical Society, James Foos, Ruth Hyland Hall, John Marshall High School Alumni Association, Kamm's Corners Development Corporation, the late Arthur Kouba, Blaine Hays, Jay Himes, Lakewood Historical Society, Timothy Lassan, Ellie Mapson, Andy Mathews, the Northern Ohio Railway Museum, Dr. Harlan Peterjohn, Earle Pfingsten, Laura Pfingsten, Homer Ramby, Vern Rolland, Howard Schreibman, the late Barbara Unterzuber, J. William Vigrass, Gayle Walter, Daniel Weber, West Park Kiwanis, Larry Worz and The Cleveland Police Department Archives, and the late Bruce Young.

For guiding me through the maze that is "Pagemaker", and, for doing most of the layout work, I am indebted to my brother Earle. To the three distinguished English teachers, Ken Latkovic, Joyce Murphy and Joy Smith, who proof read, corrected, and greatly improved the quality of this work, I extend my heartfelt thanks. I am grateful to the Trustees of the John Marshall High School Alumni Association for their moral and financial support during this long process.

I wish to thank Jim and Sally Thomas for their challenge grant for publication costs. Major support was also received from Gary Brookins and the John Marshall High School Alumni Association. Other support was received from West Park Councilmen Martin Sweeney and Michael Dolan.

FOREWORD

In 1999 John Marshall High School, formerly West Park High School, celebrated its one hundredth birthday. To commemorate that event the trustees of the Alumni Association committed themselves to produce a history of the school. Having attended Marshall for six years, teaching there for 25 years, and being Alumni Director for 11 years, I soon realized that the bulk of the task fell on my shoulders. It was a task I willingly accepted, and although it has been a great deal of work and frustration, it was a fascinating task. I discovered early on that I could not separate the history of the school from that of the community. Consequently, I began the research on the area and decided to use Rockport Township and West Park as the basis for the development of the history. As the project moved along, it became apparent that there was too much for a single work and the history of John Marshall High School would have to wait until the present work was completed.

Throughout the state most historical societies are based or focused on a single township. Since people in the Cleveland area are used to a highly urbanized environment, they are totally unfamiliar with the township concept. Nevertheless, most of Ohio still falls under this type of government and organization. Even today many of the Cleveland area historical societies are based on their original townships— Brooklyn, Parma, Strongsville, and Middleburg, to mention a few. The history of Rockport Township however, is fractured and the recording of that history is poorly organized. This is due in part to the Township's never having a permanent historical society.

The most obvious fact is that the Rocky River Valley effectively splits the township in half. In the early days travel from one side of the valley to the other was difficult under the best of conditions and impossible when the weather was bad. This problem was not completely solved until the first high bridges were built across the valley in 1890 connecting Detroit Road with Lakewood and Rocky River, and in 1895 connecting Lorain Road with West Park and Fairview Village. By that time towns and hamlets had developed independently of township influence. Consequently there was no sense of community in relation to the entire township.

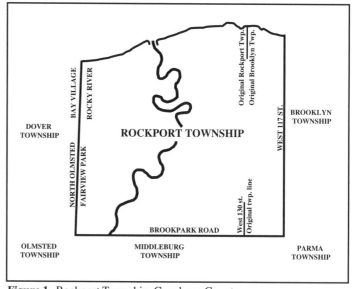

Figure 1. Rockport Township, Cuyahoga County

On the east side of the river were Kamm's, Lakewood, West Park and Linndale. On the west side were Rocky River and Goldwood (Fairview). Many of these communities had their own local historical societies that produced publications documenting their growth and development. Most of these publications were brief or anecdotal, but some were extensively researched.

The purpose of this work is not to duplicate what has already been written, but rather to correct misinformation from the earlier publications and include new material that has not been previously published.

Arthur W. Kouba 1904-1983

This volume is replete with maps, diagrams, charts, and photos. These give a much clearer perspective to the relationships between people, places and events. Many of these materials have come from the work of Arthur W. Kouba who was a long time resident of West Park.

Following his graduation from West Tech, Arthur became a surveyor for Sol Bauer, Inc. However, most of his career (33 years) was spent with the Cuyahoga County Engineer's Office under Albert S. Porter. He developed a keen interest in the development of townships in the county and constructed detailed maps documenting those events. He spoke freely and often to many community groups throughout the years including social groups, historical societies, and scouting organizations. He also produced special programs for the Metroparks. His collection of maps and photographs has been donated to the Alumni Association by his daughter, Joyce Kouba Murphy. He would have greatly appreciated seeing his meticulous work used herein.

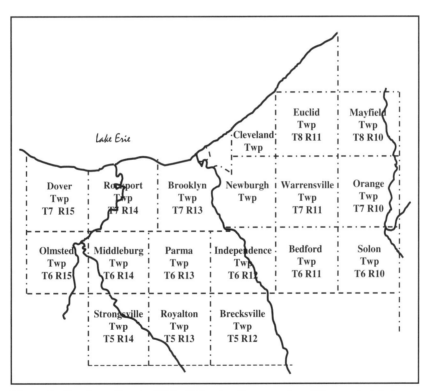

Figure 2. Cuyahoga County 1810. Following the surveying of the county into townships most were known only by their range and township numbers. Rockport, for example, was not named until 1819. *Adapted from Arthur Kouba Collection*

CHAPTER 1
THE GEOLOGIC PAST

A study of Rockport Township must start at the beginning, the geologic beginning. A look at the forces that shaped Ohio, in general, and Rockport, in particular, will show how much early life in the township was influenced by geology.

The area that is now called Ohio is made up entirely of sedimentary rock from marine deposits laid down during the Paleozoic Era 350 million years ago. Originally these sedimentary layers were level and flat, but due to pressures associated with the formation of the Appalachian Mountains, 200 million years ago, the layers were bent upward into a gentle arch with its crest near Cincinnati. Since that time erosion has removed much of this rock, cutting deepest where the rocks stood the highest. So the upper younger layers are eroded in Western Ohio thereby exposing older rocks at the surface (Forsyth, 1989). In Rockport the exposed bedrock is Devonian (Age of Fishes) Shale. Chagrin Shale is found along the lake and mouth of Rocky River. The remainder of the area is comprised of Cleveland or Ohio Shale.

Erosion of these exposed rocks took place for perhaps 200 million years by preglacial streams (Fig. 1-1). The preglacial stream system came to an end with the advance of the first of probably four glaciers 700,000 years ago. Most of the river systems were either blocked or re-routed with each glacial advance so that by the time the last glacier finally receded, about 14,000 years ago, Ohio was left with its present drainage pattern. (Fig. 1-2). Besides drainage changes, the glaciers had many other profound effects on what was to become Rockport Township.

Northern glaciers began to expand and move south when average annual temperatures dropped by only a few degrees in mid latitude areas like Ohio. Although as the ice approached, July temperatures in central Ohio were about 20 degrees cooler

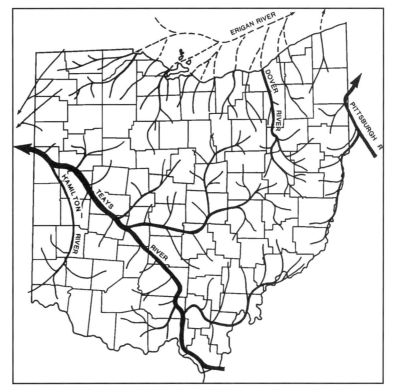

Figure 1-1. The drainage pattern in Ohio prior to the last Ice Age, about 1,000,000 years ago. The basin of what is now Lake Erie was occupied by the Erigan River. No Ohio River existed in preglacial times. The major drainage was the Teays River System. With its headwaters in the Appalacian Mountains, this river flowed northwest across West Virginia, Ohio, Indiana and Illinois to join a small preglacial Mississippi River. This pattern had remained in existence for 200,000,000 years. *Forsyth, 1989*

than today. At the same time there was probably a modest warming trend far to the north that supplied more moisture in the form of snowfall. In fact, we now know that glacial size is more a function of snowfall than low temperature (Goldthwait, 1967). Over several centuries the snow accumulated to great depths far to our north and the tremendous weight compressed snow into ice. As the "pile" continued to increase, the base of the "pile" also broadened or expanded in all directions. The depth or height of the glacier in Northern Ohio averaged about a mile in thickness and the base or front of the glacier traveled forward between 3 and 300 feet per year (Goldthwait, 1967). This tremendous mass sheared off the tops of hills and filled valleys with soil, rock, and boulders carried from several hundred miles to the north. It plowed down onto and into the bedrock, pushing all loose material and plant and animal life up and onto the glacier. Contrary to what most people believe, glaciation did not necessarily produce a vast wasteland of snow and ice. The glacier itself might not even have been visible near the front as forests continued to grow in the soil on top of the glacier.

Figure 1-2. The present drainage pattern in Ohio. Most of this has been in existence for less than 20,000 years.

The front of the glacier continued to push to the south as long as the amount of snowfall far to the north exceeded the amount of melting at the front. When the climate changed or warmed even slightly in our area, the amount of melting at the front would exceed the buildup of snow to the north, and the glacier would "retreat." If the melting was uniform, the retreat would leave behind uniform deposits of everything carried by the glacier, and then the surface of the land would be flat and level as it is in Rockport. Present day variations in the topography of the township were caused by other factors, such as erosion of the valley by Rocky River and the formation of ridges along shorelines of ancient lakes.

Figure 1-1 shows that a steam did drain an area similar to that drained by the present Rocky River. This preglacial stream and valley that passed through Rockport is shown in Figure 1-4. Core drillings show that the bottom of the river valley was 200 feet deeper than the present valley and considerably wider (Williams, 1940). This old valley was completely filled with the loosely sorted glacial material of silt, sand, pebbles, and rock called glacial till. This material is much more quickly eroded than the surrounding shale bedrock. Thus, where the new river crossed the old valley, the glacial till was rapidly carried away, and the river carved out an area much wider than the rest of the valley. It is the only area

2

large enough for the present day golf courses. Elsewhere the narrow steep sided valley was wide enough only for the river, road, and small flood plain. Slopes of the filled valley also erode rapidly and are very unstable. Therefore, homes or roads built near these slopes along the lakeshore or at the top edge of the valley (Puritas and Mastick Roads) are destined to move to the bottom of the slope! The Puritas and Mastick Road hills were each closed for several years while complicated rebuilding was undertaken.

Figure 1-3. Mastic Road hill being rebuilt. *Cleveland State University Library, Cleveland Press Collection.*

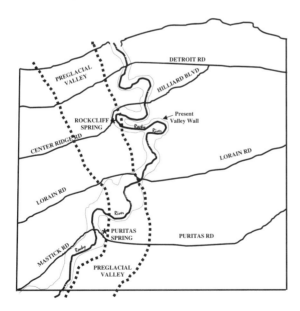

Figure 1-4. Rocky River crosses the old filled valley where the present Big Met, Little Met and MasticWoods Golf Courses are located. This is the only area of the present valley that is wide enough to accommodate these golf courses.

Because shale is the result of compression of the tiniest silt particles, it is impervious to water. When groundwater encounters the impervious shale it moves horizontally until it is exposed along a valley wall where it emerges as a spring. Where the new valley crosses the old valley there were at least two of these well-known springs, Rockcliff and Puritas, (Fig. 1-4)

The history of Lake Erie is a complicated one. Like all of the Great Lakes, it originated when water was held between the melting ice and the land to the south. The level of the lakes was at first high, but as the retreating ice uncovered lower and lower outlets, the lake levels were also lowered until the present outlines were reached. The Great Lakes now occupy valleys of rivers that existed

3

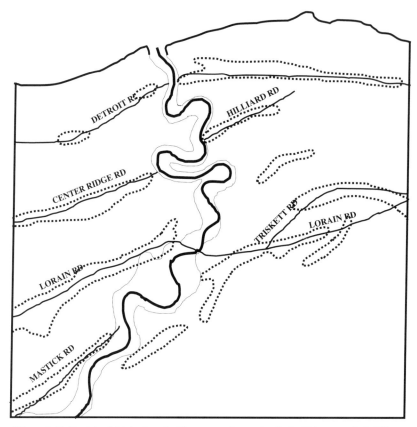

Figure1-5. Postglacial lake beach ridges were formed as Lake Erie occupied different levels. As lower and lower drainage outlets of the lake were uncovered by the retreating ice, sandy ridges were formed along the shorelines. These high, dry and relatively straight ridges were early Indian trails and later became the major east-west roads in Rockport. These ridges are still evident today as they slope 10-20 feet downward to the north along these roads. *Adapted from Goldthwait, White and Forsyth, 1961*

before glacial times. The ice that occupied them for long periods of time and then blocked their outlets with deposits of glacial material probably excavated the present lake basins. The bodies of water that preceded the final stage of the Great Lakes, at varying levels, have left their outlines as sandy ridges that formed along their shores. These ridges served as Indian trails before European settlers arrived, and they later became the route for many of the east-west roads through Rockport (Fig. 1-5).

****

CHAPTER 2
EURASIAN PEOPLES ARRIVE

At the close of the Ice Age, seas had still not completely recovered to their pre-ice levels, and the separation between Alaska and Asia was less distinct, perhaps even relatively dry land. It was at least an easily navigable water journey to the New World. Exactly when Eurasians began to move southeast across the North American Continent is unknown, but it is thought to have begun about 25,000 years ago. Whenever it happened, Eurasians had invaded most of the Americas by about 16,000-17,000 years ago. In fact, by 12,000 years ago, these peoples had made their way to the tip of South America (Hothem, 1990).

These first nomads are referred to as Paleoindians and were primarily hunter-gatherers living in small mobile groups of 25-50 individuals. Evidence suggests that these people existed in the Ohio area from about 10,000-8,000 BC (12,000-10,000 years ago). There are over 900 known small sites of Paleoindians and five large sites in Ohio (Seeman, et al, 1994). One of these large sites was discovered in 1989 in northern Medina County. Artifacts and other materials found here were radiocarbon dated at 10,000 B.C., making it one of the earliest known settlements in the southern Great Lakes (Brose, 1994).

The distinctive flint and chert projectile points used by these peoples were designed, or at least would have been very efficient, for killing large mammals. In fact, contemporaries of our Paleoindians in the Great Plains were killers of elephants. Until recently there has been no direct evidence that this occurred in Ohio. In 1989 the skeleton of a mastodon was unearthed near Newark with unmistakable Paleoindian projectile points (Fisher, et al, 1994). Nevertheless, it is possible the conifer and leaf browsing mastodons had resin tainted flesh and may have been somewhat unpalatable, while the grass eating mammoths were probably rare in northern Ohio. It is more likely that these early hunters relied more on less dangerous prey like deer, caribou, and elk-moose, and that the Newark kill was a rather rare occurrence (Hothem, 1990).

As the Paleoindians arrived in Ohio, they would have encountered a diverse mammalian fauna. Some animals like the mastodon, mammoth, peccary, and ground sloth were widely distributed and would

Paleo-Indian (10,000?-8,000 BC)	first inhabitants of the New World lived in small mobile groups of 25-50 people obtained food by hunting and gathering
Archaic Indians (8,000-1,000 BC)	economy based on hunting, fishing, collecting may have domesticated squash lived in different camps according to seasons
Woodland Indians (1,000BC-AD 1,000)	first pottery (early) trade networks (middle) mounds and earthworks (middle) some domesticated plants (late) use of bow and arrow (late)
Late Prehistoric (AD 1,000-1,600)	permanent villages, grew corn or maize, Whittlesey Tradition in northeastern Ohio, Sandusky Tradition in north central Ohio, Fort Ancient cultures in southern Ohio.
Historic Indians (AD 1,000+)	Euro-American and Native American (Wyandot and Ottawa) settlers move into northeastern Ohio.

Table 2-1. The Indians of northeastern Ohio's past. *Adapted from pamphlet on Archaeology, Cleveland Museum of Natural History.*

have been familiar. Others, like the giant beaver and elk-moose, were restricted to the eastern United States and would have been new to these Indians. While these taxa are now extinct, others such as the caribou and musk ox are still found only much farther to the north. Changes in the mammalian fauna at the end of the ice age probably resulted from changes in climate, vegetation and habitat, especially the disappearance of cold-adapted species and their replacement by southern species. While Paleoindians coexisted with these extinct fauna, it is uncertain what effect, if any, they had on the faunal reorganization (McDonald, 1994).

Prehistoric Indian cultures came and went over the next several millennia; (Table 2-1) each had its own characteristic life style and tradition. The last of them were originally recorded by Charles Whittlesey (1851) Ohio's first state geologist and founder of the Western Reserve Historical Society. He described a series of "fortified villages" located upon the isolated steep bluffs of the major river valleys of northeastern Ohio. As information accumulated over the next 100 years, it was thought that these villages were of the Erie Nations. But Brose (1971, 1976, 1978), and Lupold and Haddad (1988) have shown that the belief that the Erie occupied the entire south shore of Lake Erie is wrong. We now know that the villages between the Black River (Lorain County) and Conneaut Creek (Ashtabula County) are quite distinct from the Erie and are now referred to as the Whittlesey Tradition (Fig. 2-1).

Figure 2-1. This map, adapted from Brose, 1994, shows the locations of Late Prehistoric Indian Traditions in the Great Lakes. (A) Upper Mississippian Culture, (B) Fort Ancient Tradition, (C) Philo Fort Ancient Complex, (D) Younge Tradition, (E) Sandusky Tradition, (F) Fort Meigs/Indian Hills Complex, (G) Whittlesey Tradition, (H) Allegheny Glen Meyer/McFate Complex, (I) Iroquois Tradition, (J) Riker/Neals Landing Complex, (K) Monongahela Tradition, (L) Various Late Woodland Complexes.

One of the larger and more famous sites known as the South Park Village Site is found in the Cuyahoga Valley not far from Tinkers Creek. It has been extensively examined by professional and amateur archaeologists alike for over 100 years. The most recent investigation by the Cleveland Museum of Natural History from 1977-79 provides a detailed look at this group of people (Brose, 1994).

By about 1600 A.D. the Whittlesey Tradition had all but disappeared from northeastern Ohio. Brose (1994) suggested that they may have gradually moved to the lower Muskingum Valley or the upper Ohio Valley in response to the shorter growing season induced by the little ice age which occurred between 1450 and 1550. Brian Redmond of the Cleveland Museum of Natural History (personal communication, 1996) feels that they simply moved or drifted off to the west. The one thing which appears certain, however, is that the Whittlesey never had contact or traded with any European settlers. This marked the end of any permanent Indian occupation of northeast Ohio. It was certainly used as a hunting and pass-through area, but there were no longer any Indian settlements. In fact, this part of Ohio would remain essentially unoccupied for nearly 200 years.

The Indian history of Rockport Township is nearly nonexistent. There is no evidence of any permanent settlements anywhere within the township. A site just outside of the township known as Fort Hill is located on a promontory near the confluence of the East and West Branches of Rocky River in the Metroparks. While it is well known as an earth works, there have never been any artifacts discovered to identify its significance. It is possible that much of the area has eroded away or that it may have been some sort of ceremonial site that was only occasionally visited. The lone site within the Township, known as Dead Man's Island, is located near the mouth of Rocky River (Ohio Archaeological Inventory site # 33-Cu-153). The site is now under a paved parking lot of the Cleveland Yacht Club. Remarks from the Ohio Archaeological Inventory are as follows: "The island is known as Dead Man's Island due to the large number of Indian skeletons that have been found or plowed up since early 1800's. Apparently the Indians burned and buried their dead here. Early accounts tell of Indians arriving in winter and beaching their canoes on this island prior to an inland journey for hunting. Returning in spring, they would light fires at each grave and dance to the dead. Only part of the site was destroyed; the rest is supposedly intact under the parking lot of the Yacht Club." Unfortunately no artifacts or skeletons have ever been subject to scientific investigation so the source of the materials has never been identified.

****

CHAPTER 3
EUROPEANS INVADE

Following the disappearance of the Whittlesey there was little permanent activity in northeastern Ohio until the formation of the Connecticut Western Reserve in 1786. Things were not quiet elsewhere, however, as the French began settling the Upper St. Lawrence Valley and the British established colonies along the Atlantic Coast. As the European invaders moved inland, conflicts developed with the Native Americans, and wars broke out between the British, French, and their respective Indian allies. There were also bitter conflicts among the Native Americans, not the least of which was the obliteration of the Erie Nation by the Iroquois. And finally, there was the American war for independence and the establishment of democracy in the New World.

The beginnings of our area probably lie with King Charles II of England who, in exchange for a firm foothold in the New World, granted the first settlers of Connecticut rights to all lands between the 41st and 42nd parallel all the way to the Pacific Ocean. Part of this land, however, (New York) had already been granted to the Duke of York. Later Pennsylvania disputed the claim between the Delaware River and its present boundary (Lupold and Haddad, 1988). This claim was sustained by a federal court, and thus the Connecticut claim was limited to Connecticut and the land west of Pennsylvania to the Mississippi River (Fig. 3-1).

In 1780 the Continental Congress suggested that Colonies owning wasteland cede them to the United States. Connecticut gave up lands east of the Mississippi River up to a line parallel to, and 120 miles east of, the western boundary of Pennsylvania. The lands east of that line were reserved for themselves (The Connecticut Western Reserve). With these ceded lands from Connecticut and other colonies the Congress established the Northwest Territory on July 13, 1787.

The Northwest Ordinance of 1787 provided for the government of the entire region and was based in part on a plan drawn up by a committee headed by Thomas Jefferson in 1784. It provided an orderly procedure for the creation of new states from the territory and for the first time used a rec-

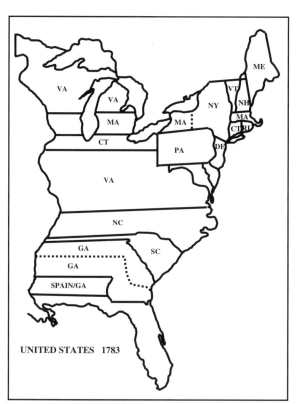

Figure 3-1. The United States in 1783.

tilinear pattern of surveying based on square townships. Prior to this time a very random survey method was used and in fact was also used to survey the Virginia Military Lands of Ohio (Knepper, 1976). As can be seen from Figure 3-2, this system created a great deal of confusion.

The survey of the Northwest Territory began at the intersection of the boundary of Pennsylvania and the Ohio River; townships were to be numbered from the Ohio River northward, and each row of

8

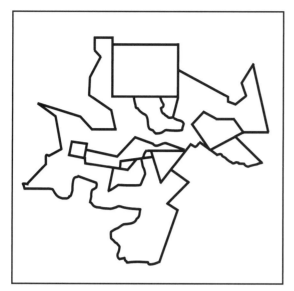

Figure 3-2. An example of how surveying was conducted in the Virginia Military Lands of Ohio. *Knepper, 1976*

townships (called a range) was to receive a number beginning at the Pennsylvania line and running westward. The Townships were to be subdivided into 36 sections of one square mile each (640 acres). Section 16 of each township was set aside for schools, and section 4 was set aside for future sale by the federal government (Roseboom and Weisenburger, 1954). The same rectilinear pattern was used in the Connecticut Western Reserve except that the grid was based on five-mile square townships. (Knepper, 1976). Since a private developer was selling the Reserve (Connecticut Land Company), no sections were set aside for schools or government.

In 1786 General Arthur St. Clair became the first Governor of the Northwest Territory, and in 1788 The Ohio Company of Associates established Marietta as the first permanent settlement. On July 27, 1788, Governor St. Clair established Washington County (Fig. 3-3), and by 1790, Cincinnati was regarded as the capitol of the Northwest Territory.

During the Revolutionary War, the British sailed through Long Island Sound and entered several Connecticut harbors burning and plundering houses and public buildings. Those suffering most were from the towns of New Haven, East Haven, Greenwich, Danbury, Ridgefield, Norwalk, New London and Groton (Wittke, 1941a). These Sufferers, as they came to be known, sought relief from the Connecticut legislature which in May, 1792, set aside 500,000 acres at the west end of the Western Reserve for those who were burned out. This became known as the Firelands, and many of the present township names within Erie and Huron Counties were derived from the names of those burned out towns.

The Connecticut Land Company (1795-1809) was authorized by the State of Connecticut to purchase and resell a majority of the Western Reserve. A syndicate of 58 individuals agreed to purchase the land on September 2, 1795 for $1,200,000 on credit. The subscriptions to the purchase ranged from $1,683 to $168,185. Each dollar subscribed entitled the subscriber to one twelve-hundred-thousandth part of the land purchased. The number of shares was fixed at 400, each one costing $3,000 (Cherry, 1920). Proceeds from the sale were to be used to form a Connecticut School Fund. The Land Company investors expected to make fortunes by the resale of the 3,000,000 acres along Lake Erie to settlers flooding the frontier following the nation's independence. Sales of property were sluggish at best due to malaria, high prices for Cleveland lots, and cheaper land elsewhere. The first directors included Moses Cleaveland who led the first Company survey party into the Reserve in 1796. Cleaveland negotiated a treaty with the Iroquois who gave up claim to all lands east of the Cuyahoga River. Moses Cleaveland also founded the settlement of Cleveland. The second survey party led by Seth Pease completed the project east of the Cuyahoga River in 1797.

Because of company mismanagement, not many of the original proprietors made profits. There were constant questions as to title to lands within the Reserve. These were not settled until President John Adams signed the "Quieting Act" on April 28, 1800, which conveyed all rights within the Reserve to the state of Connecticut. Connecticut then granted the United States jurisdiction over the Reserve, and on July 10, 1800, the Reserve became Trumbull County, a part of the Northwest Territory (Fig. 3-4). The 1809

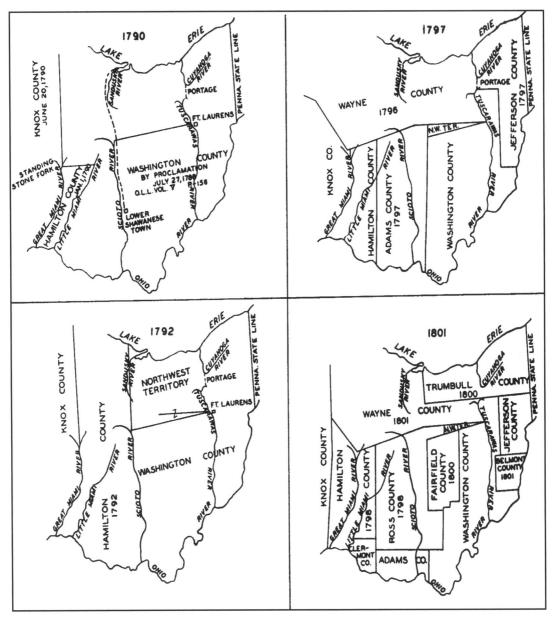

Figure 3-3. The evolution of the Ohio portion of the Northwest Territory. In November of 1800, Chillicothe became the capital of the Northwest Territory and also the first capital of Ohio when statehood was granted on February 19, 1803. *Maps adapted from Arthur Kouba Collection*

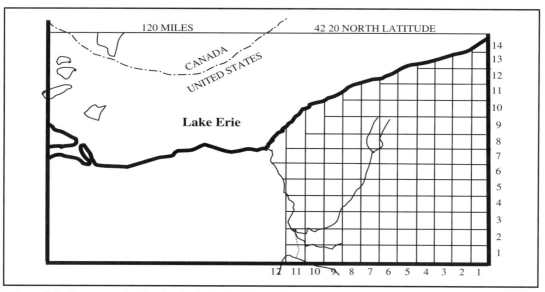

Figure 3-4. One reason for slow land sales in the Western Reserve was the constant question of title to the land. This was settled when President John Adams signed the Easement Act conveying all rights in the Reserve to Jonathan Trumbull, governor of Connecticut on April 28, 1800. Connecticut then granted the United States jurisdiction over the Reserve and on July 10, 1800, the entire Western Reserve became Trumbull County of the Northwest Territory. At this time land west of the Cuyahoga and the Portage Path (dashed line), was Indian Territory and remained unsurveyed until July 4, 1805, when the signing of the Treaty of Fort Industry moved the Indian lands to beyond the western boundary of the Western Reserve. *Map adapted from the Arthur Kouba Collection*

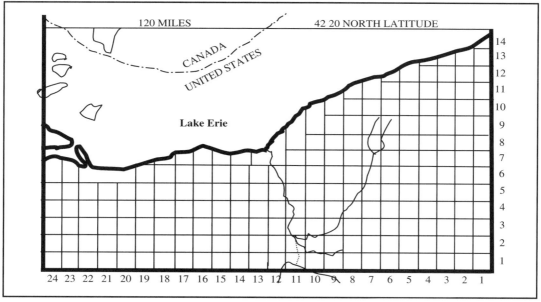

Figure 3-5. While the Treaty of 1805 cleared the title to land west of the Cuyahoga River, it only made it possible to begin surveys preliminary to sale and settlement. Another year was lost due to errors in surveying while the Connecticut Sufferers waited for their land in the Firelands. Thirty years had now passed and many of the original claimants from the Revolution were dead. When claims were finally allotted they were done so through a complicated process which caused large tracts to be scattered rather than concentrated in a single piece. There is little wonder as to why settlement of the area was so slow (Hatcher, 1991). *Map adapted from the Arthur Kouba Collection*

11

report on the Connecticut School Fund showed that a large amount of interest on the company's debt was unpaid. On January 4, 1809, the Connecticut Land Company was dissolved, and all remaining land was divided among the proprietors (Van Tassel and Grabowski, 1996).

Further complicating the problem, the Indians who remained in Northern Ohio at the end of the 18th century formed a loose confederation that was able to block settlement of the Reserve. On August 5, 1795, General Anthony Wayne defeated these Indians at the Battle of Fallen Timbers (west of Toledo) and established the Greenville Treaty Line. North and west of the Cuyahoga River remained Indian lands but south and east of the line belonged to the new settlers. On July 4, 1805 The Treaty of Fort Industry relieved the Indians of any remaining claim to the Reserve, and thus lands west of the Cuyahoga were opened to settlement (Fig. 3-5). Up to that time, land west of the Cuyahoga had been considered Indian Territory (Lupold and Haddad, 1988).

The survey of land east of the Cuyahoga was completed in 1797, and the draft (or drawing) for those townships took place prior to 1800. That draft required an ownership of $12,903.23 of the original purchase money to entitle an owner (or group of owners) to a township. Lands west of the Cuyahoga were not surveyed until 1806-07 following the Treaty of Fort Industry. The draft for the West took place April 4, 1807, and it required ownership of $26,087 in the original purchase money to entitle an owner (or group) to a township (Fig. 3-6).

Judson Canfield	$10,226.50
Judson Canfield & Co.	865.00
Timothy Chrittenden Jr.	1,000.00
James Johnston	4,322.00
David Waterman	4,128.00
Penuel Cheney	106.00
Jonathan Dwight et. al.	5,439.50
Total	$26,087.00

Figure 3-6. Fourth Draft, Drawing #15, April 4th 1807. Original purchasers of Township 7, Range 14.

After the surveys, the owners of lands took possession or placed them on the market. Settlement commenced in nearly every township almost at once rather than by a gradual east to west development. So with the draft of April 4, 1807, Township #7 of Range #14 and its owners were clearly established, paving the way for the growth that was to come.

****

CHAPTER 4
THE FIRST SETTLERS

The early settlers of Ohio followed three main routes to get to their new home. The first group originated in New England, came across New York to Buffalo and then by water or overland to northern Ohio. The second group followed streams to the beginning of the Ohio River at Pittsburgh and then down stream to Marietta and other river towns. The third group was made up of people from Kentucky, Virginia, and North Carolina who came to Ohio and settled in the southern part of the state. The southern part of the state was the most populated for a long time, and in 1803 when Ohio became a state, its laws and legislation mostly reflected the sentiments of those from southern Ohio (Davis, 1972). Early settlers of the Western Reserve were almost entirely from New England.

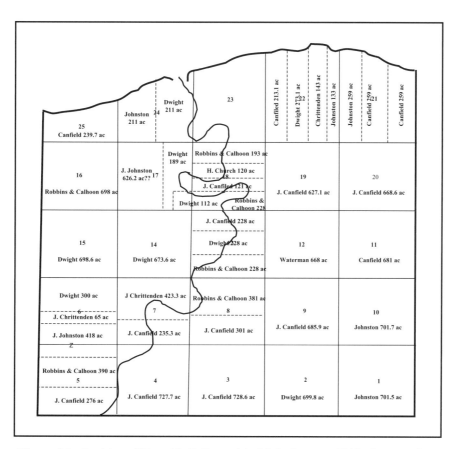

Figure 4-1. Partition of Town No 7, Range 14. Made August – 1812. Owners of Record. *Common Pleas Court Record Volume 1- Page 282   Map adapted from the Arthur Kouba Collection*

Rockport Township was not named until 1819 and prior to that time was known only as Town No. 7, Range 14. There were, of course, no roads in the township, only Indian trails so travel was extremely difficult. The southern part of the state experienced settlement about 20-30 years before the north because travel down the Ohio River was much easier than overland through the forest. In 1809, the State of Ohio appropriated money to build a road (bill actually passed in 1810) from Cleveland to the Huron River (at that time the present Huron, Erie and Lorain Counties were still a part of Cuyahoga County). They appointed Ebenezer Marry, Nathan Doan and Lorenzo Carter of Cleveland to superintend the construction.

Some of the very first settlers to use this road were George Peake, and his family. George has the distinction of being the first African American to settle in the Cleveland area and was probably the first long-term settler in the township. He and his wife and sons George and Joseph purchased 105 acres in the southwestern corner of section 23 (Fig. 4-1). Fisher Road., McKinley Avenue, Lakewood Heights Boulevard and Northland Avenue approximately bound the area of his farm. Two other sons, James and Henry followed later.

George had served in the British Army under General Wolfe at the siege of Quebec (1759). Following military service, he moved to Maryland where he met and married his white wife who was reported to be very wealthy. Following their marriage, they moved to Pennsylvania and raised a large family. At the time of his arrival in Rockport, he was 87.

In Rockport, he farmed and worked for other early settlers. His invention of the hand-operated gristmill was a great improvement over the mortar and pestle type. By all accounts, he was a highly respected citizen and passed away here at the age of 105. There does not seem to be any record as to where he was buried.

The distinction of being the first settler, however, belongs to Philo Taylor. He came from New York to Cleveland in 1806 where he met Harmon Canfield and Elisha Whittelsey, agents and owners of land in Rockport. He came to verbal agreement with them about a parcel of land near the mouth of the Rocky River. Journeying with his family in an open boat, he made landing at the mouth of the Rocky River on April 10, 1808. He built a cabin on the east side of the river, cleared land and within a year had made many changes. Soon after, Canfield informed him that he would have to move because the owners had decided to lay out a town at the mouth of the river.

As has already been noted, many of the original purchasers of property in the Western Reserve were nothing more than land speculators. Not the least of these was Gedeon Granger. He was one of the original 49 shareholders of the Connecticut Western Reserve. In 1805, Thomas Jefferson appointed him seventh postmaster of the United States. Granger was very interested in land west of the Cuyahoga and had purchased all of section 24 shortly after the township was partitioned. This was his westernmost land speculation adventure and was to be a great port of Lake Erie at Rocky River called Granger City. With Calvin Pease and John Beyer, he laid out an elaborate survey (Fig. 4-2).

He had enlisted a number of influential men including Joseph Larwell of Wooster who purchased land on both sides of the river near the mouth. The sale of lots for Granger City was widely advertised, and when the sale day arrived in 1815, a large crowd attended. Lots were sold as high as $60. Larwell figured to make a fortune as the great city began. Charles Miles built the first cabin in Grangertown in 1815. In 1816 John Dowling, George Reynolds and Captain Foster built on city lots. Growth was slow and Miles sold out to John James of Boston and moved west to a farm that would later become the home of Govenor Reuben Wood. Other settlers who came in 1816 included Asahel Porter, Eleazer Waterman, Josephus B. Lizer and Henry Canfield. Canfield of Trumbull County was the son of Judson Canfield who was one of the original large purchasers of land in Rockport (Fig. 3-6). Henry stayed long enough to be married then moved to a farm in Rockport, but he eventually returned to Trumbull County.

Some say that the city was cursed from the beginning. When Philo Taylor was forced to move from his homestead, it was reported that he was so angry that he left a curse over the city. Nevertheless, for whatever reason, Granger City was a miserable failure. The Taylors did remain long enough for their

14

A Plan For The Town of Granger

State of Ohio-Cuyahoga County. Cleveland November 2nd A.D. 1815 this day personally appeared Calvin Pearse who signed and sealed the foregoing instrument for himself and as attorney to Gideon Granger and Joseph H. Larwill who signed and sealed the same for himself and as attorney to John Bever and severally acknowledged the same to be their free act and deed for the uses purposes therein mentioned before me.
Horace Perry, Just. of Peace.

The annexed map represents a plan of the town of Granger situated on the west bank of Rocky Riverin the County of Cuyahoga and State of Ohio in Lot No 24 of Township No 7 in the 14 range of Townships as laid out by the undersigned proprietors contacting one hundred and fifty lots as marked on the annexed plan each lot being sixty feet in front and one hundred and eighty feet deep excepting lots No.s 12, 13, 14, 15, 16, 17, 18, 19, 20, 21, 22, 23 and 24 being bounded east by the River and westerly by Water ST. which is sixty feet wide. Lot 24 on the north line on Island ST. is 33 feet to the River and the line on the south side of lot 12 is 110 feet to the River; Water ST. extends from lots 4 and 12 to Island ST. and makes lot 46-160 feet on Island ST. Main ST. and Island ST. are each eighty feet wide. Blount ST. is forty feet and excepting that part which is South of Fancy ST. which is sixty feet wide. The ST. on the South side of lot No 1 is sixty feet wide each alley is twenty feet wide. The square reserved by the propitors (sic) is 280 feet on Main ST. 490 on River ST. and 455 on Island ST. and bounded Easterly by the River. Lot No 111 is given for the use of the Town to erect a house for public worship thereon, and lots No 109 and 110 are also reserved for the use of the inhabitants of the town to erect a school house thereon and for the support of schools of learning, Now therefor be it known to all people that we the undersigned propritors (sic) of said town of Granger do hereby establish said town of Granger agreeable to the foregoing description and annexed map and agreeable to the Statue Law of the State of Ohio in such case made and provided. In testimony whereof we have unto set our hand and seals at Cleveland this second day of November A.D. 1815. Calvin Pease - for himself and as attorney to Gideon Granger - for John Bever and self

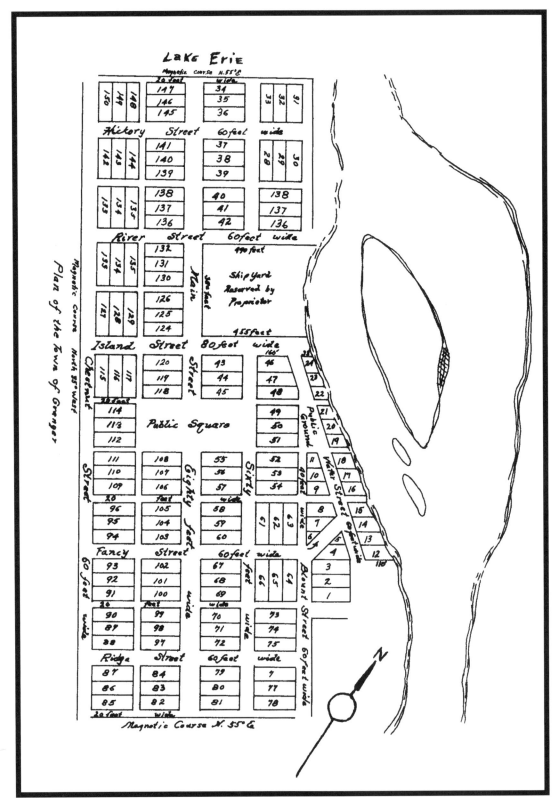

Map adapted from the Arthur Kouba Collection

son Egbert to be born in November of 1809 thereby being the first birth in the Township.

Most of the Ohio country was densely forested in 1750. Realistic estimates indicate that as much as 95 percent of the land area was covered with trees. Numerous diaries of frontiersmen, soldiers, and pioneers stress the size and apparent endlessness of the forests. Several of these people emphasized their relief by praying when at last they emerged from the dense gloom of the canopied forest into the openings of sunlight (Trautman, 1977).

There were occasional openings in the forest resulting from windstorms or tornadoes and sometimes Indians would set fires to clear an area for crops. However, since most of northeastern Ohio, including Rockport, had no resident Indians, the canopy was virtually unbroken (Trautman, 1977).

In addition, these early settlers would have encountered large predatory and game animals that were soon wiped out from the frontier including the gray wolf, black bear, mountain lion, American elk, and woodland bison. The last bison recorded in Ohio was from Lawrence County in 1803, elk were observed in Ashtabula County until 1832, mountain lions were gone by 1850, and black bears and gray wolves were gone from Ohio by the 1880s (Gottschang, 1981). However, it should be pointed out that at least one of these species, the black bear, has once again been confirmed as a permanent resident. There are at least 100 known bears in eastern and southern counties and sows with cubs have been seen during 2000 and 2001 in counties along the Pennsylvania border (ODNR, 2002).

It is hard for us to imagine the difficulties of the first settlers. However, Rummel (1998) provided a description of some of the challenges that faced the pioneers of southwestern Ohio.

"For the Brethren, as they floated down the Ohio River on their flatboat, all they could see was forest, the banks on both sides were lined with dense forest. It was an overwhelming forest, so thick, so tall. It surrounded a person, even out in the middle of the Ohio River. They were huge trees covering the sky. Trunks were often four or five through, and the limbs intertwined high overhead, so one walked in the twilight underneath. It was fairly open beneath the tall trees. The sun was virtually shut out and little underbrush grew, except in openings where one of the forest giants had fallen and along the rivers and streams. There the shrubs and brush clogged the edge of the forest, and the thorny blackberry vines grew like a wall.

When you first came to the Frontier, there was a lot of hard work that had to be done. First, the ground had to be cleared to plant a crop for food. Small trees were cut down and trimmed out. They made brush piles out of the trimmed out tops and brush, laid them around the large trees, to be burned come winter. The large trees were girdled, so the tree would die standing upright. They were too big to cut down and too big to use. The tops died, and the sun touched the ground through the dead branches. The settler broke the soil for the first time, planting around the stumps and standing trees. He planted his hills of corn by hand and hoe, and added squash, pumpkin and potatoes to produce food for next winter. At first, you couldn't use a horse to plow or break up the soil, there were just too many huge roots. The first year a man might clear 5 or 10 or maybe even 20 acres. It made a scanty crop to supply food for a family that first winter, and families were large but times were hard for everyone.

Then the cabin had to be built, it was all a man could do, even with the neighbors help. The longest maneuverable log would be 20 feet. That was the long side of the cabin. The short side would depend on how much space the settler needed and how big a family he had. The height was enough to stand, and enough more to make a loft for the children. Those small trees made the cabin logs. They were a foot, to a foot and a half thick. A man would square them off with an adze. The Tulip Tree was naturally straight and would lay tight together with only a minimum of chinking, the local clay made good chinking to stuff in between the logs. They were thick enough to give decent protection against the cold and with chinking kept the winds out. The ends were cut to overlay with special angle cuts, so they would lock together and hold fast. The angles were shaped so water would drain out and not rot the wood. The logs of the gables for the loft were cut short to give the slope, and to allow cross poles to hold the gables steady and to make a kind of rafter for the shingles. The peak was locked with a ridge pole. The roof was covered with big clap board shingles rived out of oak or ash. They were four feet long, six inches wide or more and an inch thick. They were held down with cross poles. They kept out most of the rain, partly because the roof sloped enough so the water ran off quickly. In time they warped badly and let in considerable air, but at first they were reasonably tight. Clay and flat stone built the chimney and a fireplace in one end of the cabin. The fireplace often covered half of the wall of the cabin and provided the heat and light inside the cabin.

The actual construction was a neighborly thing that would take three or four days. It took several men together to cut the logs and roll them to the cabin site. Or a man with grown sons might already have the logs cut and adzed square before the neighbors came to help put up the cabin. The logs were raised into place with hand spikes and skid poles. The higher it went the

Figure 4-3 This is what an early settlers cabin would look like. The logs are sawn, either by hand, or by an early mill. *Author collection*

more work it took, and accidents did happen. If the family were large, the log walls were raised higher, a loft gave sleeping space to the children, especially the boys. Some cabins had an outside ladder to the loft, others an inside ladder up the wall. The door and windows would be cut out of the logs after the cabin was up. A hole would be augured through the logs and the opening sawed out with a crosscut saw. Hewed lumber three of four inches thick, was fastened by wood pins to the opening in the cabin logs to make a framed doorway or window. Large clapboards would be pegged to split cross poles to make a door. It would swing on a hinge made of a pointed pole, with corresponding holes augured into the logs top and bottom A latch bar on the inside closed it shut, but the latch-thong was allowed to hang outside through a hole in the door during the day so the latch could be raised and the door opened. At night it would be drawn inside, to prohibit entry by unwanted guests. Inside above the doorway hung the rifle, on two wood hooks, or a deer's antler rack. If the family could afford to bring glass panes with them from the east, it would usually only be enough for two or three small windows. Glass in those days was to let light in, while it kept the wind out. It was not clear and you could not really see out of it. A piece of paper, or some hog guts, heavily larded, was a translucent substitute if glass was unavailable. Heavy wooden shutters, made of clapboards, like the doors, would protect the window from night or storm damage. The floor might originally be tamped clay, covered with white sand, but a puncheon floor of split logs smoothed off was a quick improvement.

Much of the furniture would be homemade. An upright post in the floor, connected by poles to walls in a corner made a bed, or covered by clapboards made a table. A split log with stick for legs made a stool or bench, and if a little larger, would make a table. Pots and kettles were opposite the window, often hung from pegs on the wall. The dutch oven with short legs, and a lipped lid (to hold hot ashes on top for the cooking food) was a necessity.

For the new settler, wild game provided a major part of the food supply. In the earliest days, the buffalo, or bison, still roamed the country. The winter of 1800 had three months of ice covering the ground. The wolves decimated the buffalo and they were seen only occasionally in the succeeding years. Venison was a good source of meat. The deer were stalked at dawn and twilight, or by a bright torch at night called "shining their eyes". They were bled, gutted and hung up, then a pack horse was brought to take them home. Again the winter of 1817 the "year that had no summer", trapped the deer, and while it made it easy food provision for settlers during that hard year, so many were killed that it was no longer a reliable food source for future years. Possom, coon, squirrel, wild turkey, pheasant, wild pigeon and ducks were continuing food. Wild turkeys roosted in the beech woods. When scairt by dogs, they would fly into a tree where they were stalked, or they might be shot at roost at daylight. They would weigh 12 to 15 pounds. Pigeons would roost at night and were hunted by torch and club. They made a tasty meat dish. Rabbits were not shot, they were caught in the deep snow, and in a couple days their meat would freeze and could be kept for a while. From the wild around were many edible plants, "greens" and roots that the settler's wife scrounged and even stored for winter.

Maybe the first winter, maybe not till the second, after the majestic trees were thoroughly dead and after the crops were all harvested and away, then the brush, the dead tops of the smaller trees piled up against the trunks of the girdled trees were set on fire. The ashes were plowed back into the soil. After the trees were down, then you could try to plow. It was hard work, tear up a man's insides as the plow hooked on roots, jerked the team to a stop, and slammed the plow handles against a man's ribs. Then it took an ax to cut the root at the stump, and maybe the yoke of oxen to get it pulled out of the ground.

There were predators on the frontier, animals, not only the Indians. The rattlesnake and copperhead were constant dangers in their respective territories. The wolf was not such a danger to man as to his livestock. Bears ate young pigs. The hunter would loose his dogs, follow and when they chased the bear up a tree he would come for the kill. Bear meat was wild but edible. Bear fat usually made several gallons of grease. The bear skin made a good robe, especially for the children up in the cold loft.

Money was a problem on the frontier. The statement that 'cash will not be refused' can be understood only when it is recalled that trade and barter were still the common mode of exchange and the currency had been so debased and discredited that indiscriminate acceptance of it was not general. Many a doctor or midwife received payment in chickens or a ham. It was normal to consider that it would be five years before the farm would supply a surplus. But the land office still wanted payment and there were the taxes. While a man might own a quarter, half or even a whole section, most of it was still in forest. A man could only do so much work, and for one man, that usually meant that he had 40 acres that he was tilling. The 40 acres raised all his food, and the extra hay for the cows, horses and sheep. Some of his land might be cleared and used as pasture. The rest of his land was still forest, used for fence poles, logs for building and firewood. Man's work started as soon as it was light enough to see, and went till it was too dark to continue.

But for the women and girls, work started even earlier, food was ready before it was light outdoors, so the men could eat before they left to work. Food was prepared and ready for them to carry with them to eat during the day. While the men were out working, the woman had endless chores to do. Feed the chickens, hoe the garden, cook dinner for those at home, get supper ready for when the men returned home. Then there was flax and wool to ready for the spinning wheel to make thread, then for the loom to make cloth.

The cloth made shirts and pants for the men, and dresses and shawls for the women. There were underclothes to make, and endless socks to knit. Deer hide or bearskins could make good robes or rugs, or even jackets and coats, but someone had to do it. Wood ashes had to be carried outdoors, even if there wasn't an ash rack. And lye had to be cooked into the lard to make soap. Apples needed to be peeled and cored before they could be cooked into apple butter. After the harvest there was still the preservation of the food. And mostly it devolved on the woman. As if this wasn't enough, there always seemed to be another baby. Those days didn't have throwaway pampers, except as dry grass or moss lined the inside of the cloth diaper, and a dirty diaper was just exactly that. Even the wash wasn't easy. The big iron kettle sat over the open fire for boiling water. Lye soap was peeled into the water and the clothes were stirred by a stick and beaten by hand until they got clean. By night all the women were tired, but they still weren't done. The men came home, expecting supper to be ready. Then after the meal there were still dishes to clean up. Even after the family was in bed, the baby always demanded attention. The best frontier families had large families, with boys to help on the farm, and girls to help in the house. The cabin was only 20 feet long and maybe 15 feet wide, but there easily were 12 or 16 children in it. Many was the home that the fair young bride had died and now, mother was the second or even third wife. Often with her previous children too.

The frontier life was a time of hard work that sometimes never seemed to show much result. It seemed like the work never stopped."

In Rockport most of the earliest activities were centered near the mouth of Rocky River along the Detroit Road (path). The inland parts of the township were slower to develop, due to dense forests, swamps and an abundance of streams. The first to settle inland was Nathan Alger, his wife, four sons and three daughters. In June of 1812 they had made their way west on the Detroit Road Indian path and turned south at Warren Road which was another crooked Indian trail and settled in part of sections 12 and 13 (Fig. 4-1) establishing what for many years was known as the Alger Settlement. Eventually this would become the center of the village of West Park. Nathan had been sent by the Connecticut Land Company to homestead in the Western Reserve. If he remained a full year, he would receive 640 acres (a full section or one square mile). The family arrived with seven cents and a few meager belongings. Among his many jobs, Nathan walked to the settlement in Columbia Township and chopped an acre of wood in exchange for 100 pounds of flour that he carried back home.

Shortly after the Algers arrived, Dyer Nichols, John Kidney and Benjamin Robinson joined them. Each of them eventually married an Alger daughter. Unfortunately Nathan died on January 21, 1813, just six months after putting up his log cabin. Consequently, the family received only 320 acres. Nathan's burial was the first in Alger Cemetery, a plot of one acre which son Henry eventually deeded to the County.

COLUMBIA TOWNSHIP

In the late winter of 1807, Columbia became the first settlement west of the Cuyahoga. By 1810 there were over 100 people in the village, nearly twice the population of Cleveland. Just south of Columbia in Hardscrabble, Liverpool Township, Seba Bronson Jr. cleared land around a salt spring that had been long known to the Indians. Salt from this type of spring was used for preserving food and was a more important commodity than just about anything else on the frontier. This salt spring would become important to settlers all over northeastern Ohio and may explain in part the early growth of Columbia.

In 1811 Daniel Kelley and his four sons Datus, Irad, Reynolds and Alfred settled west of Rocky River. Each of these men would figure prominently in the development of Rockport, Cleveland or the State of Ohio. In 1810 Datus Kelley had visited his uncle, Joshua Stow, in Cleveland and became interested in the idea of a new Granger City. He purchased a large farm one mile west of Rocky River for which he paid $3.18 per acre (Richards, 1953). He returned to Lowville, New York to marry Sarah Dean on August 21, 1811. Accompanying them on their return trip to Ohio were her sister Cynthia and brother Joseph.

Datus was a surveyor by trade and was responsible for building the first industry in Rockport. His sawmill was constructed on a creek at Detroit Road near Elmwood. It was a busy place when timber was needed by newcomers (Butler, 1949). Irad Kelley erected the first brick store in Cleveland and was one of Cleveland's first postmasters. Alfred Kelley was, at age 21, the first attorney in the Western Reserve and became the first prosecutor in Cleveland, and then in 1815 the first president of Cleveland. Daniel Kelley succeeded his son as the second president of the city. All of the Kelleys were instrumental in organizing the Cleveland Pier Company to improve Cleveland's harbor (Butler, 1949).

The first wedding in the township was between Chester Dean and Lucy Smith of Dover (township) on January 9, 1814. It was held at the home of Datus Kelley and in spite of stormy weather, everyone in the township attended that first big social event.

In 1833 Datus and Irad Kelley prospected Cunningham's Island in western Lake Erie and found high quality limestone. They purchased the western half of the island for $1.50/acre and continued to buy until they owned the entire island of 3,000 acres. Kelley's Island became famous for its red cedar, vineyards, peach orchards and limestone.

When Datus moved to the island, he sold the southern part of his farm to Chester and Samuel Dean. Samuel and his father, Joseph, then built the first tannery in Rockport just south of Detroit Road. The rest of the farm was sold to Reuben Wood, an attorney, who in 1850 would become the Govenor of Ohio.

CLEVELAND HARBOUR

On March 3 1825 Congress appropriated $5,000 to build a pier into the lake from the west shore of the Cuyahoga because a heavy sandbar impeded navigation in the channel. The channel remained precarious at best. Congress then made a larger appropriation for a second pier to the east, and the channel of the river was changed to flow between the two piers thus giving Cleveland a good harbor. This harbour and the canal system gave Cleveland a new impetus and resulted in unparalleled growth. The first boat from the Erie Canal arrived in Cleveland on October 26, 1825, while navigation on the Ohio Canal to Newark began on July 10, 1830 (Avery, 1893).

Two problems that all early settlers faced in this western wilderness were transportation and lack of organized government. Considerable progress to alleviate these problems came with the arrival of Rufus Wright in 1816. A veteran of the War of 1812, he bought 3/4 acre of land from Gedeon Granger for the exorbitant sum of $300. His property eventually became the site of the Westlake Hotel. He built and operated a tavern on this site until 1853 when it was sold to Jacob Silverthorn.

By all accounts Wright was a dynamic individual and as a tavern owner his popularity was assured. His business was not dependent on the failing Granger City because he also operated a ferry on the river. Settlers could leave their orders at the tavern for goods on the next boat to Cleveland. The tavern was the gathering place for all the township's inhabitants (Butler, 1949). With the exception of the Alger Settlement, all of the township's residents lived close to the mouth of Rocky River.

****

CHAPTER 5
ROCKPORT, THE FORMATIVE YEARS (1819-1850)

By 1819, there were 18 families in the township, and the settlers petitioned the County Commissioners to change the name from Township 7 Range 14 to Rockport. This was an appropriate choice because of the rocky cliffs and banks along the lake and mouth of the river. The request was granted on February 24, 1819, and the first election of officers was held at Wright's tavern on the first Monday of April.

List of officers elected at the first Rockport Township meeting April, 1819

Henry Alger, Trustee
Daniel Bardin
Henry Canfield, Clerk
Chester Dean
Joseph Dean, Lister, Fence Viewer
Samuel Dean, Overseer of the Poor
John James
Erastus Johnson, Trustee
Charles Johnson
Datus Kelley, Judge

John Kidney
Charles Miles, Chairman
Dyer Nichols
James Nicholson, Overseer of the Poor
John Pitts
Asahel Porter, Judge
Benjamin Robinson, Fence Viewer
Josephus B. Sizer
Rufus Wright, Trustee

Overseers of the Poor

In society today, we would probably assume that this position would be someone in charge of the welfare office. However, at the time of early settlement, ownership and title to land was not always clear-cut. Every township had problems with squatters, and it was the overseer's job to see that those settling illegally in the community were quickly moved out.

That is not to say that people did not care for the legitimately poor in their community because the opposite was true. It is just that there were so many transients settling in abandoned cabins and houses that each township actively pursued the eviction of those squatters.

For example in 1834, the following warrant was issued in Royalton:

"The State of Ohio, County of Cuyahoga, Royalton Township to any Constable of said township. Greetings. We the undersigned overseers of the poor of Royalton Township have received information that there has lately come into said township certain poor persons who are not legal residents who may become a township charge. You are therefore commanded to summon Rufus Olds, his wife and family, to deport out of this township. And of the warrant made service as the law directs Given under our hands this ninth day of October eighteen hundred thirty five."

L.B. Bosworth
Asa Norton Overseers of poor
(1992, North Royalton Historical Society)

Every work that has included something about the early history of Rockport is based in part on the recollections of Henry Alger that were published in the Cleveland Leader in 1858 (Johnson, 1879; Butler, 1949; Gobelt, 1978; Lindstrom, 1936; Morris and Boieru, 1973; Richards and Gabel, 1953; Borchert and Borchert, 1989).

One reason that this article has been so extensively cited is because it is the only source of information about early Rockport. Unfortunately, there are no official records extant for the township for most of the 19th century. I have searched at the Cuyahoga County Archives, Cleveland Public Library,

Cuyahoga County Library, Cleveland City Hall, The Western Reserve Historical Society, and the historical societies of Lakewood, Fairview Park and Rocky River. No one seems to have a clue as to where any of these records are or when they disappeared. Even Johnson (1879) in his History of Cuyahoga County noted, "the first book of township records has been lost." He did find records from 1832 and was able to list all township officials from 1832 to 1879 (below). However, those and all other records are now gone.

Township Officers 1832-1879

1832. Trustees, Dyer Nichols, Jared Hickcox, Charles Warner; clerk, Dyer Eaton; treasurer, Calvin Giddings.
1833. Trustees, Alanson Swan, Dyer Nichols, John B. Robertson; clerk, George T. Barnum; treasurer, Ira Cunningham.
1834. Trustees, Alanson Swan, Paul G. Burch, James S. Anthony; clerk, George T. Barnum; treasurer, Ira Cunningham.
1835. Trustees, Alanson Swan, James S. Anthony, James Stranahan; clerk, Isaac P. Lathrop; treasurer, Solomon Pease.
1836. Trustees, James S. Anthony, Collins French, Henry Alger; clerk, Isaac P. Lathrop; treasurer, Solomon Pease.
1837. Trustees, Epaphroditus Wells, Joseph Dean, Benjamin Mastic; clerk, Isaac P. Lathrop; treasurer, Solomon Pease.
1838. Trustees, Joel Deming, James S. Anthony, Guilson Morgan; clerk, George T. Barnum; treasurer, Solomon Pease.
1839. Trustees, Obadiah Munn, Israel Kidney, Elial Farr; clerk, George T. Barnum; treasurer, Solomon Pease.
1840. Trustees, Elial Farr, Obadiah Munn, Jonathan Plimpton; clerk, Timothy S. Brewster; treasurer, Solomon Pease.
1841. Trustees, Asia Pease, Dyer Nichols, Israel Kidney; clerk, A.S. Lewis; treasurer, Solomon Pease.
1842. Trustees, Asia Pease, J.D. Gleason, P.G. Burch; clerk, G.T. Barnum; treasurer, Royal Millard.
1843. Trustees, Eliel Farr, W.D. Bell, John P. Spencer; clerk, Timothy S. Brewster; treasurer, Royal Millard.
1844. Trustees, Chauncey Deming, Aurelius Farr, Benjamin Stetson; clerk, Aaron Merchant; treasurer, Royal Millard.
1845. Trustees, Chauncey Deming, Joseph Leese, Dyer Nichols; clerk, Theophilus Crosby; treasurer, John D. Taylor.
1846. Trustees, Chauncey Deming, John P. Spencer, O.W. Hotchkiss; clerk, Theophilus Crosby; treasurer, John D. Taylor.
1847. Trustees, Hanford Conger, Aurelius Farr, James Stranahan; clerk, Royal Millard; treasurer, Benjamin Lowell.
1848. Trustees, Hanford Conger, Chauncey Deming. Benjamin Maskick; clerk, G.T. Barnum: treasurer, F.G. Lewis.
1849. Trustees, Aurelius Farr, Osborne Case, Benjamin Mastick; clerk, G.T. Barnum; treasurer, F.G. Lewis.
1850. Trustees, Royal Millard, Aurelius Farr, William B. Smith; clerk, G.T. Barnum; treasurer, Truman S. Wood.
1851. Trustees, Aurelius Farr, Thomas Hurd, James Stranahan; clerk, G.T. Barnum; treasurer, Isaac Higby.
1852. Trustees, Aurelius Farr, Thomas Hurd, John West; clerk, John Barnum; treasurer, Lewis Rockwell.
1853. Trustees, John P. Spencer, John Freeborn, Chauncey Deming; clerk, John Barnum; treasurer, Horace Dean.
1854. Trustees, Frederick Wright, Ezra Bassett, John Blank; clerk, John Barnum; treasurer, Horace Dean.
1855. Trustees, Edward Hayward, Ezra Bassett, A. Cleveland; clerk, John Barnum; treasurer, Horace Dean.
1856. Trustees, J.T. Storey, Thomas Hurd, Benjamin Mastick; clerk, Lucius Dean; treasurer, Horace Dean.
1857. Trustees, John F. Storey, Benjamin Mastick, Obadiah Munn; clerk, Lucius Dean; treasurer, O.W. Hotchkiss.
1858. Trustees, John F. Storey, Richard McCrary, Lucius Dean; clerk, John Barnum; treasurer, O.W. Hotchkiss.
1859. Trustees, John F. Storey, Obadiah Munn, John Farr; clerk, A.M. Wagar, treasurer, O.W. Hotchkiss.
1860. Trustees, Thomas Hurd, Benjamin Mastick, James Potter; clerk, Edwin Giddings; treasurer, O.W. Hotchkiss.
1861. Trustees, Thomas Hurd, George Reitz, A. Kyle; clerk, Robert Fleury, treasurer, William Sixt.
1862. Trustees, Thomas Hurd, George Reitz, William Jordon; clerk, A.M. Wager; treasurer, William Sixt.
1863. Trustees, Thomas Hurd, George Reitz, Thomas Morton; clerk. A.M. Wager; treasurer, William Sixt.
1864. Trustees, Thomas Hurd, William Tentler, Calvin Pease; clerk, Andrew Kyle; treasurer, William Sixt.
1865. Trustees, William Tentler, William L. Jordon. F.G. Bronson; clerk, Andrew Kyle; treasurer, William Sixt.
1866. Trustees, John F. Storey, F. Colbrunn, A.M. Wagar; clerk, John Barnum; treasurer, William Sixt.
1867. Trustees, Allen Armstrong, F. Colbrunn, Alfred French; clerk, John Barnum; treasurer, William Sixt.
1868. Trustees, Anthony Cline, Lewis Nicholson, John Gahan; clerk, Andrew Kyle; treasurer, William Sixt.
1869-70. Trustees, John Gahan, Anthony Cline, George W. Andrews; clerk, Andrew Kyle; treasurer, William Sixt.
1871-72. Trustees, John Gahan, George W. Andrews, Henry Southworth; clerk, Andrew Kyle; treasurer, William Sixt.
1873. Trustees, G.T. Pease, George W. Andrews, John Gahan; clerk, Andrew Kyle; treasurer, William Sixt.
1874. Trustees, G.T. Pease, Anthony Cline, John Gahan; clerk, Andrew Kyle; treasurer, William Sixt.
1875. Trustees, Anthony Cline, John W. West, Fred Baker; clerk, O.P. Stafford; treasurer, William Sixt.
1876. Trustees, A.M. Wagar, John W. West, Anthony Cline; clerk, H.A. Mastick; treasurer, B.F. Phinney.
1877. Trustees, L.A. Palmer, John W. West, A.M. Wagar; clerk, Edwin Giddings; treasurer, B.F. Phinney.
1878-79. Trustees, A.M. Wagar, George Fauchter, George W. Andrews; clerk, E.P. Thompson; treasurer, B.F. Phinney.

Henry Alger's recognitions do contain some errors, but since it is the only source of information, I have included the entire series of articles. As you read it, I am sure you will be amazed at how primitive this wilderness was a mere 180 years ago.

CLEVELAND MORNING LEADER
NOVEMBER 8, 1858

THE FIRST SETTLEMENT OF ROCKPORT
UP TO 1821

BY HENRY ALGER

Editor of the Leader:—Agreeably to your request, I have written a brief sketch of the first settlement of Rockport. No doubt, there are some errors in my statement, but it is the best I am able to give you. If you should think it worthy of a place in your paper, you are at liberty to publish it; and if the officers and members of the Cuyahoga County Historical Society can make any use of it, or any part of it, they are welcome to as much or as little as they may choose to adopt.

CHAPTER I.

The first white inhabitants in the township were Herbertson, an Irish refugee, with his family. He settled on the east side of the river, on the top of the bank, near where the Lake Shore Plank Road turns down the hill. There was also another Irishman, Wm. McConkey, who came over from the old country with Herbertson. He came into the township probably in 1807 or 1809, and settled on what is known as the "Benschoter Bottom" He staid a year or two and left.

On the 10th of April, 1808, Philo Taylor, formerly from the State of New York but at that time from Cleveland, landed with his family from an open boat at the mouth of the river, and located on the top of the hill nearly opposite where Silverthorn's tavern now stands.

Early in the year 1809, the Legislature of Ohio made an appropriation of money to open a road from Cleveland to the mouth of Huron river, and appointed Ebenezer Merry. Esq, of Mentor, Nathaniel Doan and Maj. Lorenzo Carter of Cleveland to superintend the opening of said road. Before this time, there was no road from Cleveland to Huron.

George Peak, who was a soldier under General Wolf, and deserted from the army, found a black woman in Maryland who had a half bushel of dollars, married her, raised a family of mulattoes in the State of Pennsylvania, and came to Rockport with two of his sons, George Peak and Joseph Peak, in April, 1809; and two more of his sons, James Peak and Henry Peak, came in soon afterwards. When the old man reached Cleveland, the above-mentioned road had been cut out from the Cuyahoga river to Rocky river, and his wagon was the first one that ever came through from Cleveland to Rocky river. The Peaks settled on the farm now owned by John Barnum, Esq. some of the Peaks built a hand-mill. The stones were 18 or 20 inches across. This mill was a great improvement over the stump mortar and spring-pole pestle, in use in those days, in grinding hominy. The elder Peak died in September 1827, at the age of 105.

In 1810, Daniel Miner, from Homer, in the State of New York came in and bought out Philo Taylor, and moved into the house built by the later; and Mr. Taylor bought on the lakeshore in Dover, and kept a tavern there for a number of years. Minner commenced to keep a tavern in 1810 or '11. He also kept a ferry at the mouth of the river. He bought out Herbertson in 1811. Herbertson moved to Huron. Minor also bought the "Mill Lot" so called. In the spring of 1812 Miner lived in the Herbertson house, and kept tavern. In the summer of the same year he built a new log house adjoining and fitted it up for tavern keeping.

In 1810 or '11, Dr. John Turner, brother-in-law of Miner, came on from the State of New York, and settled on the farm now owned by Gov. Wood. In the fall of 1813 or '14, while the Doctor and his wife were in the woods gathering hickory nuts, their house was consumed by fire, together with their two children and all their worldly effects. The Doctor then left Rockport and settled in Dover.

In 1811, Jeremiah Van Benschoter and John Pitts came in from the state of New York. Van Benschoter settled on and gave name to the "Benschoter Bottom." He staid one year and then went to Huron.

In the same year (1811) Datus Kelley, and Chester Dean, his brother-in-law, came in. Mr. Kelley settled on the farm now owned by Geo. B. Merwin.

On the 7th of June, 1812, Nathan Alger and family, with his sons, Henry Alger, Heman A. Alger, Nathan Alger, Jr., and Thaddeus P. Alger and his son-in-law, John Kidney from Waren, Litchfield county, Connecticut came into Rockport and settled on Sections 12 and13, and gave name to the Alger Settlement."

Benjamin Robinson, formerly from Vermont, came in on the 9th of June 1812.

Nathan Alger, Sr, died January 21st, 1813, which was the first death in the township. He left his wife with a family of four children the oldest sixteen and the youngest nine years old.

In 1818, Horace B. Alger and Dyer Nichols settled in the township.

In the fall of 1812, Daniel Miner commenced building a mill. He had got the dam nearly completed, when there came a freshet and carried a portion of it away.

Deacon Minor died in February, 1813 which was the second death in Rockport.

In the spring of 1813, Moses Eldred moved into the township, and kept tavern at the Miner stand for a short time. After that, the widow Miner kept tavern there for a year or two.

The first white child born in the township of Rockport was Egbert Taylor, son of Philo Taylor in Nov. 1809. The second was Addison Kelley, son of Datus Kelley, in June, 1812. The third was Philuna D. Alger, daughter of Henry Alger, in December, 1812.

The first couple married who were residents of the township, were Benjamin Robinson and Amelia Alger, daughter of Nathan Alger-They were married in Cleveland by George Wallace, Esq. on the 5th day of November, 1812. The first wedding in the township was at Datus Kelley's on the 9th day of January, 1914. The parties were Chester Dean and Lucy Smith, daughter of Abner Smith, of Dover. George Wallace, Esq. of Cleveland, performed the marriage ceremony. It was a splendid wedding for olden times. There were no sleighbells jingling in Rockport then. Those who were wealthy enough to own a yoke of oxen rode on ox sleds, and those who owned no team went on foot.

In olden times the settlers claimed to be neighbors if they did not live more that eight or ten miles apart, and were well acquainted for ten, fifteen, or twenty miles around; and could you have been present when they met each other, from the hearty shaking of hands and friendly greeting you would have supposed them to have been brothers and sisters. But most of the old settlers are gone, and also that unbounded hospitality and generous feeling which was so universal among the first settlers seems to have departed with them, we fear never to return

In 1814, Samuael Dean with his sons, Joseph Dean and Aaron W. Dean, settled in the township. Joseph Dean being a tanner and currier by trade, commenced business on the North Ridge, near where Lucius Dean now lives-he was the first tanner and currier in the township.

CHAPTER II

In 1815, Joseph Larwill came from Wooster to Rockport, and bought the "Mill Lot." He also bought the land on the west side of the river, and in the fall of the year (1815,) he laid out a city on the west side, and an auction was held for the sale of city lots. Buyers were on hand from all quarters; lots sold high, and a splendid city was in prospect. The city was to be called "Granger" in honor of Gideon Granger, the original landholder, Charles Miles built the first log cabin in the new city. It stood on the bluff at the top of the hill in Silverthorn's back yard.
The next settlers that came into the city were John Dowling, George Reynolds, and Captain Foster.

In 1816, John James, from Boston, Mass, came in and bought the farm now owned by Gov. Wood. James brought on a small store of goods, and commenced trading and keeping tavern. He kept tavern until the time of his death in 1820. His widow kept on in the business a short time afterwards, say six or eight months, whilst Enopch James was settling up his brothers estate, and then she bid farewell and left.

About the year 1816, Rufus Wright came in, built a house, and commenced keeping tavern. Also, Asahel Porter, Eleazer Waterman, Josephus B. Sizer, and others, whose names I have forgotten, came into the city. Also, Henry J Canfield came in and built "Canfields Old Store," and filled it with goods; and a Dutchman named Fluke, from Wooster, came in. He was a potter by trade, and commenced making brown earthen ware. Henry Clark came in some time between this and 1820, and kept tavern at Wright's old stand for a short time.

This year (1816) was a year of business in Rockport. Speculation ran high. A man by the name of Scott, from Painesville, came in and went into partnership with Larwill in building mills. They succeeded in getting a frame dam built, and went in for winter quarters. During the winter the floods came and made a channel for the river around the south end of the dam and by the time the birds began singing in the spring, Larwill had failed, Scott had left, the lights in the city of Granger soon went out, the music and dancing ceased, and the "castle in the air" fell to the ground with a mighty crash, so heavy that they scarcely left a grease spot, and many of the inhabitants fled.

About the year 1816 or '17, James Nicholson settled in the township, on the farm where he now lives.

About 1817, Datus Kelley built a sawmill on a small creek which crosses the North Ridge near A.W. Dean's.

In 1818, Erastus Johnson and Charles Johnson came in under Larwill's claim, repaired the dam, and built a sawmill. The sawmill was afterwards burned down.

In February or March, 1819, the township was set off and named Rockport, and a notice put up for the electors to meet and elect their township officers. The first township election was held at Rufus Wright's, on the first

Monday in April, 1819, and as they had not received the laws of the State, so in the absence of all law to direct them, they proceeded as in other meetings for business-first decided how many road districts they would have, took a little of Captain Wright's good old whisky, as was the custom in those days, and commenced business by appointing a chairman and two judges, and then proceeded to the election of officers. They first elected their Township Clerk. He was sworn into the office by the chairman, and took his seat at the table; and as they nominated their officers, one by one, and voted in the old way by raising the right hand, the story was soon told. Those elected were sworn into office by the Clerk. It may be doubted whether the election was conducted in every sense of the word according to law, yet the officers performed the duties of their respective offices to the entire satisfaction of the inhabitants of the township. I think there were but nineteen voters in the township all told. All were present, and eighteen officers were needed. Every man in the township was considered competent to fill any township office; so at the close of the election about every voter in the township either held office, kept tavern, or owned a sawmill.

Almost all who voted at that election are now gone. Rufus Wright, Asahel Porter, Henry J. Canfield. Samuel Dean, Chester Dean, Joseph Dean, Dyer Nichols, Daniel Hardin, John Kidney, John Pitts, and John James are dead. Chas. Miles, Erastus Johnson, Charles Johnson and Josephus B. Sizer, uncertain. Datus Kelley is living, now resides in Kelley's Island. Jas. Nicholson, Benjamin Robinson and Henry Alger are still living in the township.

Charles Miles was the first Justice of the Peace in the township. He was elected in June, 1819, and re-elected in 1822. In 1825 there were two Justices of the Peace elected-Joseph Dean and Henry Alger. In 1828, Eliel Farr and Henry Alger were elected.

In 1819, Eliel Farr and family, his sons, Aurelius Farr, Eliel Farr, Jr., and Algernon Farr came in from Pennsylvania. Eliel Farr settled on the farm where he now lives, at a good old age, he having seen some eighty-one years.

About the same time, Augustus Porter came in and settled on the lake road, east of the river.

About 1820, Mars Wager settled in the township, on the farm now owned by the Wager family.

In 1821, the first bridge across Rocky River was built, on the lake road. It was built mostly by subscription. Capt. Rufus Wright built the bridge; and when it was raised, all hands, far and near, turned out and spent a week in putting it up; and when the "raising" was completed, Capt. Wright invited all hands up to his house; and the good and generous old Captain brought on the "oh-be-joyful" in great abundance, so much so that they had a regular time of jollification expressive of their joy at having a bridge across the river. The spree went on to such quick time that the magistrate of the township jumped up on the table and danced a jig among the bottles and tumblers about for keeping with the good old tune of "Yankee Doodle." which caused a roar of laughter, when they parted in friendship.

And here we close this chapter, in 1821.

CHAPTER III

I will give you a brief history of one family and their sufferings, whilest there are other families who could tell you about their hardships and privations in settling in this country in those days

When Nathan Alger and his wife arrived here, June 7th, 1812 all his personal property consisted of an old French watch, an axe, part of a "kit" of shoemaker's tools, and seven cents in cash, and no household goods except a bed. They had no provisions on hand, and he owed ten dollars of borrowed money to begin with. He built a log cabin 15 by 15 feet inside, one story high, with a "stake and ridered" roof, as we used to call a roof covered with wide, thin staves, and poles laid on to keep the wind from blowing them off. He split out his floor boards, and hewed out boards for door, a table, and a shoemaker's bench. (The shoe-bench is still in his possession). When they had got moved into their hut, built their fire in one end against the logs and had brought in their "catamount" bedstead, table, shoemaker's bench and a stool or two, they found their mansion to be quite roomy and convenient. To describe a "catamount" bedstead—say take four round sticks of wood of the size and length desired for posts, bore holes in them, take four poles, sharpen the ends, put them in for rails, and bottom it with strips of elm bar, and you have a fair sample of a bedstead in those days.

But I will return to the story. All the iron ware they had for use the first summer was the half of a tea kettle he found on the beach of the lake. The kettle was broken from top to bottom and the half in question had the spout on it, into which they drove a plug. They used the spout for a handle. In the fall they bought a two quart kettle and a piece of rod for a bail, at the moderate price or $1.50, which rendered them quite comfortable. (The kettle is still in the family.)

In the fall of 1812, he went thirty-six miles to Mentor, four miles west of Painesville, and thrashed wheat for Ebenezer Merry, Esq., for every tenth bushel and fanned it up in a board fan, to get bread to live on.

About the first of March, 1813, he took a yoke of oxen and a wagon belonging to his father's estate, took with him his axe and a log chain which were two indispensable articles in those days, when one went with a team; and a blanket to cover up his load; and went to Abrham Bishop, in Euclid; to get a load of provisions for his mother and her family; (the provisions had been bought by his father before his death;) and also to get some for his own use He got over 200 lbs of fresh pork, and salt to cure it with; quite a quantity of corn meal, some flour, &c; bought a bushel of flaxseed to sow in the spring, for people in olden times made their own cloth, and when he got back to Cleveland, he bought a new axe of "Uncle Abram," and run in debt for that. It had thawed while he had been gone, and he was afraid to venture on the ice to cross the river, but a man standing by said he could pilot him safely across, so on they went, and when they had got about half way across, down went the team, wagon and load, into the drink; the wagon turned wrong side up, but the good people of Cleveland soon rallied to his assistance. One ox was drowned. They got out the live ox and wagon, and three bags of meal, well wet up, this was all that was left of the load. He left the wagon and meal and started for home with the live ox When he got to Rocky River, he met a man who lived in Euclid, sold the ox to him, received a little money, and was to have the balance in provisions.

Among the dainties in the line of meals were raccoons and woodchucks. You may be inclined to ask why he did not kill a deer, as they were plenty in those days. The fact is, he was not a hunter. At one time they lived five weeks without one mouthful of bread, meat, butter or milk in their house, and two weeks of the time they had no salt. Perhaps you may ask what they lived on! The answer is potatoes and beans.

In the fall of 1813, he went to Cleveland and tried to find a chance to work and get a little salt. He spent the day without success. At night he met with S.S. Baldwin, of Newburgh, who offered him salt for work. He then laid himself down on the bar room floor at Wallace's until morning, and then went to Newburgh and worked nine days for fifty pounds of Onondaga salt. Work was then worth one dollar per day. On the eleventh day, (Sunday excepted,) he carried the salt on his back sixteen miles from Newburgh to Rockport and not a little rejoiced to get it at that. Then it was ten miles, the way they had to go, from the Alger Settlement to Cleveland.

In the summer of 1814, he went to old Capt. Hoadley, in Columbia,-who offered to give 100 lbs. of flour for chopping an acre of heavy timber and piling the brush, the logs to be chopped from 14 to 16 feet long, and rail timber 11 feet. He then on the strength of the contract took about 50 lbs. of flour and carried it home on his back, ten miles, five miles of the distance through the woods where there was not even a marked tree to guide his way, and said to his wife, when he got home "We shall not want for flour any more, for I have found a place where I can get 100 lbs. of it for chopping an acre."

We have now given you a part of their history for the first two years and a half they lived in the township. They kept house almost two years before they owned a cow, and then he ran in debt for one. Soon after they bought a cow, they bought a small dinner pot that held about six quarts, and they not only boiled their dinner in it, but made a lid and a dasher to it, and churned their butter in it. He had no team until he had been here five years, and then he ran in debt eighty dollars for a yoke of oxen, and knew not where their first dollar was coming from to pay for them with.

To close this chapter, I will say that they are still living on the farm they first settled on, at the advanced age of three score years and ten, possessed of the good old Yankee feelings and principles that characterized them in their youth, and invite their friends and acquaintances to give them a call.

CHAPTER IV

I had thought that I would say nothing about the war of 1812, but seeing in the Leader of Aug. 25th, an account of an officer in the army getting frightened at a dead Indians bones. I have concluded to say a word about some of the first settlers, and how they got frightened in the summer of 1813, when the British and Indians were prowling about Fort Stephenson, and the feeling and fears of the people were on tiptoe, expecting every day that the fort would be taken and the Indians would be upon them. One night when they were all asleep, they were awakened from their slumbers by a terrible yelling and screaming as they thought, and at once concluded that the Indians were murdering some of their neighbors. They soon ran together to one house, and found that there none missing. They then in their fright concluded that the Indians must be near by and torturing some captive they had taken, which caused the yelling and screeching that has awakened them. So they once prepared for defense, fastened the doors and windows, put their women and children into the chamber, and took down the ladder. Each woman had a good shillelah, and the men with axes, loaded guns and fixed bayonets, stood prepared for battle the balance of the night, expecting every moment that the Indians would be upon them. Daylight came and no Indians in sight, and they concluded that it must have been the yelling of wolves that awoke them, and each of them went to his daily labor.

The wolves, bears, deer, wildcats, raccoons and snakes were very plenty when the first settlers came into Rockport, and occasionally a straggling panther came along.

WOLVES

The wolves would frequently follow people when they were in the woods, and sometimes attack them. Benjamin Robinson was in the woods one morning, about one hundred rods from his house, when all at once he was surrounded by ten or a dozen wolves. He picked up a club and gave them battle, rushing upon those that were nearest whilst those behind followed him up, and when those behind came too close he turned upon them. He fought them in this manner for some time, when they sat down around him to rest; and hearing another wolf howl at a distance, they left him, and he ran for home at the best of his speed.

At another time Robinson and his brother-in-law set a trap for wolves. Robinson went to the trap one morning and found a large black wolf in it. He took a club and knocked the wolf down, and supposing that he was dead, he took off the trap, and seizing the wolf by the hind legs, he slung him over his shoulder and started for home. His wolfship revived and gave quite a howl while Robinson had him on his shoulder. Robinson soon had him on the ground and gave him another killing.

BEARS

Some of the early settlers concluded to have a hunt and kill a bear. So when it had been very cold for several days, and the snow was six or eight inches deep, five of them started out—Each one took a blanket and three days' provisions, resolved to kill a bear before they returned. They had not been out long before they discovered a track. The bear had been gone a day or two, but they concluded to follow him. So they went on, crossing the river several times, and going through gullies and swamps, when just at night they found his bearship in a large stub about fifty feet high. They commenced chopping it down, when the bear made his appearance, coming out at the top of the stub—They shot him and he fell back. They cut down the stub, put a withe in Bruin's jaws, and fitted two sticks into the withe, so that four of them could draw him on the snow, and one carried the axes and guns, in this way they started for home. They had eight or ten miles to go and got home the next day about 10 o'clock. The bear weight 340 lbs when dressed. They sold the skin for $3.75 and each of them had seventy-five cents in cash once more, and they feasted on roasted bear's meat and cakes fried in bear's grease.

At another time Henry Peak shot a bear and wounded it and came into the Settlement to get help to kill it. Four or five men started off with their guns and two dogs, went to the place, started the bear, and gave him a chase for about half a mile. They shot him three times on the run; the last shot brought him to the ground, when they all rushed around him, each one eager to kill a bear, and shot four or five balls into his head in about as many seconds, while his bearship laid dying.

At another time Benjamin Robinson and John Kidney killed four bears on one tree at one time.

DEER

Deer were very plenty, and a good hunter could kill one at almost any time, and those who were not good hunters might spend a week or two and not kill one.

RACOON

The 'coons were very plenty. Dyer Nichols, Benjamin Robinson and Henry Alger, at a time when it was thawing in the winter, went into the woods, tracked the ' coons into trees, cut down the trees and killed forty of the "varmints" in two and a half days.

RATTLESNAKES

The rattlesnakes were so plenty that if a man did not kill half a dozen in a day, he did not claim to have done but a small day's work in killing snakes.

George Peak killed the largest and fattest rattlesnake ever killed in the township. His snakeship measured over ten inches in the girth, and was between five and six feet long. He was so big ... twentyfour rattles on his tail. He was supposed to be one of the first settlers.

Joseph Peak and Henry Peak, in one pitched battle with the snakes around the roots of a hollow tree, killed twenty rattlesnakes and four copperheads, and the same day destroyed eight or ten more rattlesnakes.

One of the old settlers, when he was in the woods hunting for his cows, stepped over a raattlesnake. The snake made a pass at his heel, and struck his fangs into the bottom of his buckskin pants. The man gave a bound, and finding the snake hanging on, he went at the best of his speed for fifteen or twenty rods, when the snake broke his hold to the great satisfaction of both parties -- the man that he was not bitten, and the snake that he was no longer whirling in the air; but the man in his wrath turned upon the snake and slew him.

If this story is doubted by any one, it is a very easy thing to prove it, for the man himself is still living.

FISH

The fish were also very abundant in Rocky river when the township was first settled, and for a number of years afterwards, so much so that one man would catch with a spear in one night from twenty-five to fifty or sixty large pike, and sometimes one hundred. A man by the name of Root caught one hundred and fifty large pike with a spear in one night. People came from all quarters to Rocky river to fish. They used to have great times on the fishing grounds. One night they concluded to gather together all the men in the company whose names were the same as those of wild beasts, and found they had a Painter from Medina, a Bear and a Coon from Wooster, a Wolf from Dover, a Lyon and a Fox from Rockport. They would go into the river and fish until their torches burned out, and then come out and stay by their fires an hour or so for the fish to come up. During that time they would drink whiskey, tell stories, sing songs, and have all manner of fun going on; but at the words, "Light Torches!" all the torches would be stuck into the fire, and in a minute or two the men would be jumping into the river, a lighted torch in one hand and a spear in the other, and then what a scrambling there would be for the fish. Sometimes there would be fifty or sixty blazing hickory bark torches in sight in the river at one time, making about as pretty a torch light procession in a dark night as people get up in our big cities now-a-days

But I am getting my story too long. Suffice it to say, if the fish were as plenty in Rocky river now as they were then, the fishermen would be thicker in Rockport in fishing time than the gold diggers are in California.

BIG HUNTS

I will now say a word or two about the big hunts which were gotten up in early times in this vicinity, as the people of Rockport participated largely in them.

In December, 1818, all hands, far and near, turned out and surrounded the township of Hinckley in Medina county. They marched towards the center of township killing the bears and deer as they went; and when they reached the center, and had killed the game they circled, and had gathered in all they had killed, their day was far spent. So they chopped down the trees, built large fires, and encamped for the night. Some one brought into the encampment a barrel of whisky, and we had a great time in roasting venison, &c. But to give a full description of the affair, and how the Clevelanders roasted a bear, and what a spree they had would extend this chapter to too great a length. It is sufficient to say that we killed between three and four hundred deer, seventeen bears, seven wolves, and some smaller game—In the morning, after paying off the officers, the corporals and the soldiers, those who lived near by had all the venison they could carry on their backs out of the woods, and those who lived a distance took each a good deerskin and started for home.

The Hinckley hunt having turned out so well, we soon started another hunt, and surrounded the township of Parma, in Cuyahoga county. Benjamin Robinson, of Rockport, was one of the captains at this hunt. The officers took the greater share of that game that was killed.—However, we built our fires and encamped for the night. Keeler, from Tinker's Creek, brought in a barrel of whisky. There was but one bear killed and that was by one of the Rockport boys. One of the captains of the hunt living near claimed the bear for his services—went home got his oxen and sled and returned to the camp just after dark, loaded on his bear and started for home. Some of the boys thought he ought not to have the bear, so they went along with him as though they belonged out his way. He went on his oxen's heals "gee Buck" and "haw Brigh," so as to dodge the trees. Part of the company kept him busy in conversation about the hunt, when the bear slid off the sled, and he went on a half mile or so before he missed it. All hands returned to the camp in search of the bear, but it was nowhere to be found, and no one knew anything about the affair. In the morning they all started for home, faint and tired, but not burdened with game.

CHAPTER V

We have now given you a brief history of the first settlement of Rockport up to 1821, according to the best of our recollection and what few memoranda we have on hand; but we don't claim to be perfect. As we have only brought our history up to 1821, we leave the last thirty seven years of Rockport for those who have more time to write and are better acquainted with the affairs of the township.

We wish to make a few comparisons between what in the township was then, in 1821, and what it is now, in 1858. Then there was one bridge across the river in the township, now there is four; then it was an almost unbroken wilderness and timber was of but little value, and now it is a cash article and firewood is worth from fifty to seventy-five cents per cord standing; then there was perhaps thirty families in the township, all told, now there are three or four hundred; then they all lived in log cabins, with two or three exceptions, now they live in houses and some have splendid mansions; then they had forest trees and mud around their cabins, now many of them have beautiful ground, graveled walks, splendid evergreens, with shrubs, flowers and vines, and all that taste could wish; then, I think, we had no schoolhouse in the township, now we have good school houses, built at a cost of from four to twelve hundred dollars each; then we had no regular preaching or religious society in the township, the first Methodist society being organized in 1822, the first Baptist church in 1832, the first Congregational Church in 1835, and the first Freewill Baptist Church in 1840; then there was no meeting house in the township, now there is six—two Methodist (one has a steeple and a bell), one Baptist, one Freewill Baptist, one Sweedenborg and one Roman Catholic; then there was but a few roads in the township, and some of them so bad that an empty wagon was a load for one team, now there are good roads running in every direction and two plankroads and two railroads running through the township; then letters and newspapers were carried through the township on horseback at a slow pace, now the iron horse takes them along at the rate of forty miles an hour, and as several telegraph wires run through the town, if you wish to hold converse with your friends east or west, the lightning is at your command to carry your words. Then there was not a buggy in the township, and I believe there was not even a one horse wagon, now take the buggys and all descriptions and they are to be counted by hundreds, then our wives and daughters thought it no hardship to walk two and even three or four miles on an afternoon's visit, and home again at night, now if they have a mile to go they need a conveyance; then our young men thought it no hardship to take a knapsack on their back and start off on a journey of four or five hundred miles on foot, now if they have a few miles to go they must have a horse and buggy to go or go on the railroad; then our wives and daughters could spin and weave, milk cows, make butter and cheese, cook our dinners, wash the dishes, work in the garden and raked hay if occasion required, now they can play on the piano or melodeon, do fine needle work, and all of them can read novels, dress fine, wear hoops, ride out for pleasure, and make calls. But perhaps I am drawing too close a comparison, if so, I will beg pardon and will forbear.

In the 20's and 30's many new settlers arrived, including Isaac Warren in 1822 who settled near the present Madison and Warren Road area. In 1830 Jonathan Spencer bought 125 acres in the southwest corner of the township but would not move to the area until five years later. By 1830 John West owned 700 acres south of Lorain and east of West 140 where in 1842 he built his home, operated a stock farm and built a pond with rowboats and a picnic grove. It would become known as West's Park and eventually be the name of the community. In 1835-36 the first settlers west of the river in what would become Fairview Park established their homesteads. This included Jonathan Spencer in the far west, Stephen Jordan in the eastern part, Benjamin Mastick in Mastick Valley, and Russell Hawkins in the center.

Land for Sale.

The subscribers offer for sale 3,917 acres of land, situated in Rockport, Cuyahoga County, which will be sold in lots convenient for farms, at reasonable prices, and upon accommodating terms. From the quality and situation of these Lands, it is presumed they will please those who wish to procure farms.

For particulars, inquire of the subscribers, in Cleaveland, or of Henry J. Canfield, in Rockport.

Samuel Cowls,
Leonard Case.

"Cleveland Herald", Nov. 16. 1827
Western Reserve Historical Society

Although it is not known for certain, it appears that only the very first settlers built real log cabins. Among the earliest pioneers, there were several attempts to construct a mill. At least one sawmill was in operation before the township was erected in 1819. This provided a source of cut lumber at an early point in the development of the township.

Log cabins were room size square or rectangular units made of horizontal log walls. The strength of the structure was dependant on the four corner joints. These joints could have been notched, dovetailed, lapped, saddle jointed or tenons inserted into slots of an upright post. The principal problem with the log home was the difficulty in adding on to the structure when more room was needed. Framed additions and porches were commonly added to log homes as sawmills supplied a source of cut lumber.

In some areas, log homes continued to be built even after cut lumber was available. In these cases the logs were covered with shingles or weatherboard. However, it does not appear that any of these "second generation" log homes were ever built in Rockport.

1833 marked a breakthrough in home construction in America. "Balloon frame" construction was developed in the Chicago area and rapidly spread throughout the frontier. This construction was based on precut two-by-four studs positioned 16 inches apart held together by factory-produced nails. It no longer took skilled craftsmen and large crews to hew logs and joints and erect walls. Simple carpentry skills and a couple of men could erect a home relatively quickly. Most of the homes built in Rockport from about 1840 on were of this type of construction.

Figure 5-1a.. Tracks of the Cleveland and Southwestern Interurban pass in front of a "cabin" located on the north side of Puritas Avenue at about West 142nd Street. The date of the photograph is approximately 1920, and it is apparent that the home has been abandoned for some time. *Dr. Harlan Peterjohn Collection*

Figure 5-1b.. A closer view of the cabin reveals that there is an inside vertical support between the door and the window to the right. It appears that the exterior rough sawn boards on the front are left to extend and interlock with boards on the side of the cabin. Given the gaps between the outside boards, it is possible that there may originally have been another layer such as shingles on the outside. Because Puritas Road predates 1835, it is possible that this structure was one of the earliest frame homes in Rockport perhaps even predating "balloon frame" construction. It is unknown when the home was torn down. *Dr. Harlan Peterjohn Collection*

Dr. Jared Potter Kirtland   1793-1877

No history of Rockport would be complete without mention of its most famous citizen, Dr. Jared Potter Kirtland.   Although well documented in many other works (Lindstrom, Butler, Borchert and Borchert, Grabowski), a brief profile of his life in Rockport bears inclusion.

He was born in Wallingford, Connecticut in 1793. His father was the General Agent for the Connecticut Land Company and conducted loads of surveyors, emigrants and provisions to the Western Reserve. When his family moved to Poland, Ohio (Youngstown area), he remained behind living with his grandfather, Dr. Jared Potter, who introduced him to the studies of Medicine, Natural Sciences and Horticulture. He was a member of the first class of medical students at Yale College and received his M.D. in 1815. That same year he married Caroline Atwater. In the early 20's an outbreak of typhus claimed his wife and one of his daughters. With his remaining daughter, he moved to Ohio intending to enter business with his father. However, when typhus broke out in Trumbull County, he was immediately called upon as the recognized authority and quickly became known as Ohio's best and most beloved doctor. In 1825 he married Hanna Toucey. Beginning in 1828 he served three consecutive terms in the state legislature and was instrumental in prison reform. Throughout this time he continued his studies of the natural sciences.

When his second wife died in 1837, Kirtland moved to Cleveland to live with his daughter and her husband Charles Pease. This same year he purchased 200 acres in Rockport. The property was bounded by what is currently Bunts Road, Madison Avenue, and the Lake. Here he spent many hours in horticultural pursuits and delved into the Natural Sciences with vigor. He was asked to take charge of zoological research in the first Geological Survey in Ohio. Due to lack of funds in the State Treasury, the

Figure 5-2. Home of Dr. Jared P. Kirtland. *Atlas of Cleveland 1874*

survey was abandoned the next year, but he continued the research on his own. His final report listed 585 vertebrates including a catalogue of birds, reptiles, fish, mollusks and insects. That same year he accepted a Professorship of Medicine at the Ohio Medical College in Cincinnati which was the leading medical school in the West.

In 1839 he built his home from sandstone cut from a quarry on Cook Avenue. In 1841 he became professor of Medicine at Willoughby Medical College which was split in 1843 to form new Medical Schools in Cleveland and Columbus. He retained his Professorship in Cleveland until 1864. This college eventually became the Medical School of Western Reserve University.

In 1844 he helped organize and was the first president of the Cleveland Horticultural Society. In 1845 he organized the Cleveland Academy of Natural Sciences and served as president for 25 years. This would eventually become the Cleveland Museum of Natural History.

In 1847 he was elected as President of the Ohio State Medical Society and presented a paper on the connection between impure drinking water and typhoid fever. He was instrumental in the eventual shift of Cleveland drinking water to Lake Erie rather than the contaminated ditches and streams of Cleveland. For three years beginning in 1850 he helped establish and edit the *Family Visitor*, a weekly newspaper relying heavily on articles about natural history.

His knowledge of Rockport soils and horticulture led to the creation of many hybrid plants suitable for local conditions, and was primarily responsible for the development of the tremendously successful fruit industry of Rockport. He developed 26 varieties of cherries, 6 of pears, and his name is borne by a strawberry, raspberry, a fossil plant, mollusk, snake and warbler. He made perfect wax imitations of flowers and was an excellent taxidermist.

If he came into possession of a rare fruit or plant, his first thoughts were to share it so others could enjoy it with him. He was especially fond of the neighborhood children, and if any became interested in natural history, he would go to their homes and help. There is little doubt as to why he was referred to as "The Sage of Rockport."

On the national level the boom and bust cycle inherent in capitalism did not have much effect on the newly arriving settlers. They were simply too busy trying to eke out an existence. The war of 1812 made Cleveland a trading center, but the exchange of goods was mostly through bartering. There was little hard money (gold and silver coins) in the frontier, and paper money had little value.

In 1819 a financial panic swept across the country. The growth in trade following the war of 1812 came to an abrupt halt, and banks failed throughout the country including some in Cleveland. Following recovery from that "panic," 1837 marked the end of a period of wild speculation. Everyone was getting rich on paper. Many people expected to make a fortune by buying land, holding for a year and selling at exorbitant profits. When the crash came in 1837, almost every bank and businessman in Cuyahoga County failed. Building and railroad construction came to an immediate halt (Kubasek, 1976). Early banks, exchange brokers and insurance companies had note-issuing privileges. As a result, with each financial panic or depression, these institutions and their currencies failed. It was not until 1863-64 that a national currency was established. Government bonds to finance the Civil War secured the currency. In 1865 state bank notes were no longer issued, and the value of paper money was finally stabilized.

The census figures for 1830 show that 368 people were living in the township and 44 of them were free colored. By 1840 the number of residents was 1235 of which 46 were free colored. For several decades there were more African-Americans living in Rockport than anywhere else in the county. This was probably due to the influence of George Peake. There were at least two African-American families living on the Kirtland Estate including Andrew Farmer who managed Kirtland's extensive farm and gardens (Borchert and Borchert, 1989). The census also lists eight schools and 516 scholars in the township.

To keep up with the growth, new roads were being built. The County Road Records indicate that in 1824 Warren Road was laid out, and in 1832 Fischer Road and Spencer Road (West 220th Street) were built along with an extension of Riverside Drive to Lake Road. In 1835 Puritas Road was extended from the West Bank of the river to intersect Wooster Road in the southwest corner of the township. Butler (1949) indicates that Warren Road was built as a center line in the township east of the river.

ROADS-THE ESSENTIAL TO COMMERCE

Even before settlers arrived they were complaining about the lack of roads into and through the new Western territories. Once they arrived they complained about the lack of roads to get their goods to market. Easterners had heard stories about the forested wilderness, but few could appreciate how isolated they were from the settled communities of the East once they were on the other side of the Appalachian barrier.

They felt neglected by the federal government which was not building any roads or canals connecting them to the eastern markets. Their only outlet to national and foreign markets was via the Ohio and Mississippi Rivers to New Orleans. This produced a glut and spoilage of goods on the docks of that port (Gieck,1988).

However, the federal government did have one project called the National Road which was started in Cumberland Maryland and by 1817 had reached Wheeling. However it would be another 16 years before it was pushed on toward Columbus.

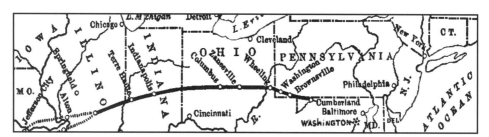

Figure 5-3. In 1806 Congress ordered the construction of the National Road. By 1815 it would extend from Cumberland, Maryland to Wheeling, but would not reach Columbus, Ohio for another 16 years. *Gregory and Guitteau, 1929*

Early roads were only slightly wider than the original paths cut through the wilderness. They were wet and muddy six to nine months a year, frozen ruts in the winter, lacked bridges, were full of stumps and rarely, if ever, were they smooth, flat and dry. The first improvements were probably the corduroy roads where logs were simply laid across the road side by side. Later improvements included splitting or sawing the logs length wise and placing the flat side of the half logs on the ground. The surface had the obvious appearance of corduroy and provided a wagon ride of unbelievable jostling proportions. Other disadvantages included floating logs during a rainy spell or the wet season and gaps between the logs where many a horse suffered a broken leg.

Even though the Federal Government gave little support to the west, help would come from the state of New York. In 1817 they began construction of the Erie Canal, connecting Lake Erie with the Hudson River and the markets of New York City. By the time the Erie Canal was finished in 1825, Ohio had begun construction on its own canal system (Gieck, 1988).

Once the Ohio canals were completed in 1827, the State seemed to abandon the burden of laying out state roads and gave private corporations the right to improve certain roads and charge tolls. In 1838

The Plunder Act committed the State to assist any private company that would build a canal, railroad or turnpike by investing in one third of the capital stock of the company. Although the act was repealed in 1840 to save the state from bankruptcy, turnpikes and plank road companies sprang up all over the state (Rose, 1950).

Every community needed good roads. Turnpikes and plank roads were the next step. They evolved almost simultaneously, and in fact the terms are sometimes used interchangeably. In either case they were both toll roads. A turnpike was usually just a graded right of way with stumps removed. It may have been covered with gravel but more often was not, and in some cases existed alongside a plank road (Butler, 1949).

The turnpikes were private enterprises financed by stock subscriptions set up to pay dividends. The roads were built with earth and gravel and were usually 15-40 miles in length. Few ever paid any dividends due to several problems. First of all many people objected to paying tolls and simply bypassed the toll houses. Secondly, many roads were built in advance of development and didn't have any traffic to support them. Then, there was the governmental requirements and regulation of tolls which made it almost impossible to make a profit. Finally, the turnpikes were not much of an improvement over early roads and were themselves often a sea of mud.

Plank roads were organized like turnpikes and promised a smooth, cheap alternative to turnpikes. Promoters predicted that they would last eight years before needing to be resurfaced. But iron covered wagon wheels, metal horse shoes and weather rot usually wore them out in half that time. (Libertyhaven.com). These "Farmers Roads," as they were called, consumed millions of board feet of lumber. The sale of timber helped to pay for many farms and speeded up the clearing of the land for crops (Holzworth, 1970). Plank roads were in use much sooner, perhaps by 10-15 years, in southern Ohio than in the north. It was almost the middle of the century before construction of a plank road was begun in northern Ohio.

The base of the road consisted of large logs flattened on top and bottom. Two parallel rows were laid lengthwise in the roadbed, spaced about the width of a set of wagon wheels. The ends of the logs in each row were staggered to give more stability. The ground was then graded level between the rows of logs and tapered away on the outside. Two inch planks were then nailed across this base. Wherever possible, the road-bed adjacent to the planking was graded for lighter vehicles. Short passing places were made at intervals by doubling the width of the planking. Nevertheless, disputes frequently arose when an oncoming rig was met over who had the right of way and who had to take to the dirt (Butler, 1949).

Figure 5-4. Plank road toll house at Warren and Detroit Roads. *Lindstrom, 1936*

The Detroit Plank Road extended from West 25th to five miles west of Rocky River. Toll houses were set up at West 65th, West 117th and at Warren Road. By 1852 the entire 188 miles from Cleveland to Detroit was planked (Cleveland Plain Dealer, Sept. 3, 1940).

Maintenance of the toll roads was the responsibility of the proprietors. When roads were taken over by the state, they were maintained by laborers hired with road tax money or by farmers who preferred to work off their road tax with their labor (gev.org.maps/toll-house). By 1870 most Turnpike and Plank Road companies had disappeared which left the upkeep to the counties. A local exception was the toll house at Warren Road which remained until 1901 when Detroit became a free road (Butler, 1949).

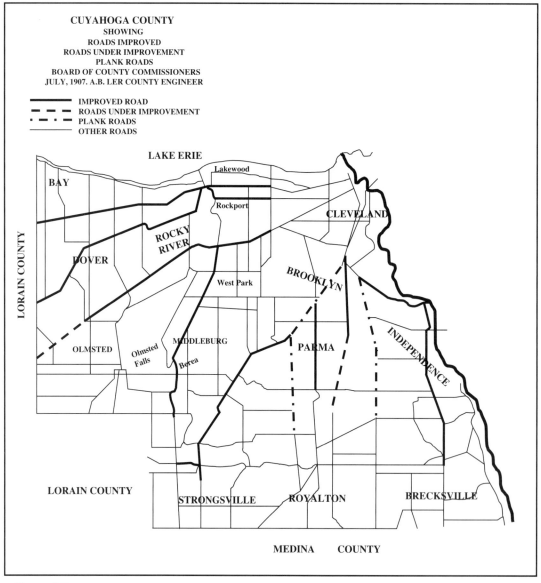

Figure 5-5. A county road map of 1907 shows that plank roads still exist on parts of Pearl, York, and Broadview Roads. *Adapted from Arthur Kouba Collection*

36

With more roads came more travel and in the early 20's the stagecoach was beginning to make its influence felt. The first line was established in 1809 from Cleveland to Painesville. By 1820 lines were being organized to Columbus, Norwalk and Pittsburg. The Norwalk route would pass through Rockport on Lorain Road.

In the summer, the big coaches moved along with relative ease. However, a ride in late winter or spring was a much greater adventure. The male passengers would usually walk alongside to help push and pry the coach from one mud hole to the next. Moreover, they still paid their regular fare. The stagecoach was heavily constructed and could carry eight to nine passengers. Top speed with a four horse team was about eight miles an hour but they generally covered about 10 miles in a day. The establishment of freight wagon lines followed the successful stagecoach lines. Both types of lines carried mail (Kubasek, 1976). By the 1840's, the stage lines would be the primary means of travel with daily service from Cleveland to Columbus, Pittsburgh and Detroit. By 1890 there was hourly "bus" (stagecoach) service between the Cleveland city line at West 98th and Kamm's Corners.

On the Lorain Road turnpike there were toll gates set up at West 117th Street, West 130th Street, West 143rd Street, Triskett Road, and Rocky River Drive. One of the local investors in this venture was a German immigrant by the name of William Sixt. In 1849, he built a large inn and tavern on Triskett at Lorain by the toll gate. This landmark stopping place for weary travelers would later be named the Sherman House after the Ohio Civil War General, William Tecumseh Sherman.

Figure 5-6. The Sherman House 1999 is today the West Park Masonic Temple. *Author photo*

William Tecumseh Sherman (1820-1891)

Sherman was born on February 8, 1820 in Lancaster, Ohio, and educated at the U.S. Military Academy. At the outbreak of the Civil War in 1861, he was put in command of a volunteer infantry regiment as a brigadier general. By 1864 he was made supreme commander of the armies in the West and was ordered to move against Atlanta. He did not capture Atlanta until almost three months later. After ordering the burning of the military resources of the city, he launched his most famous military action, known as Sherman's march to the sea, in which, with 60,000 men he marched from Atlanta to Savannah. He then set out to join forces with Grant in Virginia by marching through North and South Carolina. After three months of fighting he reached Raleigh, North Carolina as the war came to an end.

Following Grant's election to the presidency, Sherman was promoted to full General in 1869 and given command of the entire U.S. Army.

Figure 5-7. The Lorain Street House. *Cleveland State University Library, Cleveland Press Collection*

The Lorain Street House at 15535 was opened in 1860 by Louis B. Harrington. It was located almost directly across from the Sherman House. These were two of the many roadhouses which once ringed the city, within horse and buggy distance of Public Square. Later it became The Rockport Inn and finally in the 1940's, it was Paddy Barrett's Old Homestead. There were small bedrooms on the second floor for summer borders or cattle drovers on their way home from markets in Cleveland. There was a low round building in the back that was originally a stable for trotting horses training at the Rockport Driving Park. This eventually became a dance hall/beer garden (see Figure 9-31e) and finally an auto repair shop (Cleveland Press 2/19/46). In 1913, owner Anna Fishcher exchanged land with the Village of West Park thereby allowing the Village to build their town hall next to the Inn (Figure 11-6a).

During the 1840's Rockport had two Justices-of-the-Peace. One of those was Royal Millard whose first of three terms of office began on June 24, 1843. His journal, found at the Western Reserve Historical Society, seems to be the only official record of any kind still in existence from Rockport Township.

For the most part the Justice dealt with squabbles over simple bad debts. I have included his complete record of one of his more interesting cases. I think you will agree that legalese jargon is not a recent invention. Spelling, grammar, and punctuation are retained in the original.

State of Ohio Cuyahoga County SS.

James L Bowman

vs

Jacob Becker.

Proceeding under the act to regulate the action of forcible entry and detainer had before me Royal Millard a Justice of the Peace in and for the Township of Rockport in said County.

March 18th. 1845. The said James L Bowman made complaint in writing to me the foresaid Justice and which complaint is in substance as follows-

To Royal Millard a Justice of the Peace in and for the Township of Rockport in Cuyahoga County and State of Ohio-

The undersigned James L Bowman a resident of Brownsville in Fayette County and State of Pennsylvania doth hereby make complaint to you against one Jacob Becker for this—That the said Jacob Becker hath enssine the 15th of April in the year 1844 and doth still unlawfully and forcibly detain from the undersigned possession of the following premises situate in the Township of Rockport in said County of Cuyahoga and described as follows-about twelve acres of land in section seventeen in the original division of said Township with a cabin thereon bounded North East and South by the line of said section seventeen and land owned by Calvin Giddings and west by the old road leaving south from the mouth of Rocky River. The said Jacob Becker entered upon said premises as the tenant of the undersigned. The Lease therefor expired about the time herein first mentioned. and from that time, the said Jacob Becker hath unlawfully and forcibly held over his said time-On the first day of February in the year 1845. the undersigned duly served upon the said Jacob Becker as required by law. Notice in writing to leave said premises.

The undersigned asks possession and restitution Rockport March, 18.th 1845 James L Bowman by his Agent Calvin Giddings.

The said Plaintiff being a non resident of the County aforesaid a Bond with Theophillus Crosby as his surety was duly taken of Plaintiff bye the said Royal Millard and filed with him and Royal thereupon on the same day March 18th 1845 at the said Justice issued a summons to the Defendant an said complaint duly filed by me for appearance and trial at my office in the Township of Rockport in said county. on the 27.th day of March 1845-@ 11:O'Clock AM March 27. 1845. 11" O'Clock AM. at the time and place above designates for trial the parties appeared Summons returned by the Sheriff of said County endorsed "Rockport March21. 1845. served this suit on Jacob Becker by leaving a true copy of the same this day at his place of residence

fees - service 35 cents   Hearon Beebe Sheriff

milage 50 cents   by E I Root Deputy

copy 25 cents

at the same time on application of the Defendant the cause was adjourned until March 31.th 1845 at 11'O'Clock AM March 29.th 1845 subpoena issued on the part of the defendant for Hamilton Stockham (and) Harlow Landphair witness served by deft.

March 31.st 1845 11'O'Clock AM parties and witnesses present recd an application of the defendant issued a warrant for a jury to appear at said time and place of trial an delivered the same to the sheriff of the County. aforementioned warrant returned by the sheriff office endorsed "Rockport March 31.st 1845. Served this venire by summoning Benjamin Spencer Russell Hawkins John sweet John P. Spencer Jonathan Spencer Dennis Dow as jurors in this Case

fees-service $2.00. Milage 60 cents   Hearon Beebe Sheriff

attendant on Court 75 cents"   by E I Root Dept"

All the said Jurors appeared ant the said Benjamin Spencer was chalanged by the defendants and Harry B Millard a talesman were duly impaneled and Sworn and the parties proceeded to trial. Calvin Giddings produced a power of Attorney as witnessed entered by James L Bowman instructing him his agent James L Bowman of the Borough of Brownsville Fayette County Pennsylvania have made constituted and appointed and by those presents do make and appoint and in my place and sted put and depute— Calvin Giddings <u>Farmer</u> of the town of Rockport, County of Cuyahoga and State of Ohio my true and lawful attorney for me and in my name to take charge and possession of a tract of land which I own adjoining the residence of said Giddings in the said Town of Rockport County and State aforesaid and in my name to yearly rent on ——the same in whole or in part to suitable and good tenants and to have a supervision over the same and in my name and for my use to ask demand due for and recover and receive any rents dues on demands coming to me as proceeds from the same And further in my name and on my behalf to prosecute according to law for trespasses committed on the said tract of land and if necessary to employ an Attorney at low for the better? prosecution of the same. Giving and granting? with my said Attorney by these presents my full and whole power in and about the premises as herein before specified, to have use and take all lawful ways and means in my name for the purposes aforesaid and upon the recipt of any such dues or sums of money recipts or other sufficient discharges for me and in my name to make and deliver.

Hereby ratifying and holding for firm and effectual whatsoever and said Attorney shall lawfully do in and aborit the premises by virtue hereof - in witness whereof I have hereunto set my hand and seal this seventh day of January AD One Thousand Eight Hundred and forty five

James L Bowman   seal

Pennsylvania
Fayette County

Notamal   seal

Personally appeared before me the subscribers a Notary Public in and for said County duly commissioned and sworn. James L Bowman who signed the within letters of Attorney and acknowledged the same to be his act and deed for the purposes therein stated. In witness whereof I have thereunto set my hand and affixed my notanal seal this seventh day of January AD 1845

Henry Barkman NR

Also - the Plaintiff produced a written notice duly served on the defendant - to leave the premises as evidence. - The complaint was law before the Jury - William Giddings and Solomon White were sworn and Examined on the part of the Plaintiff. Calvin Giddings was sworn but not examined. Hamilton Stockhorn and Harlow Lanphair were sworn and examined on the part of the Defendant and after hearing the evidence the jury repaired to a room by themselves under ——— of the sheriff and returned their verdict to the aforesaid Justice as follows. We the Jury do find that the defendant is guilty in manner and form as the Plaintiff hath in and by his said complaint set forth - we do further find that the Plaintiff did notify the
defendant ten days prior to the issuing of the writ in the course - to leave the said premises as required by law

Russell Hawkins	John P Spencer
John Sweet	Dennis Dow
Jonathan Spencer	H. B. Millard

It is therefore considered by me the said Justice that the said plaintiff have restitution of the premises mentioned and described in his said complaint and recover of the said defendant the costs herein taxed at Nine Dollars and fifty cents. Defendants costs is one dollar and thirty four and one half cents

Justice fees Plttff Sherriffs fees Plttff   Witness fees Plttff
Summons $0-25   service on summons $0-35`   Solomon White $0-50
venrie $0-25   milage $-50   William Giddings 0-50
swearing 6 jurors 0-24
swearing 3 witnesses 0-12 milage   venrie   2-00 Defts-costs-Justice
court fees   0-75   0-60   Justice fees-subpoena -12 1/2
trial   0-25   Attending court   0-75   1 add- witness   0-04
satisfaction   0-10   swearing 2 witnesses 0-08
                                                                    continuance   0-24 1/2
Transcript 0-31 1/4 Deft. April 1985   0 -10
                                                                    Defts Costs witnesses 0-34 1/2
Jury fees
Russell Hawkins 0-50   Dennis Dow 0-50   Harlow Landphair 0-50
John P Spencer 0-50   Jonathan Spencer 0-50   Hamilton Stockham 0-50
John Sweet 0-50   H B Millard   0-50

Royal Millard Justice of the Peace

****

CHAPTER 6

Wilderness No More (1850-1900)

Ohio Governor Reuben Wood Lives in Rockport

Reuben Wood was born in Middletown, Vermont, in 1792 or 1793; he was the oldest son of the Rev. Nathaniel Wood, who had served as a chaplain in the continental army during the Revolution. He received his early education at home, but after his father's death, he went at the age of fifteen to live with an uncle in Canada, where he pursued studies in the classics and the law. At the outbreak of the War of 1812, he was conscripted into the Canadian Army but made his escape in a hazardous crossing of Lake Ontario in a small boat with another American. He served for a short time in the American army and at the close of the war returned home to aid his widowed mother on the farm. He also taught school and completed his legal studies in Middletown.

In 1816 Wood, married Mary Rice and two years later moved to Cleveland, Ohio. He is said to have arrived in town with his wife and infant daughter and only a dollar and a quarter in his pocket. So poor was he that, when qualifying for admission to the bar, he walked form Cleveland to Ravenna, where the supreme court was in session to receive his certificate. Cleveland at that time was a village of six hundred and had only two other practicing attorneys, Alfred Kelley and Leonard Case. Wood was elected President of Cleveland in 1821.

Through his energy and ability, Wood soon gained a wide reputation and was drawn into politics. He was elected to the state senate three times serving from 1825-1830. In 1830 he was elected by the general assembly president as judge of the court of common pleas for the third judicial circuit. In 1832 and again in 1839 he was elected a judge of the state supreme court serving until 1847.

When Wood was inaugurated as governor in December of 1850, the constitutional convention was in progress. The new constitution was adopted the following year. This document provided for the election of officials in odd-numbered years, thus limiting the incumbent governor's term to one year. He was reelected by a wide margin to a second term.

Of great significance is the mass of new legislation passed by the assembly during his second term to carry into effect the provisions of the new state constitution. In 1853, Governor Wood resigned to become the American consul in Valparaiso, Chile, where he remained until 1855 when he returned to Cleveland to practice law. Soon thereafter he retired to his beautiful farm, "Evergreen Place" (160+ acres on the lakeshore just west of the Rocky River) and engaged in farming until his death in October of 1864. He was buried on his farm, but the body was later removed to Woodlawn Cemetery in Cleveland.

As an individual, Reuben Wood was energetic and forceful. He was a capable lawyer, a conscientious legislator and an excellent trial judge. His tall, lean frame gave him the nickname, "Old Chief of the Cuyahogas." As judge and governor during a critical period in the state's history, he served Ohio well (S. Winifred Smith, Ohio Historical Society).

One hundred and forty one years later, Rockport would send another native son to the Governors Mansion when Richard F. Celeste would be inaugurated in 1983. Could Rockport be the "Cradle of Governors"?

The census of 1850 reveals that 1441 people lived in the township in 261 "dwelling houses." In 1854 the first detailed maps of Cuyahoga County appeared. These atlases, drawn from plat maps, (Fig. 6-1) show the property owners in the township as well as the roads. The Rockport map shows a brand new feature in the area. For the first time two railroads cut diagonally across the southeast portion of the township. These would have great economic impact on things to come. The arrival of the railroads soon had an effect on some of the plank road companies. In Strongsville, for example, the arrival of the trains to nearby Berea caused an immediate decline in traffic on the Wooster Pike (Rt. 42), and the stage line was discontinued. Because of the decreased toll revenues on the Pike, there was not enough money to maintain the plank road so the planks were torn out from Albion back to York Road (Strongsville Historical Society, 1967).

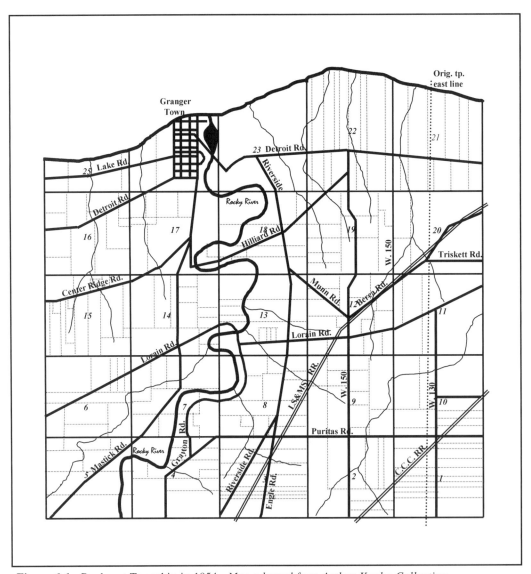

Figure 6-1. Rockport Township in 1854. *Map adapted from Arthur Kouba Collection*

Figure 6-1. Rockport Township Owners Of Record 1854

Section 1. W. Tortwine, F. Bonner, C. Vanger, J.W. & F.H., J. Gorman, Codun, State of Conn., C. Mack, W. Mack, J. Mack, Johnson, J. Blank, J.K., J. Morott.

Section 2. Stickland & Gaylord, F. Granger, J.G.P. Reitz, Shuster & Inglehart, J.G.C., J. Peterson, F. Oakly, H. Smith.

Section 3. J. & A. Moan, S. Gardner, D. Sloan, S. Flewelling, B. Baker, E. Bassett, M. McMuller.

Section 4. B. Mastick, E.R. Rockwell, N. Rockwell, S. Flewelling, E. Bassett, N. Foley, B.F. Andrews, A. Dunham.

Section 5. J. Spencer, B. Spencer, H.D. Johnson, B. Stetson, M.C. Baker, Dan & Dan Dennison, Thomas C. & C.F. Ruggles.

Section 6. F. Granger, A. Potter, J. Sweetzer, L. Hawkins, R. Hawkins, J.L. Anthoney, J. Spencer, J.B. Spencer, B. Spencer, H.D. Johnson.

Section 7. L. Rockwell, M. Jordon, Royal Millard, B. Mastick, B.A.&E Mastick, A. Mastick, Robert Fife.

Section 8. J. Stranahan, A. Colburn, N. Dykes, E.M. Dykes, G. Copeland, W. Reeves, R. Wood, W. McCay, Wm. Jordon, H. Moore, P. Lanhoff.

Section 9. G. Copeland, T.E. Warren, T.L. Warren, B. Bly, S. Flewelling, J.M. West, S.&J. Bitterman, J.H.D., L.B. Harrington, C. Rheim.

Section 10. Foot & Hoyt, Robert Hicks, J.W. Day, J. Doerr, J.H., C. Myers, State of Conn.

Section 11. Leonard Case, J. West Jr., R. Hooper, Osborn Case.

Section 12. Wm Brown, C.H. Higgins, J.M. West, J. West Jr., D. Harrington, W. Coon, J.S. Coon, D. Lafler, H.H. Alger.

Section 13. E.C. MacCay, F. Granger, A. Colburn, H. Alger, J. Stranahan, J. Phillips, P. Jordon, H. Lamphier, S. Flewelling.

Section 14. Heirs of Gideon Granger, W. Story, B.W. Brown, C. Giddings, T.S. Brewster, H. Lamphier A.&F. Lewis, F. Granger.

Section 15. H. Clark, N. Schondrof, T. Foot, Heirs of S. Pease, A. Lamphere, R. Hawkins, A. Bentley, John D. Taylor, I. Highby, S. Lowell, J. Dailey.

Section 16. A. Farr, E. Farr, C.H. Olmsted, C. Deming, A. Dean, George C. Merwin, J. Bidwell, J. McMahon, A.S. Farr.

Section 17. R. Kennelly, Gov. Reuben Wood, L. Dean, D. Myers, Calvin Giddings & Benjamin Finne, Calvin Giddings, S. Jordon.

Section 18. H. Barnum, J. Gleason, P. Mackivit, Heirs of N. Churches, S. Flewelling, F. Granger, D. Lafler.

Section 19. A.M. Wager, James Kidney, Thomas Warren, Wm. Brown, J.B, Warren, J.E. Warren, I. Warren, D. Lafler, E. Ackley, J.E. Giddings, M. Barnett.

Section 20. H.L. Whiteman, Leonard Case, R. Hopper.

Section 21. T.S. & R.H. Hurd, H.&A.E. Fowler, W.B. Smith, Stone, James Nickerson, Dr. J.R. Kirtland, P. French, R.G., T. & H.B. Hurd, Heirs of D. Carter.

Section 22. J. Brown, Richard Hilliard, Julia E. Flewelling, S, Flewelling, Heirs of Mars Wagar, John Honan, Delia Paddock, J. Nickerson, Dr. J.P. Kirtland, James Kidney, J. Hall, I. Kidney, M. Barnett.

Section 23. J. Cannon & J. Colahan, F. Granger, Joseph & Sarah Hall, W.D. Beall, S. Flewelling, H.D. Johnson, Leonard Case, Heirs of G. Fitch, T.P. Mays, H.D. Johnson.

Section 24. E. & P. Wright, Gov. Reuben Wood.

Section 25. Gov. Reuben Wood, George B. Merwin, J. McMahon.

In 1850 the Cleveland, Columbus, and Cincinnati (eventually known as "The Big Four Railroad") was the first Railroad to arrive in the township with a train from Wellington on its way to Cleveland. The Lake Shore and Michigan Southern Railroad arrived in the township in 1852 via Sandusky, Elyria and Berea. A switching yard was built between West 150th and Lorain, which would become known as the West Park Yard. A passenger station was built just north of Lorain Avenue. These two railroads would eventually become part of the New York Central System, and each would have a major influence in the development of the township.

Figure 6-2. When this photo was taken on May 24, 1906, the West Park Yard of the Lake Shore and Michigan Southern Railway was 17 tracks wide. We are looking east. The watchman in the tower on the right controls the gates guarding West 150th Street. The L.S. & M.S. became part of the New York Central System which became part of Penn Central, then Conrail, and today it is a part of the Norfolk Southern System. In the 1940's, before the overpass was built on West 150th Street, the switching activities in the yard were a constant source of irritation to motorists. Today only seven tracks remain in the yard. *Timothy J. Lassan/ John E. Eles Collection*

The Big Four tried to promote allotment developments as commuter communities to increase revenue. One such community, known as McKinley was located on the southeast corner of Smith and Brookpark Roads. It even had its own post office from 1891-1903. The 70-acre allotment had 400 lots. However, it was a complete failure as very few lots were sold and fewer homes built. Almost everything was eventually sold for delinquent taxes (Holzworth, 1970).

Steam engines were not only being used to move railroad trains, but stationary engines were beginning to appear in a variety of uses. In 1855 William McAllister set up a sawmill near the intersection of Triskett and Lorain. His use of a steam engine for power was the very first in Ohio. By 1906, his son,

Claude, moved the mill to Woodbury Avenue. (Woodbury would eventually be taken by the construction of the West 150th interchange with I-71). Claude's son, Clyde, took over operation of the mill in 1935, and, in 1946 moved it to West Richfield. Finally in 1969, Clyde moved the mill to Jeromesville (near Ashland). At that time it was one of the last operating steam powered sawmills in the state (Vittek, 1981).

1850 opened with the planking of the Detroit Road and a new bridge across the river. Meanwhile, farming had become the largest industry in Rockport. In 1852, Thomas Hern on his (Lakewood) farm produced the best wheat grown in Ohio (Rose, 1950). Kirtland's study of the underlying shales of Rockport led him to the conclusion that the soils were most suitable for grapes. Farmers along the lakeshore throughout the county were specializing in orchard fruits. By mid century, cherries and peaches were being shipped by boat and rail to eastern and midwestern markets, and grape production was increasing every year. There was little wine production as most of the crop was shipped as table grapes. By 1860, Ohio would lead the nation in the value of agricultural products. The railroads obviously provided faster access to the eastern markets for Ohio farmers. The railroads had quickly replaced the canal system because of their greater speed and their general east-west orientation rather than the north-south orientation of the canal system. In this same year, Ohio had more miles of railroads than any other state. By 1870, Cuyahoga County was the grape capital of the country. In Rockport, fruit and grapes were the most important source of revenue, and in 1872 the value of the crop was estimated at $50,000 (Lindstrom, 1936).

After the Civil War when commercial orchard production was declining due to insect and fungus damage, most of the orchardists turned exclusively to the production of grapes. By 1890 there were 5000 acres of grapes in the county concentrated along the shoreline east and west of Cleveland.

A rather innocuous shipment of raw material arrived at the port of Cleveland in 1853. This half dozen barrels of iron ore would portend things to come. By the end of the century, Cleveland would be one of the largest steel producing areas in the world, and the industrial revolution would be in full swing. Even so, Rockport would remain basically an agricultural community. In 1860 the population had only increased by about 350 since the last census bringing the number of residents to 1794 (930 males and 864 females). The population would continue to be concentrated along the lakeshore (Lakewood) and near the mouth of the river (Rocky River).

With its well-manicured estates, orchards, vineyards and farms, Detroit Road would become a favorite place for "Sunday drives" by city dwellers. The 1874 Business Directory for Rockport reflects the agricultural nature of the community. No less than 14 of the 42 listings are agriculture related including nurseries, fruits, vegetables, vineyards, orchards, farming and dairy farming, cattle and horse breeding.

Cleveland Herald June 1, 1861
ROCKPORT OMNIBUS

Mr. A. French of Rockport has put a "bus" on the line from City Hotel, in this city, to The Rockport House, in Rockport. It will run each way once a day, and twice each way Saturday. The "bus" will take packages and parcels and the driver will execute commissions in the city.

Mr. French is one of the most responsible citizens of Rockport, and if the people of that Town properly appreciate his efforts, the "bus" will become a permanent "Institution".

1874 Rockport Township Business Directory

Lewis Nicholson & Co., Proprietors of Lake Erie Nursery, grow every variety of Fruit and Ornamental Trees, Grapevines, Shrubs, Evergreens, &c. In their Greenhouses are kept a complete stock of Flowering and Hothouse Plants. Flowers furnished for Parties, Weddings, &c., at all times. East Rockport.

Wm. Sixt, Propr. of Sherman House. A fine Hall for the accommodation of Balls, Parties, &c., in connection with the house.

John French, Builder, P. O. East Rockport.

C. W. Ranney, Fruit Grower. Every variety of small Fruit in abundance during the season. East Rockport.

Wm. Maile, Propr. of Brickiln and Drain Tile Works, keep constantly on hand every size of Tile at bottom prices, East Rockport.

J. C. Hall, Grower of Fruit, East Rockport.

G. F. Krauss, Rocky River, Propr. Of Restaurant; also, extensive grounds and buildings in connection for Picnics, Excursions, &c., cor. Elm and Detroit Sts.

M. C. Hall, Grower of Fruit and Vegetables; also Plants for sale in season, every variety; East Rockport.

Benno Martinetz, Propr. of greenhouse. All Kinds of Cut Flowers. Wreaths, &c. made up to order in the best manner, at low rates. Detroit Street, West Cleveland.

J. A. Parsons, Contractor and Builder, East Rockport.

Frederick Wright offers for sale a number of choice Lots in what was known as the Granger townplot, Rocky River.

P. S. Clampitt, Painting and Graining. East Rockport.

Gideon T. Pease, Township Trustee.

G. A. Bebee, Propr. Of Rocky River Nursery, grows and has for sale every variety of Fruit and Ornamental Trees, Grapevines, Evergreens, Hedge Plants, Roses, and Flowering Shrubs, East Rockport.

Beech Grove, the most romantic Picnic ground, at Rocky River, close to the Lake. Dining Hall, Confectionery, Bowling Alley, Shooting Gallery, Bath-houses, Flying Swings, &c. in connection. John N. Knoll, Proprietor.

Williams Brothers, Proprs. of the Rocky River Boat House. Steam Yacht, Sail and Row Boats to let. Picnics, Fishing Parties, &c. supplied at all times.

O. P. Stafford, Dealer in Flour, Feed, Groceries, Provisions, and Notions generally, Rocky River.

D. Webb, Butcher, runs a wagon. Meat delivered to any part of town free of charge. Also, Fruit and Vegetable Dealer. East Rockport.

Frederick Mimut, Proprietor of Hotel, one mile south of Lorain St. Plank Road. Large Hall on second floor, fitted especially for accommodation of Balls, Parties, Concerts, &c.

Joseph Z. Filiere offers his Farm for sale, consisting of 39 acres of choice land, located on L. S. and M. S. R. R., six miles from city. Fair buildings, Timber, Orchard, small Fruits, Vineyard, and living Water. For terms, apply on premises.

J. W. Williams, Stock Dealer; also, furnishes milk to Hotels and Families.

Peter Smidt, Propr. Of Grocery and Dealer in Flour, Feed, and general Groceries; also, a fine Hall in connection for Balls, Parties, &c., one mile south of Lindale, on C. C. C. and I. R. R.

John Gahan, Township Trustee.

Andrew Kyle, Postmaster and Justice of the Peace, Rockport.

Henry Beach, Grower of Fruit and Vegetables, East Rockport.

George G. Mulhern, Superintendent of Rocky River R. R.; Office at Murch House.

A. T. Jordan, Grower of Vegetables of every variety, Rockport.

C. R. Jordon, Milk Dealer. Pure milk at wholesale. Rockport.

H. A. Mastick, Postal Clerk of L. S. and M. S. R. R. P. O. Rockport.

D. W. Hogan, Agent for Singer Sewing Machine; P. O. Rockport.

J. A. Potter, Bricklayer and Plasterer, Rockport.

W. E. Eggleston offers his Farm for sale, consisting of 60 acres, desirably located in Rockport. on Coe Ridge; two good dwelling houses, with suitable barns, sheds, and outbuildings, living soft water in abundance, a good orchard of choice fruit, 30 acres of fine garden land. Will sell in whole or part at favorable terms. For particulars apply on the premises.

J. W. & F. J. Spencer, Proprs. of Brick and Drain Tile Works. Every size of Tile on hand at rates to suit the times.

Andrew Worshing. Propr. of Steam Sawmill. Lumber for sale of all kinds. Custom sawing done to order.

D. Dardinger, Proprietor of Summer Boarding House at Tisdale Point. Boat Landing and Extensive grounds in connection for the accommodation of Picnics, Excursions, &c. Rocky River.

John Granger, Farmer and Stock Dealer.

H. Dreyer, Veterinary Surgeon, treats Horses and Stock generally at reasonable rates, Rockport.

G. W. Andrews, Contractor and Bridge Builder.

F. H. Wagner, Dealer in Real Estate and small Fruit Grower, East Rockport.

A. N. Clark, Real Estate Dealer and Breeder of fine blooded Horses.

Smith Woodbury, Fruit and Vegetable Grower, East Rockport.

J. P. Kirtland, M.D., LL. D.

Figure 6-3. Gates Elevator and Mills in South Brooklyn was built in 1893 to serve farmers in surrounding communities including Rockport. *1897 photo from Cleveland The Metropolis of Ohio*

At times the Census Bureau would conduct a special census and provide information about manufacturing and agriculture. One of those was conducted between June 1, 1879, and May 31, 1880, and provided the following information about Rockport businesses.

Special Census June 1, 1879-May 31, 1880

Lumber Mills

Edmund Stroud	6 hands	10 hour days	200,000 feet of lumber
Andrew Wershing	4 hands	10 hour days	100,000 feet of lumber

Brick Yards and Tile Works

John Spencer	3 hands	25,000 common brick	25,000 pressed brick
William Maile	2 hands	200,000 common brick	20,000 pressed brick

Blacksmith

William Crabb
Joseph Scrimshaw
Mark Mitchell

Wheelright

Joseph Scrimshaw

Mill

Edmund Stroud   10,000 bushels wheat, 2,000 bushels other grain, 2,000 barrels wheat flour, 500 barrels rye flour, 10,000 lbs cornmeal, 50,000 lbs feed.

Figure 6-4. Oswald Kamm
Kamm's Corner Development Collection

Oswald Kamm was born in Switzerland in 1845. After comming to this country as a young man, he worked in a grocery store/saloon at West 49th and Lorain. When that business closed, he moved to Rockport and bought four acres of land on the southwest corner of Rocky River Drive and Lorain from Fred Colbrunn. He also married Lena Colbrunn who was a granddaughter of Fred. In 1875 he built his general store which soon became the hub of the community. He was appointed postmaster of the new post office located in his store. Outgoing mail was postmarked Kamm's, Ohio. Every day he had to walk across the valley to the railroad station in Rocky River to pick up the mail. At the turn of the century, the store was also the station for the Cleveland and Southwestern Interurban.

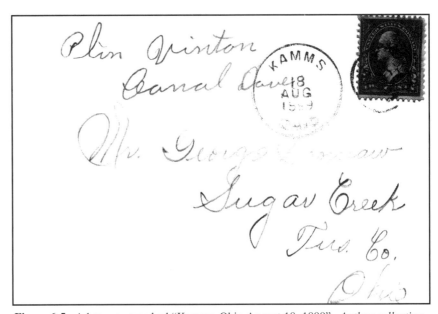

Figure 6-5. A letter postmarked "Kamms, Ohio August 18, 1899". *Author collection*

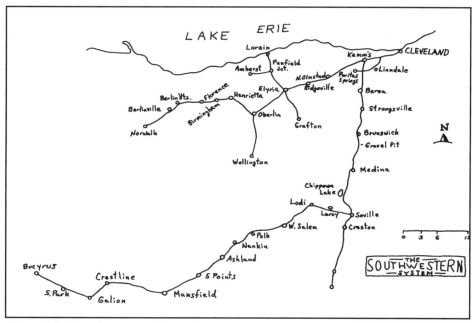

Figure 6-6. Kamm's store was also a station for the Southwestern Interurban Line. Kamm's Corner was a major junction point on the line. *Map adapted from Wilcox, 195?*

He built his three-story home just to the west of the store. In 1937 it was moved to 17134 Fernshaw Avenue. In 1909 he built an apartment building known as The Terraces at 3890 Rocky River Drive. The building remained in the family until 1950. It still stands today and is used as a series of offices.

Figure 6-7a. "The Terraces"(circa 1910). *LaVerne Landphair-Buch Collection*

Figure 6-7b. " The Terraces" today. *Author photo*

49

Mail Spurs the Development of Transportation

From Revolutionary times to the present, the Postal Service has constantly tried to improve transportation of the mail. The Postal Service has helped develop and subsidize every new mode of transportation in the U. S. and experimented with inventions that offered potential for moving the mail faster.

As mail delivery evolved from foot to airplane, mail contracts ensured the income necessary for contractors to improve equipment and build highways, rail lines and airways that eventually spanned the continent. At the turn of the 19th century when post roads were established (any road on which the mail traveled), the Post Office Department purchased stagecoaches and encouraged design improvements for passenger comfort and safety in carrying the mail. They used steamboats 10 years before waterways were declared post roads and awarded mail contracts to railroads two years before railways were declared post roads. In 1896, they experimented with "horseless wagons", and in 1911 the first mail was carried by airplane.

In the early part of the 19th century a customer had to take a letter to the post office to mail it, and the addressee had to pick it up at his local post office. Postage stamps did not come into usage until 1847, but the mailer still had the option to prepay or let the recipient pay or refuse the letter. In 1855 prepayment became compulsory. By 1858 street mailboxes began to appear in larger cities, and in 1863 free home delivery was instituted in 49 of the country's largest cities. By 1890 most post offices were making free home deliveries. However, Rural Free Delivery would not arrive for another 10 years. Like the impetus provided by the Postal Service to modes of transportation, RFD provided an impetus for infrastructure improvement. Hundreds of petitions for rural delivery were turned down because of unserviceable or inaccessible roads. So local governments had to improve and extend those roads. (www.usps.com/history).

Figure 6-8. Rocky River Post Office. This photo from the Cleveland Press Collection at Cleveland State University is undated. In the window next to the post office is a movie poster advertising "Girl Shy." A quick search on the Internet revealed that this silent film, starring Harold Lloyd, was released in 1924.

Rockport	1820-1902
East Rockport	1852-1888
Kamms	1866-1920
Linndale	1873-1873
North Linndale	1873-1899
Rocky River	1877-1925
Lakewood	1888-1901
McKinley	1891-1903
West Park	1894-1919
Clifton Park	1898-1904
Goldwood	1899-1902

Name and date of Rockport Township Post Offices (does not include Cleveland Branch Offices)

By mid-century community conscious-ness was beginning to ex-press itself as residents between Brooklyn Town-ship and the Rocky River requested a separate Post Office for their area. Since 1827 all of Rockport Town-ship was served by a single Post Office near the mouth of the river. In 1852

Figure 6-9. Rockport Township 1880. By this time plots of land were being rapidly divided into smaller and smaller parcels. *Adapted from Arthur Kouba Collection*

51

the Post Office Department created a new Post Office designated East Rockport. Lucious Dean was appointed postmaster, and the office was located in his store near Warren and Detroit Roads (Lindstrom, 1936).

In 1890, Detroit was still the only road to the hamlet of Rocky River so the County Commissioners authorized Lakewood to open Lake Road and Madison Avenue to the river. (Rose, 1950). These newly planned roads would effectively cut the lush lake shore agricultural community into bite sized pieces. The handwriting was on the wall, and by 1892 real estate men were beginning to buy vineyards, orchards and farms to split them up into allotments. One advertisement for the sale of lots included the unique financing plan whereby the buyer could make his first payment from the sale of grapes that were on his land (Lindstrom, 1936).

Meanwhile, at the south end of the township, another type of development was taking place. In the early 1870's the Peterjohn family sold a large portion of their property between Puritas and Brookpark Roads to the American Agricultural Chemical Company. They began to build their plant next to the Big Four Railroad tracks near Brookpark Road.

Edward Peterjohn

Edward Peterjohn, who holds the responsible and important preferment as foreman of the Cleveland Dryer Company's establishment, in Rockport Hamlet, Cuyahoga county, Ohio, was born in that place, November 22, 1865. He is a son of John Michael and Margaretta (Englehardt) Peterjohn, old and honored residents of Rockport Hamlet. Both are natives of Germany and both passed the early years of their lives in the fatherland, the father being seventeen years of age and the mother sixteen when they came to America with their respective parents. The were married in Cleveland, Ohio, March 14, 1844, and shortly after that memorable event they settled in that part of Rockport township which now bears the name of Rockport Hamlet. Here they have ever since continued their residence. John M. Peterjohn has developed one of the finest farms in this section of the State, having been engaged in agricultural pursuits from the time of his advent in the township. The farm comprises thirty-eight acres and all is under a high state of cultivation, while the permanent improvements in the way of buildings are of most excellent and attractive order.

These well known and honored residents of Rockport Hamlet have had ten children, of whom eight are living, namely: Mary A., the wife of Henry Dorr; George J., who married Kate Baumgartner; Anna, the widow of William Barthelman; Fred T., who married Louisa Smith; John M., Jr., who married Julia Brunner, Louisa, the wife of William Renz; Edward, subject of this sketch, and Henry C. The two deceased children are: John who died at the age of three years, and Henry, who lived until his thirteenth year.

Edward Peterjohn grew to manhood beneath the parental roof, securing his education in the common schools of the locality. He early manifested distinctive business and executive ability and to this endowment is doubtless due the preferment he now holds.

He was married, in Parma township, November 12, 1891 to Miss Anna Hoehn. They have one son, Alvin C.

Memorial Record of the county of Cuyahoga and city of Cleveland, Ohio. 1894

Figure 6-10. The Peterjohn home in 1968. *Barbara Unterzuber photo*

The facility opened in 1874 producing fertilizer and commercial acids and provided employment for many workers in the surrounding areas of Rockport and Middleburg. The place was sometimes referred to as "The Stink Factory". Plumes of sulfurous yellow smoke billowed from its stack into the 1950's. This type of manufacturing facility flourished before anyone gave any thought to environmental effects. Ore was brought in by rail. Acid was extracted from the ore leaving a waste product of red slag. This was used to pave many of the roads in southern Rockport and northern Middleburg. It was soon ground to dust by horses hooves and wagon wheels and made an excellent surface in dry weather. As a result these areas were known as the "red road burgs" (Holzworth, 1970, 1973).

Figure 6-11. American Agricultural Chemical Company (circa 1925). Dr.Harlan Peterjohn, who supplied this photograph, is the grandson of Edward who worked here until 1930.

53

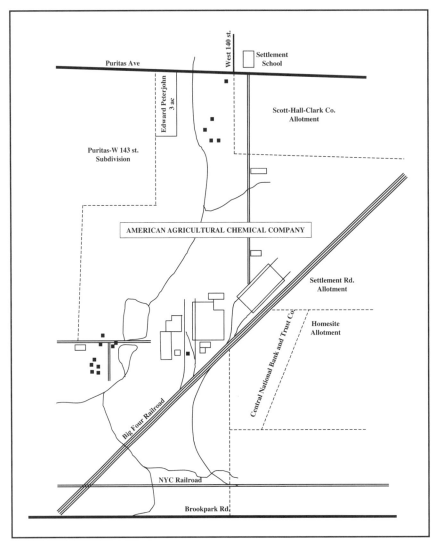

Figure 6-12. The Cleveland Dryer Works plant was located on 160+ acres making it perhaps the largest manufacturing facility in the township.

"During the past two years a number of allotments have been opened along the Puritas Springs car line in and around Rockport. These sections, however, have not yet experienced a building boom. It is to be feared that these allotments will not attract a desirable class of citizens.

One reason for this is that the fertilizing plant is in their vicinity. This nuisance is one to which even the ordinary American cannot be reconciled. Only a certain class of foreigners seem proof against its obnoxious odors and so are able to live and labor within its precincts". Ohio Correspondent June 25, 1910.

Another name for the facility was the Cleveland Dryer Works. The company widened the creek on the porperty to create two small lakes. Several generations of kids sneaked into "Dryer's Ponds" to swim in the summer. Whether or not these ponds were as polluted as some suggest is speculation; however, their original purpose was to provide a source of water for fire protection.

It is probably no small coincidence that in the 1960's with an aging facility and heightened awareness of the Silent Spring by Rachael Carson, this major polluter saw the handwriting on the wall and closed forever. As of this writing, a new business is being built on this factory site (see Figure 16-5). It is now part of an industrial park on West 143rd south of Puritas.

Schools

The first schools in the Western Reserve were the responsibility of local residents, and classes were held in the homes of early settlers. Classes were supported by the few residents and enrollment varied from one to several of the local children. The curriculum was readin' writin' and 'rithmetic, and school terms were of varied duration. The teaching was done by a man or woman for little or no pay. In the early days many of the teachers were married women. However, when the Ohio Public School System was established, married women were not considered eligible to teach (Holzworth, 1966).

The public school system was started in 1821 when the state legislature authorized township trustees and village officials to establish schools and levy taxes for their support. However, the order was not mandatory, and local taxpayers often protested that the cost of education should only be borne by parents of children attending school. The requirements for a teaching certificate were not very great. There were no high schools in the early days, so any person with the basic knowledge of the 3 R's and of good moral character was qualified (Holzworth, 1966).

This system changed in 1837 when state legislator Harvey Rice promoted the free public school system supported by compulsory taxes instead of voluntary contributions. The Common School Education Law gave power and authority to the office of State Superintendent. Schools were established in each township, and following the Ohio custom (as well as all of the Northwest Territory), the name of the township was also given to the school district. These districts were the concern of the voters and were supported by local taxes. The size of the district or sub district was established as five square miles. It was felt that this was a reasonable walking distance for any school age child to travel. Since the school was generally located near the center of the sub district, it meant that some pupils had to walk over two miles of trails, lanes, roads and woodlands to get to school (Holzworth, 1966).

In Rockport, a few schools began to appear in the 1830's and 1840's. Each was built near a settlement. One was built near Grangertown (western Lakewood). A second was built at Phinney's Corners (Center Ridge and Wooster) and a third near Triskett and Lorain.

Around 1846 compulsory school attendance laws were enacted, but in rural areas, these were not strictly enforced. Many farm boys made slow progress due to absenteeism in helping with farm work. By the time they reached the upper grades (of elementary school), they were old enough to marry their teacher (and often did) who might still be in her teens (Holzworth, 1970).

In 1853 a law was enacted which created a local Township Board of Education of three directors. This Board was allowed to hire teachers and maintain property. This system remained until 1904 when rural districts were expanded to five members and given the authority to hire a superintendent who would oversee all the sub districts in the township (Holzworth, 1970).

The exact number of districts or sub districts within a township varied. In Olmsted Township there were eight (Holzworth, 1966), in Middleburg Township there were 10 (Holzworth, 1970), and by 1879 there were nine districts in Parma Township (Kubasek, 1976). As hamlets and villages began to form within townships, they established their own school districts. In 1869, the Ohio General Assembly passed a law which provided that a village must provide an adequate number of primary schools before a high school could be built. As more advanced subjects were added to curricula, teaching requirements became more stringent. "Normal School" training or attendance at a teaching institute followed by an examination was required to obtain a teaching certificate (Holzworth, 1970).

In Rockport, the exact number of districts is not known. There were at least ten, because in 1871 the voters of subdistricts 6, 8, and 10, in East Rockport (Lakewood) voted to establish their own school district. At that time, number six was known as Middle School and located near Detroit and Warren Roads; number eight was near the present West Clifton and Detroit Roads, while number 10 or East School was near Detroit and Cohasset. In 1879, a new school in this district would be called East Rockport Central School. In 1889 when East Rockport became the Hamlet of Lakewood, the name of the school was changed to Lakewood High School (Butler, 1949).

The atlas of 1880 (Figure 6-9) shows the location of other schools in the township besides those listed above for East Rockport: section 3, on Puritas just west of Rocky River Drive; section 5, on Mastick Road near center of the section; section 10, at Puritas and West 130th; section 12 on Lorain Avenue near Triskett and section 13, Rocky River Drive just south of Munn Road.

Figure 6-13. District School No. 1, of Rockport Special School District was built in 1867. Grades were taught on the first floor and the high school was conducted on the second floor. The town hall office was also on the second floor. When the new school opened in 1899 at West 152nd and Lorain, this building was no longer used as a school (Clingman, 1932). However, it was used as the town hall until 1913 when it was badly damaged in a storm. A new town hall was authorized in that same year. *LaVerne Landphair-Buch Collection*

Figure 6-14. Early elementary school (circa 1900) located at Munn Road and Rocky River Drive. *James Foos Collection*

Figure 6-15. Goldwood School in 1912. Located at West 210th Street and Mastick Road. *Fairview Park Historical Society*

Figure 6-16. The Fairview Park Historical Society lists this building as "the second school on Lorain" built in 1860. *Fairview Park Historical Society Collection*

Figure 6-17. Wooster School located on Wooster Road at the intersection of Wooster and Center Ridge Roads was built in 1902. A large sandstone marker identifies the vacant lot today. *LaVerne Landphair-Buch Collection*

****

CHAPTER 7
CROSSING THE RIVER

Today no one gives a single thought to crossing the valley at 70 miles per hour. However, less than 200 years ago the journey from the top on one side of the valley to the other may have required careful planning and half a day's effort. The very first pioneers (around 1800) traveled mostly on foot along the Detroit path and could obviously only cross the river during low flow.

With the signing of the treaty of Greenville in 1800, the land west of the Cuyahoga was opened, and settlers began to trickle westward in ever increasing numbers. In 1809 with the erection of the township and the establishment of local government, it soon became apparent that a more reliable form of river crossing would be necessary. The first tavern owner at the month of the river provided a ferry service across the river. By 1820 Rufus Wright was instrumental in organizing the construction of the first bridge across the river on the Detroit Road. Although an improvement over the ferry service, there were still the treacherous hills to negotiate on either side of the river.

By the 1840's the canal system was in full swing, and the Cleveland area was rapidly gaining in population and commerce. The demand for more and better roads was being heard everywhere as there were repeated complaints about mud and generally dangerous conditions.

The first breakthrough in road surfacing was provided by private enterprise in the form of plank road companies. In March of 1848, The Rockport Plank Road Company was incorporated with George Merwin, President, and M.L. Whitman, Secretary. They had their work cut out for them as the old bridge crossing Rocky River had two stagecoaches capsize in November of that year. In January of 1849 County Commissioners closed the bridge and advised travelers to ford the stream near its mouth.

Two years later, the plank road company completed the new bridge. It was 492 feet long, 42 feet above the water line and approaches were now easier because of the new plank road. Thousands of two-inch planks were sawed by Orville Hotchkiss in Rockport from logs cut in local forests. By 1852 the entire 188 miles from Cleveland to Detroit was planked (Cleveland Plain Dealer, September 3, 1940).

Figure 7-1. This undated photo shows the Rockport Plank Road Company Toll Bridge that was completed in January 1851. The bridge was 24 feet wide with terminals half way down the hills. Toll was 7 cents for one horse, 10 cents for a team and 15 cents for a double-team . *Cleveland State University Library, Cleveland Press Collection*

As the end of the century approached, the Industrial Revolution was in full swing; the population of the Cleveland area had exploded, and most of Rockport had been settled. Farming was still the major activity of residents of the township, and there had been little improvement in roads and bridges since the plank road era. The plank roads were high-maintenance and short lived and in Rockport, most of the roads were still dirt.

With the arrival of the interurbans in the suburbs, the valley again presented a problem. However, by this time the technology and materials were available to build the high steel bridges connecting the tops of the valley walls. The Nickel Plate Railroad built the first of these bridges in 1882. The railroad had to build many bridges on their Buffalo to Chicago main line, and this one was built in record time.

The Cleveland and Southwestern Interurban Company built the first high bridge connecting Lorain Road in 1895. The steel trestle viaduct was 1,219 feet long with nine spans on

Figure 7-2. Test run of the Nickel Plate Railroad over its new multiple-span Bollman-Truss Bridge across the Rocky River in June of 1882. The first through train would arrive in the Village of Rocky River on August 31, 1882. The bridge was 673 feet long and 88 feet high. *Lakewood Historical Society Collection*

metal towers. The 32-foot wide deck was 130 feet above the river. The trusses were connected and assembled on the ground and hoisted into place (Watson and Wolfs, 1981).

Figure 7-3. A Cleveland and Southwestern Interurban freight motor crosses the Lorain Bridge at the turn of the century. *David Schafer Collection*

Figure 7-4a. Top photo is a view looking east towards Rockport. The smoke stack on the left is from the power generating station located at the car house of the Cleveland and Southwestern. *David Schaffer Collection* **Figure 7-4b.** Bottom photo is the same view in 1989 on the new bridge. *Author photo*

The Lake Shore Electric built the first high bridge connecting Detroit Road in 1889. It was actually the fourth bridge built here. The first was in 1821 built by the early settlers, the second was the toll bridge of the Rockport Plank Road Company in 1850 (Fig. B-1), the third was a timber trestle bridge with two iron girder spans that crossed the river at low level, and the forth was the high level Baltimore deck truss bridge with trusses 28 feet wide with an oak-plank floor and stone abutments. Use by newer heavy interurban cars would soon necessitate its replacement (Watson and Wolfs, 1981).

Figure 7-5. The new Detroit Road Bridge is under construction probably about 1909. The original high bridge is still in use on the right. *Northern Ohio Railway Museum Collection*

Bridge and Rocky River, Largest Concrete Bridge in the World, Cleveland

Figure 7-6. Opened in 1910, the new Detroit Road Bridge held the world's record for the largest single span of concrete of 280 feet. The overall length of the bridge was 708 feet. *Author collection*

Figure 7-7. This photo from about 1917 shows a two-car Lake Shore Electric train crossing the bridge. *Cleveland Metroparks Collection*

There were two footbridges that spanned the valley. The first was located near the end of Detroit Avenue and was commonly known as the Cable Bridge. The second, known as "The Grape Vine Bridge," was located near Hilliard and Riverside Drive. Each was a public walkway of planks fastened to two cables for the base and two more cables for hand rails. When they were built or torn down is unknown, but during the first decade of the 20th century they were popular ways to cross the valley. Lakewood children living near the west end of Hilliard used the bridge daily to get to the little red school house at Center Ridge and Wooster Roads (Chabek, 1998).

Figure 7-8. Although no one is certain which bridge this is, from the surrounding slopes it appears to be the footbridge at the end of Detroit Avenue. *LaVerne Landphair Buch Collection*

THE LAKEWOOD POST

LAKEWOOD, O., THURSDAY, JULY 19, 1923

Hilliard Ave. Bridge May Be Placed on Fall Ballot

WILL HAVE A SPAN OF 875 FEET WITH AN 80-FOOT ROADWAY, ENOUGH FOR TWO STREET CAR TRACKS

It will cost Close to One Million; Expert Realtors and Bankers Claim it Will Have Unbounded Influences on Development of City

---

There will be much rejoicing in Lakewood over the announcement that the county commissioners are planning to submit this fall to the voters of Cuyahoga county the authorization of a bond issue, approximately for $900,000 for a new river bridge over Rocky River at Hilliard avenue. The project has been urged persistently by Lakewood and Rocky River people for years, but the announcement that its consummation is virtually in sight will come rather as a surprise.

County Engineer Frank R. Landers submitted designs and specifications for the new structure at the meeting of the county commissioners last Friday, with the recommendation that the measure be placed on the ballot this fall. "Such relief seems imperative," said Engineer Landers in presenting his recommendations. "It would relieve traffic over the Rocky River bridge at Detroit avenue, which is jammed with a constant congestion of vehicles. This congestion is reaching its height this summer".

Official Conference Next Week

The commissioners, in accepting the report, decided to hold a conference with the city officials and civic associations of Lakewood and Rocky River before taking final action to put the matter on the ballot, for the approval of the voters of the county this fall. This joint meeting will be called next week to get individual expressions of opinion. If the final decision rests on the opinions of Lakewood and Rocky River officials, however, there seems no chance that the commissioners will fail to give the project their cordial and official approval.

Figure 7-9. Opened in 1926, the Hilliard Bridge is 896 feet long with three large arches and 135 feet above the water. It is an open-spandrel, ribbed-arch bridge (Watson and Wolfs, 1981). *(Author photo).* In 1999, Ohio Division of Wildlife personnel discovered a nest of peregrine falcons high in the arches of the bridge, one of only 13 nests in Ohio. This bird was removed from the federal endangered species list in August of 1999 but remains on the State endangered list. *Ohio Division of Wildlife*

In the early 30's residents of Fairview and West Park were trying to secure state money to replace the Lorain Road Bridge. The state, however, would only replace such a bridge on state highways. So in 1934, Lorain Road officially became State Route 10. Shortly thereafter, plans for replacement were underway.

Figure 7-10. The old Lorain Road Bridge is being torn down. *Cleveland Plain Dealer, Gayle Walter Collection*

Figure 7-11. The Lorain Road Bridge opened to traffic in 1936. It is 1260 feet long, consists of four parabolic, two-hinged steel arches, and is 130 feet high. All cross bracing was eliminated or concealed to enhance the architectural beauty of the structure. Most of the rivets were countersunk, chipped and ground. The railing design of welded shapes and open malleable iron panels is unique. The colors of the bridge compliment those in the natural setting, a gray for the masonry and a pale green for the steel. It was awarded the title "Most beautiful steel bridge in its class erected in 1935" by the American Institute of Steel Construction (Watson and Wolfs, 1981) *Author photo*

About this same time, residents near Broopark Road were clamoring for an easy way to cross the valley without having to go all the way to Lorain Avenue or into Berea.

RIVEREDGE TOWNSHIP AND THE BROOKPARK ROAD BRIDGE

Although Ohio's smallest township lies within Cleveland, most of its history lies within the boundaries of Middleburg Township, Olmsted Township and the Village of Brookpark.

To understand the evolution of this strange case, we must begin with a look at the development of Middleburg Township (immediately south of Rockport). The first partitioning of Middleburg occurred in 1850 with the incorporation of Berea. The Middleburg Township government continued to operate out of Berea, but residents of the township soon developed a sense that they were being left out of just about everything. Residents on the north end of the township were much more aligned with Rockport and Cleveland since most of them had moved to Middleburg from those communites. There was also a larger market to the north for their goods than there was in Berea.

Dissatisfaction continued until April 18, 1914, when the residents of the north end of the township voted to secede and form the Village of Brookpark.

Meanwhile, on the eastern border of Olmsted Township, there is a strip of land on the east side of Rocky River along Ruple Road of about 150 acres. Children living in this area had to negotiate the hill of Cedar Point Road or Spafford Road in order to attend Olmsted Falls Schools. Furthermore, mail for these residents came from Olmsted Falls. In the early part of this century, these daily journeys were difficult at best and impossible at worst. Given the circumstances, Olmsted Township was willing to turn the area over to Brookpark and make it easier for everyone. There was no objection from the Brookpark Council, so on February 9, 1919, the county commissioners set the township line in the middle of Rocky River thereby allowing students to attend Berea Schools and mail to be delivered from Berea.

Olmsted Township had provided little or no maintenance of roads in this area and unfortunately Brookpark proved no better. So following the November 2, 1923 elections, several residents of western Brookpark (presumably led by the Ruple Road area people) petitioned to secede from Brookpark and form a new township called Riveredge. The petition was intended to remove about three fourths of Brookpark. On December 8, 1923, an election was held, and the separationists lost. Undaunted, another petition was circulated, and a second election was held on January 12, 1924. They lost again. On February 14, 1924, a third vote was held, but this time for an area of reduced size. Once again, defeat. On February 24, another election was held, and this time they lost by only three votes, 100 to 97. Still another vote was held on December 19, 1924, once again, defeat (Holzworth, 1970).

Eastern Brookpark then took matters into their own hands, and an election was held to restore the original township line, which would have left the Ruple Road residents to fend for themselves. This passed overwhelmingly but did not deter the secessionists. Finally at a seventh election on March 13, 1926, they won, at least temporarily. The results placed 3,370 acres in the new township and left the village with 2,935 acres. However, to make matters worse for Brookpark, the new township had the lion's share of the tax base including the lucrative railroad properties (Holzworth, 1973).

The victory was short lived, however, and both Berea and Brookpark had filed petitions with the County Commissioners to delay this action. The Commissioners, obviously tiring of the mayhem, granted the petitions of both communities and returned most of the new Riveredge Township to Berea and Brookpark. The only part that was left was the small part along Ruple Road.

In 1950, these residents voted 22 to 21 to return to Brookpark, seemingly ending a bizarre episode in county government. However, that is not the end of the story.

In the early 30's, Brookpark, Cleveland and the County had been involved in negotiation to pave Brookpark Road and extend it west with a high bridge across the river. In 1932 in a move by the County Commissioners to gain federal support for the project, a 60 acre strip of land on the north side of Brookpark Road, on the east side of Rocky River in the city of Cleveland was legally made a part of Riveredge Township. As the Airport acquired more land from the township on the south side of Brookpark Road, this strip of land became isolated from the rest of the township. N.A.S.A. took part of the land for research

Figure 7-12. This October 1935 photo show the Brookpark Road Bridge shortly after it opened in 1933. The parabolic arches are two-ribbed, with open spandrels. Six of the spans are 192 feet and two are 176 feet. The overall length of the bridge is 1918 feet. It received The American Concrete Institute award for its outstanding design. *Cleveland Metroparks Collection*

buildings, and with the return of the Ruple Road area to Brookpark in 1950, only 48 acres remained of Riveredge Township on the north side of Brookpark Road. Therefore, while the original Riveredge Township was formed out of Middleburg Township, it ended up within the boundaries of the original Rockport Township. However, it was still a part of the Berea School System (Holzworth, 1970, 1973).

In 1956, John Baluh purchased land in the township, and the area became a privately owned trailer park with 477 residents in 243 trailers. With its own fire and police department, Riveredge became a notorious speed trap. In 1978 the township went into default, and in 1983 the airport purchased the remaining land. It has been uninhabited since 1986. A legal battle of annexation to Cleveland or Fairview Park went to the Ohio Supreme Court twice (Van Tassel and Grabowski, 1996). Finally, the two sides reached an agreement and formed a joint economic development corporation to the benefit of both communities (personal communication, Lucian Rego, 2004).

In addition to the high bridges, there were low level crossings at Lorain, Puritas and Cedar Point Roads. These roads were simply valley crossings until the 30's when the parkway was constructed through Rocky River Reservation.

Figure 7-13. The Puritas - Mastick Bridge. *Author photo*

Figure 7-14. Cedar Point two-span bowstring Whipple truss bridge circa 1917. *Cleveland Metroparks Collection*

Figure 7-15.
1936 photograph of the five span reinforced concrete replacement bridge at Cedar Point. *Cleveland State University Library, Cleveland Press Collection*

During the Depression, the Park Board authorized a number of large projects to provide work for the throngs of unemployed through the WPA. One of these was the construction of a Parkway from Detroit Avenue to Cedar Point Road. This project entailed straightening the river, moving fill, constructing of the roadway, and crossing the river at several places.

Figure 7-16. This is the first ford north of Lorain Avenue in May, 1931. *Cleveland State University Library, Cleveland Press Collection.*

69

Figure 7-17. The low fords made the crossing of the river and use of the park impossible whenever the river rose. This photo shows why bridges have replaced all of the fords from Detroit Avenue to Cedar Point Road. *Author photo*

Figure 7-18. On January 15, 1964, the Clifton-West Lake Bridge was opened to help alleviate the crush of commuters to the burgeoning communities of the far West Side. It had been 35 years since the first plans were drawn up for this bridge. Residents of the exclusive Clifton Park area of Lakewood fought hard to keep the bridge out of their neighborhood and no less than ten lawsuits had to be settled before construction began. *Arthur Kuba Collection*

In 1968 contracts were signed for the construction of the I-90 and I-480 bridges. Since both cross the Metropark, pains were taken to make the bridges aesthetically pleasing and satisfying to harmonize with their environment. So with the completion of these bridges in the 1970's, commuters could rush across the valley at 70 miles per hour without any concept of the valley even being present or any knowledge of the history which brought them to this point.

Figure 7-19a. I-480 bridge. *Author photo*

Figure 7-19b. I-90 bridge. *Author photo*

****

71

CHAPTER 8
THE VALLEY

As has been noted earlier, most of the early settlement of the township was centered near the mouth of the Rocky River. The reason for this settlement was that the only westward route from Cleveland and crossing of the Rocky River was near the mouth. Taking advantage of the situation were the earliest tavern owners, Daniel Miner on the east bank and Rufus Wright on the west bank. Miner's 18-24 foot log cabin opened around 1810. His tavern license was issued in 1811 about a year after he was cited for illegal whiskey sales. Miner died in 1813, but his widow continued to run it for a few years after that. (Butler, 1949)

The most famous watering hole belonged to Rufus Wright. His large frame tavern was opened on the west bank in 1816. He operated the tavern continuously until 1853 when he sold it to Jacob Silverthorn who then sold to the Patchen Family. They operated it as the Patchen House for some time until Silverthorn reacquired it. The tavern then became a favorite Sunday place for chicken dinners until it was torn down to make room for the Westlake Hotel in 1920. Of course the Silverthorn name reemerged as the Restaurant in the Westlake Hotel.

Figure 8-1. Silverthorn Tavern March 7, 1917. *Cleveland State University Library, Cleveland Press Collection*

By the middle of the 19th century the area around the mouth of the river was becoming a popular summer picnic grounds and resort area. Ezra Nicholson (son of Lakewood's first permanent settler, James Nicholson) bought a large parcel in the northwest corner of what would become Lakewood, overlooking the lake and extending along the east bank of the river. It encompassed much of the land of today's Clifton Park section of Lakewood. At one time Nicholson volunteered to give his grove to the city of Cleveland for a public park. He was turned down because it was too far out in the country, and newspapers referred to the proposition as "Nicholson's Folly".

Undaunted, he formed a syndicate with Elias Sims, Daniel Rhodes, John Sargent, John Spalding, Joseph Barber, George Hartwell, George Washington Jones, and Thomas Dixon. It was incorporated as the Clifton Park Association. Sims and Rhodes built the elegant Cliff House, Lakewood's most notable and notorious tavern-hotel. It was a popular place for balls, weddings, conventions and outings. Its large, three-story frame building had many guest rooms, a first-class bar on the first floor; a dining room on the second floor (famous for its chicken dinners and creamed potatoes) and a third floor ballroom reputed to be the most beautiful in the entire Cleveland area. There was a veranda along the second story, and a captain's walk observation tower on the roof affording an uninterrupted view of Lake Erie and the mouth of the river. A landscaped front offered a pond with fountains, and two bison were kept in an enclosure for children to see. Soon, attractive picnic groves, beer gardens, clean bathing and a scramble of boating activity drew great numbers of summer fun seekers from Cleveland. The inn opened January 28, 1869 and soon was to become a very popular place (Chabek, 1989).

Figure 8-2. The Murch House in 1876 and the occassion is the newsboys' picnic. *Cleveland State University Library, Cleveland Press Collection*

These real estate investors also built a railroad to carry patrons from Cleveland to their front door. The Rocky River Railroad had its first run on September 1, 1868. It was a single-track narrow gauge line. It started at West 58 Street and Bridge Avenue, which was then the city limits of Cleveland, ran through Lakewood and came right to the rear of the Cliff House. There was a roundhouse and machine shop at Nicholson Avenue with passing sidings at Nicholson, Summit and Hird. There were three 12-ton locomotives and 12 coaches with seats along the sides. The popularity of the park was so great on Sundays that the railroad could not handle the crowds. Liquor was plentiful along the route and at both ends, which may help to explain why it was not unusual to see several wrecked buggies on Detroit Road to and from the park (www.lakeword.org/history).

By 1874 the syndicate sold the Cliff House and turned its attention to developing the Clifton Park Association. The syndicate began to develop about 80 lots in the Clifton Park subdivision. Most of the early homes were summer places that were designed with servant's quarters.

The buyer of the Cliff House was Canadian Joseph Murch who changed the name to the Murch House. He made many improvements including the addition of four bowling alleys. Bowling was the latest rage as the first alley in the area was built just two years earlier in Cleveland on West 6th. The Murch House was at its height of popularity in 1882 when a devastating fire broke out, but it was never rebuilt. (Chabek, 1989).

Figure 8-2. One of the more spectacular promotions of the Cliff House occurred on July 12, 1871 when a professor Jenkins walked on a 900-foot tight rope across the valley 150 feet above the river. These entertainers often anointed themselves as professor. *Lindstrom, 1936*

Despite the summer crowds, the railroad never produced a profit for its shareholders because winter ridership was virtually nothing. The Nickel Plate bought the Rocky River Railroad on Sept. 9, 1881 thus giving the Van Sweringen brothers railroad access to Cleveland from the west. Ironically Cornelieus Vanderbilt could have bought this line very cheaply and kept competition with his New York Central Line out of Cleveland (Van Tassel and Grabowski, 1996).

High on the West Bank was Tisdale Point operated by D. Dardinger. There was a summer hotel, concessions and a boathouse in the Rocky River basin. Its career as a picnic ground was brief as Mr. Eels purchased the 200 acres in 1880. However, this was not to last as the development of Clifton Park and the Cleveland Yacht Club effectively eliminated any access to the lakefront by weekend picnickers. In 1905

Figure 8-4a. Postcard view of Rocky River Harbour. *Author collection*

Figure 8-4b. Postcard view of Rocky River Harbour. *Author collection*

Figure 8-4c. Postcard view of Rocky River Harbour. *Author collection*

Figure 8-4d. In the 1880's The Forest City Ice Company of Superior Street in Cleveland had a large ice cutting and storage facility at the mouth of the river. *Cleveland Yachting Club Yearbook*

Eels sold it to a real estate company who developed the Oakwood allotment. In addition, the Cleveland Yacht Club occupied the basin. At the turn of the century, the area around the mouth of the river was so popular that at least ten postcards were produced showing a scenic view of the river basin.

The Cleveland Yachting Club was founded in 1878 in an effort to save some of the lakefront for the people. By 1888, a dock building was erected near the mouth of the Cuyahoga River. In 1895, a new clubhouse was completed on the lakefront at the foot of East 9th Street. Meanwhile, a number of members began to use Rocky River as their summer anchorage. By 1900, they organized the Lakewood Yacht Club. Their one story clubhouse was built on the east bank at Clifton Park Beach. In 1906, the club bought the island in midstream and moved the clubhouse to this new site.

Figure 8-5. Moving the CYC clubhouse from Cleveland to Rocky River in 1914. *www.cycrr.org*

In 1913, the CYC and LYC merged. In 1914, the CYC clubhouse was moved via barge to Rocky River where it was attached to the LYC building. The club became known as one of the finest in the nation. A dance hall and movie building were erected. There were also tennis and handball courts.

76

In 1921, the post war depression led to bankruptcy, and the club was sold at auction. A group of loyal members secured a lease on the island and reorganized as the Cleveland Yachting Club. The Junior Barracks were converted to

Figure 8-6. The Cleveland Yacht Club as it appeared from 1914-1925. *Cleveland Yachting Club Collection*

a clubhouse, and the large clubhouse was sublet as a nightclub called Blossom Heath. It was here that Guy Lombardo and the Royal Canadians started on the road to fame.

Figure 8-7. Eddies Boathouse, a popular landmark in the 40s and 50s. *Cleveland Metroparks*

In 1927, Blossom Heath was destroyed by fire. The depression years were difficult, but by 1949 the island had been repurchased, and in 1964 a new clubhouse was erected.

Meanwhile on the west bank from 1915 to 1919 The Rocky River Dry Dock Company operated on the Rocky River between the old Detroit Road Bridge and the Nickel Plate Railroad Bridge to the north. This small operation built and serviced a variety of boats.

This company mainly constructed boats with wooden hulls. Several ships were built for duty during World War I. Following the war these vessels returned for service in the U.S. Coast Guard. Steamers built for the Army Quartermaster Corps were commissioned in and around The Great Lakes and as far away as the Panama Canal.

Figure 8-8. Building sub-chasers at Rocky River Dry Dock Company during World War I. *Cleveland State University Library, Cleveland Press Collection*

THE LAKEWOOD POST
September 12, 1918

TWO MORE SUB CHASERS LEAVE ROCKY RIVER THIS WEEK; HAS A NEW SHIPBUILDING PLANT

Not much publicity has been given to the work of the builders of the U-boat chasers at Rocky River, but the workers keep persistently on the job and two more destroyers are ready for use this week in hunting the Hun submarines. One of the new boats was tried out Tuesday and sent on its way down towards the Atlantic Ocean. The second chaser will start eastward before the end of the week. That will make four submarine chasers completed at the Rocky River plant this year, in addition to several boats that were constructed there last year.

These boats are nearly 100 feet in length-the long, rakish narrow type of speed boat, that can outrun anything in the way of U-boats that are afloat on top or under the water. These boats can turn within the radius of their length, going at full speed.

Twenty-two men constitute the crew of a submarine chaser and the women of the Federal War Emergency Board of Lakewood have been busy this week looking after the comfort and social welfare of the 44 young men who have been sent here by the government from the Great Lakes training camps to take the new boats down to the ocean. Whether the crews who take the boats to the ocean will continue their trips, as they did last year until the boats with the same crews they started with in Lakewood get in action on the coast of France and England is not known.

Earlier in the season a country home on the lake front was thrown open for the entertainment of the crews of the boats, who went out with the first chasers. This week, the women are giving little parties, dinners and entertainments, so that the 44 young men have been made to feel very much at home here. The church parlor of the Congregational church has been open for the entertainment of the visitors and the hospitable ladies of that church have constituted themselves a committee to make the sailors comfortable, during their stay at Rocky River.

A New Shipbuilding Plant

But submarine chasers are not the only vessels that will be turned out at Rocky River to help win the war. The Lakewood Shipbuilding Company, organized several weeks ago and, asked permission from the city council to use, during the war period, some portion of the banks of the river, belonging to the city. This permission was granted. It is proposed to build scows and coal barges for the government in the new ship yards, that are located far from the yards of the submarine chasers.

The Mathews Company has a large plant for turning out ornamental wood work for buildings, located at the east end of the big bridge. The demand for house building materials has dropped off in the past two years and the company will engage in more essential war work. The change can be made, while retaining the effective organization the company has built up. Work on the new ship building yards is already well under way. It is expected a number of scows and barges will be completed this season.

Farther upstream farming became the main activity of the rich bottomlands. However, in the early years, trying to get up and down the slopes with equipment and crop harvests, and frequent flooding of the river made farming very difficult. In truth, most of the valley was probably too narrow to farm except where the preglacial valley crosses the present valley (see chapter 1). However, these wide areas were home to four significant families in the history of Rockport.

The first was that of the Mastick brothers, Benjamin Jr. and Asahel. Benjamin was born in Connecticut in 1795 and Asahel in Vermont in 1800. Benjamin had fought at the battle of Bunker Hill at the age of 14. He came to Geauga County, Ohio in 1817 and married Eliza Tomlinson in 1821. He received a commission as a Colonel of the Militia from Govenor St. Clair and moved to Rockport in 1831.

He and his brother made several purchases of contiguous land in the valley surrounding what is now the Puritas Road crossing of the river. They bought 235 acres from Herman Canfield for $960 on July 8, 1833, and 46 acres from Royal Millard on April 26, 1834. Benjamin built a cabin on the west side of the river while Asahel built on the east side.

One of the first things they did was construct a dam and sawmill. (Kiwanis built a YMCA cabin here as a WPA project). Among other things the mill supplied lumber for the plank roads at $6.00 per thousand feet. Until a small bridge was built, the Masticks ferried travelers across the river in a small flatboat. They also rented out teams and wagons to carry folks to Ohio City at a charge of 30 cents a round trip for a double yoke of oxen. They also carried eggs on foot ten miles to the market in Ohio City and each returned with a 50-pound bag of salt.

Figure 8-9. By 1924 Benjamin Woods had purchased some land from the Masticks. His farm was located in the area that is now Mastick Woods Golf Course. *Cleveland Metroparks Collection*

The Mastick families were known for their gracious hospitality as well as being a stop on the Underground Railway. Brigham Young was one of the Masticks' most famous houseguests. Young, of course, became leader of the Mormon Church in 1844, established Salt Lake City in 1846, and became the first governor of Utah in 1850 (Neighbors, March 1993).

Figure 8-10. The Patriot. *Atlas of Cuyahoga County 1892*

The next large farm, perhaps the largest (455 acres) was just to the north and belonged to William J. White. It was called The Two-Minute Stock Farm based on the speed of his most famous horse, "The Patriot", who was the winner of 21 first prizes and four championships.

His 52-room mansion, Thornwood, was situated overlooking the valley on the southwest corner of Mastick and Lorain Roads. The farm included almost all land in the valley as far as the eye could see and included a half-mile track and several stables.

White made and lost his fortune in the chewing gum industry. In 1884 he was operating a candy store where he mistakenly bought a barrel of Yucatan Chicle. He discovered it could be softened, flavored and made chewable. His "Yucatan" chewing gum was an immediate success. By 1893, he teamed up with local physician Dr. Edwin Beeman who had been marketing pepsin as a cure for stomach ailments. Beeman's Pepsin Chewing Gum made a fortune for both men.

White moved to West Cleveland and was elected mayor of that city in 1889. In 1892 he was elected to the U.S. House of Representatives. His personal tastes were extravagant to say the least. He had a large steam yacht built on which he sailed to England. As a Congressman he was able to get an audience with King Edward VII whom he introduced to "Yucatan."

> *"The Country place of Hon, W.J. White is well known not only because of its products, but from the fact that countless social events have taken place at the Villa which has been considered a most important part of the farm. Long before the electric railways conveyed passengers westward from the city, tall-ho parties, coach parties and picnics at the Two-Minute farm were numerous. With the advent of streetcars, however, the fact that a trip to the farm was a matter of only fifty minutes was taken advantage of and the many visitors increased. The farm is well equipped and is one of Mr. White's most valued possessions", (Knight, 1903).*

He divorced his first wife in 1906 and married a divorcee the next day. Around 1916 he moved to New York where business difficulties made him penniless. He started a new company, which lost his next fortune due to litigation with his original company. In 1922 he returned to Cleveland where he built another company. Unfortunately in 1923 he slipped on a sidewalk and died a few weeks later.

Figure 8-11. Overlooking the Two-Minute Farm from the junction of Wooster and Lorain Roads. *Fairview Park Historical Society collection*

Figure 8-12. Some of the original structures remain today as storage facilities for Metroparks maintenance crews. *Author photo*

The next sizable farm to the north was that of Leonard Jordan shown in photo about 1900.

Figure 8-13. Making hay on the Jordan farm. The man on the left is a salesman from White's Yucatan Chewing Gum Company. *Fairview Park Historical Society Collection*

The final large estate/farm to the north was that of Washington S. Tyler. Born in 1835, he was one of Cleveland's most successful businessmen and founder of The Tyler Company, a pioneer in the production of wire specialties. In 1892, he began building the family summer residence known as "Woodside," a country estate overlooking the valley in the area around Munn Road. The farm was over 200 acres extending from Saint Joseph Academy on the south to Niagara Avenue on the north. It extended across the banks of the Rocky River and included land between Munn Road and Edgecliff Avenue on the east side of Rocky River Drive. Tyler died in

81

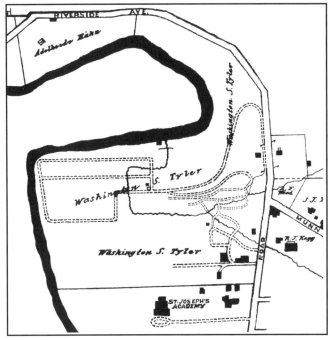

Figure 8-14a. The Tyler Estate. *adapted from Arthur Kouba collection*

1917, but his wife continued to live there until her death in 1934. In 1921, a 75-acre parcel on the valley bottom was donated to help establish the Metropolitan Park District.

Woodside was a working farm, including poultry houses, bull pens, livestock, pastures, greenhouses, vineyards, orchards, lily ponds, and formal flower and vegetable gardens. In addition to the Tyler Mansion, the estate included a large home for their daughter. There was also an Olympic size swimming pool, creamery, florist cottage, carriage house, workers houses, an octagonal barn and water towers. In the early 1940's, the family had no interest in living at the estate and the property was purchased by William E. Asplin who developed several home sites as well as Amber Drive (Foos, 1999).

Figure 8-14b. Much of the farm was located in the valley and reached by a trail that we kids referred to as the "cowpath" in the 50's. Little did I realize that it probably was just that, a cow path. The trail entrance was at the end of this wall near Munn Road. The trail cut a gentle slope along the valley wall to the bottom. It was great for a daredevil bicycle adventure. *Author photo*

Figure 8-14c. In 2000, a large portion of the wall collapsed. In 2001-02, Rocky River Drive was completely rebuilt along with the wall. The new wall became part of a memorial walkway to fallen West Park Police and Firemen. *Author photo*

Figure 8-14d. Main entrance to Woodside. The stone pillars can still be seen at 3300 Rocky River Drive. The octagonal barn is in the background. *James Foos Collection*

Figure 8-14e. The driveway to the main house ran along the edge of the valley. *James Foos Collection*

Figure 8-14f. The driveway to the main house ended in a carriage turn around at the front door. This place commanded a spectacular view of the valley. *James Foos Collection*

Figure 8-14g. This home was built for the daughter of W.S. Tyler. *James Foos Collection*

Figure 8-14h. The Carr and Blackman families lived in homes on the estate and were in charge of the day to day operations. Both families gather on November 17, 1912 for the wedding of Marjorie L. Carr and Arthur W. Blackman. *James Foos Collection*

Figure 8-14i. Most of these hand built stone walls are still in place and can be seen from the valley floor in winter. *James Foos Collection*

Figure 8-14j. The Tyler barn in 1920. *Cleveland Metroparks Collection*

Figure 8-14k. The Tyler Barn today. At the spot where this photo was taken, the road down to the barn can be seen in winter. *Author photo*

The Tyler Barn is one of the very few remaining structures from the days of land acquisition by the Metroparks.

Unoccupied buildings are of course an open invitation to vandalism and destruction. Even though this building is of no particular significance, structurally or architecturally, it was completely restored in 1998, perhaps as a small reminder of the roots of the Metroparks.

THE METROPARKS

William Stinchcomb--Founder of the Metroparks

William Albert Stinchcomb was born on June 5, 1878 in a farmhouse on what is now Denison Avenue near Lorain Avenue in Cleveland. He left West High School when he was 16 to work for the National Iron and Wire Company but became a self-taught engineer (International Correspondence School). In 1895 he joined the Cleveland Engineering Department as a surveyor. He was appointed city park engineer by Mayor Tom L. Johnson in 1902 and the following year was elected Cuyahoga County Engineer. While serving as county engineer, he directed numerous large projects, including construction of the Detroit-Superior and Brooklyn-Brighton Bridges.

As early as 1905 he pushed for an outer park and boulevard system. This finally paid off in 1917 when the State Legislature created a vehicle by which local governments could establish independent park boards "for the necessary edification of city folds." The Park Board immediately began to acquire land to make his vision a reality. In 1921 he was appointed park district director-secretary, a post he held until his retirement 36 year later. At the end of his 58-year public service career in 1957 he had amassed around the perimeter of our metro area a 100-mile chain of parks, comprising 14,000 acres and valued at $17 million. It has been estimated these same lands today, would be over a billion dollars in value.

Completion of his vast accomplishment required thousands of land purchases from early-settler families, farmers and other property holders. This involved four decades of intensive negotiations. It also meant tireless campaigning to convince county taxpayers of the worthiness of his prodigious program, so they would support levies to provide funds for the acquisitions.

Nine months after his death in January 1959, at age 80, a 30-foot-high concrete monolith was dedicated to Stinchcomb. It was erected on a high point that juts out from the east bank of the Rocky River off Hogsback Lane, just south of the Hilliard Road Bridge. It looks down on the first parcel of land purchased by the park system in the Rocky River Reservation. (Chabek, 1993)

He was humble: however, it was his courage, determination and imaginative realism that did it. Few people have the talent to move in such a direct line, and few accomplish so much. (Cleveland News, editorial, 1959).

Since its very inception in 1918, The Rocky River Reservation has played a role in the lives of just about everyone who has lived in Rockport. The popularity of the Metroparks is greater than any time in its history, attested by the fact that a tax levy for the parks has never been defeated.

Figure 8-15. Looking north from the low level Lorain Road Bridge on July 10, 1918 at the time of the very beginning of the park system. *Cleveland Metroparks Collection*

"The West Park boys have a good time swimming in the Rocky River near the south Rocky River bridge. The river is on one place 10 to 11 feet deep. Some one could make good money if he erects on that place a bathing house." *Ohio Correspondent July 2, 1910.*

Figure 8-16. In 1925 there was no park drive so these skaters below Madison Avenue probably hiked down the 99 steps at the end of Madison Avenue. There was a stairway at that point (builder unknown) of concrete steps with a pipe railing that led down the embankment to the valley floor. *Cleveland Metroparks Collection*

Ninety-nine Steps

There was a 99 step flight of stairs that once led down into the valley from the end of Madison Avenue. It was used to get to the "Lodge" built by the Lakewood Kiwanis in 1925 for the YMCA. Youth groups from the Y would take the Madison street car to the end of the line, walk down the steps, and then hike through the woods to get to the lodge near the base of the Hilliard Road Bridge (Chabek, 1990).

Figure 8-17. In 1926 Big Met golf course was opened. It was the first public course on the West side of Cleveland. This photo shows a line of workers weeding the course on May 12, 1926. *Cleveland Metroparks Collection*

Figure 8-18. In 1927 there is a long wait at the number one tee at Big Met. Over 75,000 tickets were sold that year and it is just as popular today. *Cleveland Metroparks Collection*

Figure 8-19. June 8, 1926. This cabin was built by the Lakewood Kiwanis in 1925. They raised $5,000 to construct a lodge for underprivileged boys and turned it over to the YMCA. Materials had to be carted to the site near the present Hilliard Road Bridge before any river fords were built. The cabin was reached by the same stairway mentioned in Figure 8-21. It was closed in 1970 at the request of the Park Board. *Cleveland Metroparks Collection*

Figure 8-20. Not to be outdone, the West Park Kiwanis built two cabins in the late 30's and early 40's. This one was located in the present Willow Bend Picnic area north of Berea. This photo is dated May, 1940. *Cleveland Metroparks Collection*

Figure 8-21a and b. The second West Park Kiwanis cabin was located near the Mastick Picnic Area. Both of the West Park Kiwanis Cabins were burned by vandals but both were enjoyed by thousands of kids for summer camping experiences. *West Park Kiwanis Collection*

Figure 8-22. It was June 29, 1928 and two rangers were watching or helping this fossil collector on the bank of the river near Little Cedar Point. *Cleveland Metroparks Collection*

Figure 8-23. It was in this area the fossil of <u>Dunkleosteus terrelli</u> was found. This model is now mounted on the outside of the Rocky River Interpretive Center. The original fossil is located at the Cleveland Museum of Natural History. *Author photo*

Figure 8-24. In the 20's you took your "machine" on the dirt road down Puritas Hill in dry weather only. *Cleveland Metroparks Collection*

In the early 30's the park system was able to take advantage of the many skills of WPA workers as the country was mired in the Great Depression. One of the major projects was the construction of a road from Detroit Avenue to Cedar Point Road. The project started in 1933 and required straightening of the river in many areas.

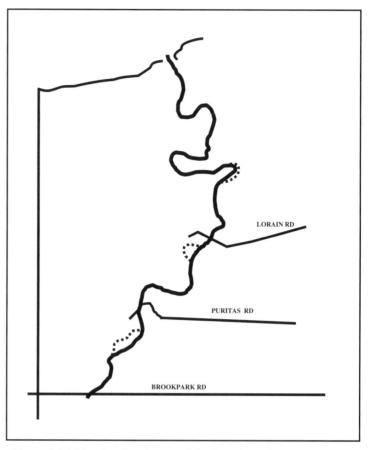

LORAIN RD

PURITAS RD

BROOKPARK RD

Figure 8-25. Map showing changes of the river channel to accommodate the new parkway drive. Dotted lines indicate old river channel.

Figure 8-26. This August 21, 1931 view of the park drive is just south of the airport. The drive is built on fill in the old river channel. *Cleveland Metroparks Collection*

Figure 8-27. January 31, 1930. A concrete retaining wall is under construction just north of Tyler field. *Cleveland Metroparks Collection*

Figure 8-28. Many of the retaining walls were built by master stonemasons working on WPA projects during The Depression. *Cleveland Metroparks Collection*

Figure 8-29. In 1931, a park ranger overlooks the construction of a new entrance to the park at Rock Cliff Drive. *Cleveland Metroparks Collection*

Figure 8-30. The Rocky River Trailside Museum at Mastick Picnic Area in 1938. This facility was used from 1936-1971. *Cleveland State University Library, Cleveland Press Collection*

Figure 8-31. The concession stand was located nearby in the Mastick Picnic Area. *Gayle Walter Collection*

Figure 8-32. In the 20's the YMCA, YWCA, Alta House, Phyllis Wheatley Association and Playhouse Settlement all established summer camps in the parks. This view looking north shows both the low level and high level bridges and dates the photograph in the early 30's. Young women of the Phyllis Wheatley Association enjoy a warm summer day. *Cleveland Metroparks Collection*

Figure 8-33. Boy Scouts at Mastick Field in July of 1938. *Cleveland Metroparks Collection*

Figure 8-34a. August 1937. The wading pool at Mastick Picnic Grounds. *Cleveland Metroparks Collection*

Figure 8-34b. Labor Day 1999. The same pool, but today health board regulations do not allow unguarded or unchlorinated pools like this. The sign on the far side reads "Decorative Fountain-not for swimming or drinking". *Author photo*

Figure 8-35. Compare and contrast. The same view separated by almost a century. The top photo, looks down on the hayfields of the Jordan family farm. This photo probably taken from a glass slide, is so fine grained that with the use of a hand lens horses or cattle can be seen grazing on the slopes of the hogback hill. The old Lorain Road crossed through the valley and came up the hill on the north side of the present Lorain Road across from Mandley-Vitrosky Funeral Home. Also note there is no road travelling through the valley. (David Schafer Collection). The bottom photo shows that the hogback hill has completely reverted to forest. *Author photo*

MASTICK MEMORY

Sunday October 6, 2002, 3 pm. I was heading back home to Berea after helping a friend move in Lakewood. I decided to take the leisurely ride through the Rocky River Reservation. It was a beautiful day, and it seemed like everyone was taking advantage of the nice weather. There were walkers, bikers, rollerbladers, fishermen, picnickers, and people just out for a Sunday drive. (The Browns were not playing until 8 p.m.). Ribbons of sunlight played through the trees that were beginning to show their first tinges of color. As I passed Mastick Park, I heard a sound that transported me through a time warp to 1948. The simple clanging of horseshoes against the stake caused me to look into the picnic pavilion and to see a family picnic more that 50 summers ago.

There was my Dad with a peck basket of kindling split from 8" pieces of 2x4 and a can of kerosene. (More often than not the burgers and dogs had an unmistakable flavor of kerosene, but I was eight, and they tasted great to me.). My mom and her mom were unloading the picnic basket. My grandfather and some of the uncles were starting to pitch horseshoes. The younger kids were already trying out the wading pool. Uncle Al Aufmuth had his car radio on (not too many cars had radios then) and soon most of the men gathered around the car to listen to Jack Grainy and Jimmy Dudley call the Indians double-header. We kids popped in from time to time to check on the score, but most of the cousins brought their gloves, and it was not too long before a bat and ball appeared and a game of some sort was under way. My dad, grandfather, and Uncle Al Thomsen (former second baseman for the Cleveland Spiders) were usually among the first on the field—it all flashed through my head with the clang of a horseshoe, is it really 50 years?

* * * * * * * * * *

97

CHAPTER 9
RECREATION

Recreation was and always will be an important part of everyday life. Before the days of video games, computers, television and even radio there was still a need for recreation. In the early frontier, the hardship of day to day living and lack of transportation afforded little opportunity for recreation, and any that did occur was centered in the home. Travel was done on foot because the earliest settlers simply could not afford the luxury of a horse much less a wagon or carriage. In fact, the first farm animals were usually oxen or cows, and the horse and carriage would not become commonplace for several decades.

It is no small coincidence that the first commercial establishments in any settlement were taverns. These provided a place for whiskey and the inevitable gathering of men. More importantly, taverns were places for lodging and commercial exchange. Early tavern owners were generally well respected leaders of the community.

By the 1840's with the establishment of churches and the gaining popularity of the horse and carriage, recreational activities became more formalized. The church social and community picnics afforded the opportunity for people to gather from a considerable distance.

Toward the end of the nineteenth century, dramatic changes occurred all over the country. The industrial revolution had a full head of steam; machines of all kinds were doing work previously unheard of, and people were leaving the farm for more dependable jobs. Railroads were connecting distant places at incredible of speeds of 30-40 miles per hour, and gas and electric lighting meant that more and more people were not tied to a dawn to dusk existence.

Entrepreneurs in Berea were experimenting with electricity and streetcars. This phenomenon would soon put many horses out to pasture and introduce the era of the electric interurban streetcar.

Figure 9-1. A speeding westbound Cleveland & Southwestern car has just cleared the Lorain Road Bridge and is entering Fairview Village on its way to Oberlin in 1910. *Fairview Park Historical Society*

Interurban lines sprang up everywhere, as investors were not in short supply to provide capital for purchase of right-of-way, materials and supplies. Many lines never got off paper; many went bankrupt quickly, and others went bankrupt slowly. Many lines only traveled short distances while others traveled long distances with insufficient ridership. Within a few short years however, consolidations provided five major lines radiating out of the city of Cleveland. The people of Rockport were fortunate to be served by two of these lines. The Lakeshore Electric ran from Cleveland through Lakewood to Toledo with connections to Detroit and Chicago. Meanwhile the Southwestern ran out Lorain Road to Kamms where it split running west towards Oberlin, Norwalk, Lorain and Wellington or south along Rocky River drive to Strongsville, Wooster, Mansfield and Bucyrus with connections to Columbus.

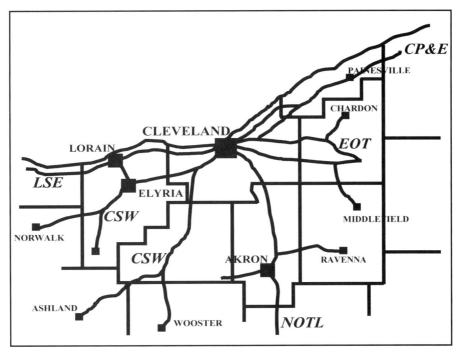

Figure 9-2. Map of Interurban lines radiating out of Cleveland including starting and ending dates. Cleveland Painesville and Eastern 1896-1926. Cleveland and Southwestern 1895-1931. Lake Shore Electric 1893-1938. Eastern Ohio Traction 1899-1925. Northern Ohio Traction and Light 1895-1932.

People began to commute to work in the central city, and they could visit relatives in faraway towns with the speed and comfort of these five major lines. Baseball teams could travel to rival cities, and charters were run to Cleveland and elsewhere for special events. The Cleveland and Southwestern, for example, ran an opera special from Oberlin to Gray's Armory in Cleveland in 1904. Freight business was soon added and this became especially important to areas not served by the steam railroads. Milk, produce, newspapers, and mail contracts became important income producers. Ridership was brisk during the week but the companies were always seeking ways to make more money on the weekends.

THE AMUSEMENT PARKS

The Interurban lines introduced the era of the "Trolley Parks." Every line from Cleveland bought, created or served and promoted one or more of these parks to increase their business. The Southwestern built a branch line to Puritas Springs Amusement Park, and promoted Seccaium Park in Bucyrus, Fleming's Falls in Mansfield, and Chippewa Lake Park in Chippewa Lake. The Lake Shore Electric provided direct access to its own Beach Park in Avon Lake, and to Crystal Beach in Vermilion and Cedar Point in Sandusky. These parks continued to operate long after the automobile put an end to the Interurbans.

CHIPPEWA LAKE PARK

Chippewa Lake is situated on the Southern Division of the Southwestern Lines and is an ideal vacation spot, with every facility for rest and recreation, including fishing, boating, bathing and all sorts of up-to-date amusements. There is a large pavilion with splendid dancing floor and a first-class orchestra furnishes good music afternoon and evening.

Chippewa Lake Park is an historic place where many years ago the Indians of the Chippewa tribe held forth and roamed through the woods and fields surrounding the beautiful lake. The grounds and adjacent woods and fields are still in their natural state yet the hand of time has improved the general aspect so as to make it ideal for the summer vacationist.

At this resort the busy man or woman finds restoration of strength and buoyancy of brain and body which are required to meet successfully the demands of modern life. Life is worth living here, whether in Hotel Chippewa, in log cabin, cottage or camp, and to those from the city or country the outdoor attractiveness of the place at once makes itself felt.

For hotel rates, picnic booking and other information address A. M. Beach, Mgr., Chippewa Lake, Ohio. Cleveland Agent, Alfred Henriques, 6801 Euclid Ave. Telephone Central 6707W.

FLEMING'S FALLS

Fleming's Falls Resort is situated between Ashland and Mansfield on the Southwestern and is an ideal spot for Sunday school, Church, and family picnics. This resort possesses great natural beauty and has a dancing pavilion and many other attractions.

SECCAIUM PARK

Seccaium Park derives it name form a tribe of Indians that held forth there many years ago. It is situated between Galion and Bucyrus on the Southwestern and is a very popular park for Church, Sunday School and lodge picnics and family reunions. Seccaium Park has a first-class dance hall, base ball grounds and numerous other attractions.

PURITAS SPRINGS PARK

On the Puritas Springs Division of the Southwestern Lines is located Cleveland's finest resort, Puritas Springs. This beautiful picnic grounds is located seven miles southwest of Cleveland on grand bluffs, overlooking from Point Puritas, the magnificent and picturesque garden valley of Rocky River, south of Lake Erie, away from the smoke and dust of the busy city, where the air is clean, the waters pure, and the scenery grand.

These beautiful grounds, the property of the C.S. & C. Ry. Co. comprise sixteen acres of forest shade, romantic glens with modern spring houses, the famous flowing spring of Puritas, cool and sparkling mineral waters, shady groves, up-to-date merry-go-round, bowling alleys, billiard and pool rooms, base ball parks, dining hall, lunch and check rooms, palace pavilion and grand ball room, the finest in the state which can be rented for private parties-dancing afternoon and evenings, except Sunday. Splendid camping grounds and has no superior for church, school, society reunions and family outings. For picnic bookings call on or write J.E. Gooding, Manager, 367 The Arcade, Cleveland, O. Telephone Central 6006W.

Cleveland and Southwestern ad from Brashares, 1982

PURITAS SPRINGS

In 1894, the Puritas Springs Bottling Plant was built to meet the demand for spring mineral water. In 1898, John E. Gooding of Painesville built Puritas Spring Amusement Park on the grounds of the Puritas Springs Bottling Plant at the edge of the Rocky River Valley. Taking a cue from the recently opened Euclid Beach Park, Gooding did not charge an admission fee. The Park remained in the Gooding family until it closed in 1958. The Dance Hall (1898-1943) was destroyed by fire in 1946 along with many of the early historical records and photographs of the park.

Figure 9-3. A unique feature of the dance hall was the large porches which allowed "outdoor" dancing in good weather. *William Chambers Collection*

The Lost Photo and the Kiwanis Connection Until this photo surfaced I had never seen or heard of a picture of the dance hall. Two long time members of the West Park Kiwanis Club are Howard Schreibman (Schreibman's Jewelers) and William Chambers (Chambers Funeral Home). While I was talking with Howard the subject of Puritas Springs came up and he said that there used to be an antique store next to his store and that one day he saw a large framed picture of the dance hall which he purchased and gave to his friend Bill Chambers. Bill graciously brought me the picture, which was hanging in his recreation room, for me to copy.

Figure 9-4. Ironically one week after developing the Chambers picture, my brother (Earle) and I were looking through the old family album and found this 1907 photograph of our grandmother (Ida Roth Peterson, front row, second from right) taken at Puritas Springs which clearly shows the dance hall to the left. *Earle Pfingsten Collection*

101

Figure 9-5. In 1905 the Cleveland and Southwestern built a branch line to serve the amusement park at Puritas. The line ran from the Cleveland border at West 98th then south on West 105th to Bellaire, Puritas and the park. This 1915 photo taken at Puritas and Rocky River Drive looks towards the Southwest with the car on the right headed towards Puritas Springs. *David Schafer Collection*

Figure 9-6. By the late 1920's automobiles were driving the interurbans to financial ruin. In an effort to stem the tide, less profitable lines were abandoned. This 1928 photo shows the interurban line being torn out on Puritas Road. This view looking east is near West 150 Street at the New York Central Railroad crossing. Note the trolley wire is still in place *David Schafer Collection*

Figure 9-7. The billboard near the southwest corner of Puritas and Rocky River Drive indicates that we are not far from the park. *Ross Bassett Collection*

Figure 9-8. May 10, 1953. An aerial view of the park as most of us remember. *Cleveland State University Library, Bruce Young Collection*

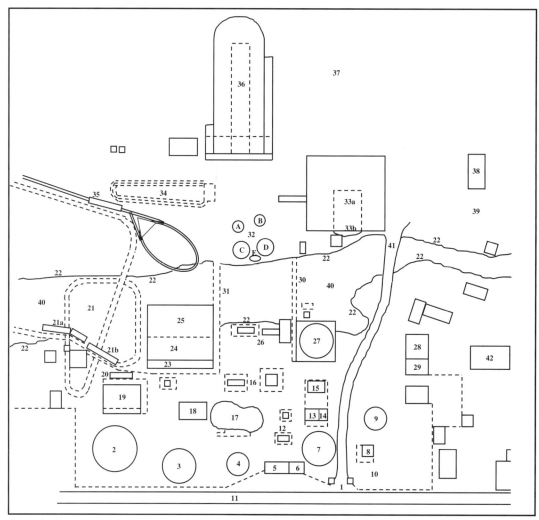

Figure 9-9. Adapted from the Sanborn Fire Insurance Maps of the early 50's. Unnumbered buildings are storage. 1. Entrance, 2. The Bug, 3. The Octopus, 4. Flying Scooters, 5. Waiting Room, 6. Photo Booth, 7. Moon Rocket, 8. Office, 9. Sea Plane, 10. Miniature Golf, 11. Puritas Avenue, 12. Concessions, 13. Lunch Room, 14. Office, 15. Drinks, 16. Concessions, 17. The Whip, 18. Restrooms, 19. Dodgem, 20. Basketball Toss, 21. Cyclone, 21a. Car Shed, 21b. Landing Area, 22. Top edge of bank, 23. Concessions, 24. Rumpus House, 25. Penny Arcade, 26. Concessions, 27. Merry-Go-Round, 28. Ride Equipment Storage, 29. Storage, 30. Bridge, 31. Covered Bridge, 32. Kiddie Rides, A. Merry-Go-Round, B. Aerial Swing, C. Rocket Plane, D. Auto Rides, E. Organ House, 33a. Dance Pavilion, 33b. Band Shell, 34. Small Roller Coaster, 35. Miniature Train Shed, 36. Roller Skating Rink, 37. Parking, 38. Shelter House, 39. Picnic Grounds, 40. Ravine, 41. Driveway, 42. Maintenance Shop.

A very exciting, as well as interesting game between the Rockport Baseball Team and Puritas Campers, was played last Sunday morning at Puritas Springs Park. The Puritas team, composed of some of the best amateur players in the state, defeated the Rockports by a score of 6 to 3. *Ohio Correspondent June 11, 1910.*

Figure 9-10a. It's the annual West Park Kiwanis Ox Roast at Puritas Springs in 1952. Each year this event raised money for civic projects. Entrance. *West Park Kiwanis Collection*

Figure 9-10b. Rocket Ships. *West Park Kiwanis Collection*

Figure 9-10c. Flying Scooters. *West Park Kiwanis Collection*

Figure 9-10d. Dodgems. *West Park Kiwanis Collection*

Figure 9-10e. Moon Rocket. *West Park Kiwanis Collection*

Figure 9-10f. Kiddie Rides. *West Park Kiwanis Collection*

Gooding introduced the first horse drawn and steam powered carousels in Ohio, and when Luna Park closed, he purchased their famous carousel and moved it to Puritas in 1929. When the park closed, the carousel was moved to Russell's Point Ohio. Finally, in 1971 it was sold to Six Flags Amusement Park in St. Louis where it was restored and remains in service today (http:history.amusement-parks.com). However, Puritas Springs will always be remembered for its' Cyclone Roller Coaster which was the highest, fastest and most dangerous in the Cleveland area. Designed by the most famous coaster designer of the time, John A. Miller, the Cyclone opened in 1928. The station was accessible from a boardwalk that led across a small side ravine of the Rocky River Valley. It was located directly under the lift hill and first drop.

Miller utilized the terrain to the fullest, and the Cyclone roared in and out of the ravine twice throughout its course. The train left the station around a left-hand turn, under the boardwalk and down a straightaway into another left turn. The track then passed under the second hills' ascent into a third left turn and hit the chain lift 20 feet down in the ravine. The lift ascended 85 feet and a u-turn at the top coupled with a fast chain lift gave the coaster plenty of momentum going down the first drop! The drop passed over the station platform and plunged 90 feet into the ravine. The train then climbed out of the ravine into a hard-banked left turn 55 feet above ground. This was followed by three camelback hills of 46 feet, 41 feet and 36 feet followed by a 30 degree high turnaround curve on the edge of the 100 foot valley wall. Then it was up again 22 feet into a 45-degree right hand drop curve. At this point a single light bulb provided the only lighting on the entire ride.

The train then climbed another 20 feet only to plummet riders 90 feet into the ravine again. The track at the bottom rested right on the ground. It then climbed up a 70-foot hill, went into a right hand turn, passed under the lift and returned to the station. (Dan MacKellar, coasterglobe.com).

Cleveland Plain Dealer July 26, 1946
Was the Puritas Springs Cyclone Dangerous?
Park Ride Closed After 3 Are Hurt
By Walter Lerch

Shutdown of the Cyclone, high-speed roller coaster at Puritas Springs Park, was ordered today by the Cleveland Police Department following serious injury there of three young women riders within a one month period. Latest victims, now confined in Lakewood Hospital with fractured spines, are Miss Dorothy Kazmer 19, of 16003 Saranac Rd., and Mrs.Margaret Lucas, 24 of 6216 Wakefield Ave.

Third casualty attributed to the steep dip in the amusement park thrill ride is Miss Mary Slaminka, 23 of 9917 Dunlap Ave. She still is under a physician's care after spending nine days in Lakewood Hospital.

Capt. John L. Palker of the Lorain Ave.-Triskett Rd. Precinct put the "stop" order on the roller coaster ride as a safety measure when told by the writer of the latest mishaps.

Other injuries to Cyclone riders have been reported over a period of years, including a serious mishap in August, 1942, which nearly cost the life of Daniel Schroeder, then living at 3445 East 65th St. Schroeder was catapulted out of his seat as the car swung around a sharp curve and he plunged 40 feet to the ground.

Medical men said it may be a "matter of months" before Miss Kazmer and Mrs Lucas are able to leave the hospital. Both will have to wear a brace to support their backs for a long period of time.

A.J. Ilg, secretary of the Puritas Springs Co., operators of the amusement park, said the ride was "safe,' and had the "best mechanical inspection available." "The women that were hurt had weak backs," he added.

Following notification of the police department order, representatives of the park said their insurance company had recommended that the speed of Cyclone cars on the drop be slowed down. This will be done immediately, they said.

The park carries a $50,000 insurance coverage on each accident it was reported.

Figure 9-11. The Cyclone. If you rode it, you know! If you never rode it, no one can explain it! *David Schaefer Collection*

From 1947 to 1963, my dad owned and operated a small drive-inn restaurant in Fairview Park. My brothers, sister and I all had our respective opportunities to work there on weekends. We usually didn't close until 1 am on Friday and Saturday nights. In the mid 50's, Jungle Larry and Safari Jane would occassionally stop in for a bite to eat after they finished up at Puritas Springs. Their arrival was always interesting because they would bring in whatever animal they had in their car- sometimes it was a lion cub, sometimes a large boa. It always made for an interesting closing.

Figure 9-12. "Jungle Larry" Tetzlaf readies his three pals for a short trip around Puritas Springs in June 1957. When the park closed in 1958, Larry went to Chippewa Lake until 1965 when it closed. Then he went to Cedar Point in 1966. *Cleveland State University Library, Cleveland Press Collection*

Figure 9-13a. For those ambitious enough, remains of the Cyclone can still be found on the hillside in the Metroparks. *Author photo, 1999*

Figure 9-13b. In 1969 the footbridge to the rear of the park was still standing though not for long as developers would soon be building an apartment complex on the former park property. *Author photo*

CHIPPEWA LAKE (1875-1978)

Sometime between 1870 and 1875, a druggist from Seville, Ohio, purchased land at Chippewa Lake with the intention of creating a summer resort. Its success was immediate as indicated by the over 1,000 wagons and carriages parked in the field on July 4, 1875 (Krynak, 1993). As it evolved into an amusement park, the crowds continued to grow. Adjacent to the park the Townsend family owned a large parcel of land. They were the managers of the Cleveland, Lorain and Wheeling Railroad (later to become part of the Baltimore and Ohio). They had a siding built from the main line to the lake. In 1903 the Cleveland and Southwestern laid tracks through the park and a round trip ticket to Chippewa Lake could be purchased for 50 cents. On a summer Sunday 20,000 to 40,000 people would enjoy an outing in the park.

Figure 9-14. 1906 post card view of park grounds. *Author collection*

Figure 9-15. The Cleveland & Southwestern Interurban station and entrance to the park is just off to the right in this circa 1930 photo. The dance hall is the large building on the right. *Cleveland State University Library, Bruce Young Collection*

Figure 9-16. This early 1920s photo shows people getting off the train (right side of photo) at the main gate. Many trainloads of parkgoers came from surrounding cities and states by way of the Baltimore and Ohio Railroad. *Northern Ohio Railway Museum Collection*

Figure 9-17a+b. In the winter of 1999 the main entrance, roller coaster and dance hall stood silent against the snow. Most of the park remained just as it did when the park closed in 1978. However, in June of 2002, one week after school was out for the summer, the dance hall was completely destroyed by a fire set by a teenage girl who was "bored". Because nearby homes were threatened, the owners of the park gave permission to local officials to burn the remaining structures under controlled conditions. As of early 2004 this destruction has not taken place. *Author photos*

CEDAR POINT

In 1870, Cedar Point in Sandusky began a career that would eventually make it the most famous amusement park in the country. In 1898 when the Hotel Breakers was built, Cedar Point became a major summer resort destination.

Figure 9-18. 1908 postcard view of the Midway at Cedar Point. *Author collection*

Figure 9-19. The New York Central Railroad often ran special trains to Cedar Point from as far away as New York City. They stopped right at the docks for the short ferry ride to the park. *Author collection*

Figure 9-20. Rockporters could board a Lake Shore Electric Car for the 90-minute ride to Sandusky just a block from the Cedar Point Pier and a short ferry ride to the park. This postcard view of the Sandusky Station is from about 1910. *Author collection*

Figure 9-21. The old station is scheduled for a historic restoration in the near future. This 1999 photo indicates that much of the exterior remains as it did in 1910. *Author photo*

114

Figure 9-22-23. For those who preferred a more leisurely trip, the C&B Lines (Cleveland and Buffalo Transit, 1892-1939) or the D&C (Detroit & Cleveland Steam Nav. Co. 1869-1951) ran Lake Steamers to Cedar Point from Cleveland on a regular basis in the summer beginning in 1914. *Author collection*

Figure 9-24. D & C Steamer City of Cleveland in 1909. *Author collection*

MEMPHIS KIDDIE PARK (1952-)

Figure 9-25. The first encounter with an amusement park for many Westparkers was with Memphis Kiddie Park. Just south of the township, in Brooklyn, the park opened in 1952. It is still owned by the same family and has essentially the same original rides. *Author photo*

Euclid Beach (1895-1969)

Although several books have been written about Euclid Beach, I would be remiss if I didn't at least mention the favorite amusement park of Rockporters and just about anyone who was ever there. "On Nickel Day and a dollar you could catch a streetcar to downtown, transfer at the square to Euclid Beach, spend the entire day and still have a dime left for carfare home" ("Big Chuck" Shadowski).

Figure 9-26a. The American Racing Derby built in 1921was sold to Cedar Point in 1966 three years before the park closed. The cost of maintenance had become too high (Bush et al, 1977). *Author collection*

Figure 9-26b. Built in 1930, the Flying Turns was truly a unique ride. With no steel or track, it had just rubber wheels in a half moon shell of wood, *Author collection*

117

Figure 9-26c. The Rocketships were designed and built in the park's own shops in the 1930's taking advantage of the public's fascination with Buck Rogers and Flash Gordon (Bush et al, 1977). *Author collection*

Figure 9-26d. One of the rocketships made an appearance at the West Park Fourth of July parade in 2004. *John Papay photo*

Figure 9-26e. Although it seemed much higher, the Over-The-Falls was only 37 feet tall. *Author collection*

118

Figure 9-26f. A favorite of young and old, the Sleepy Hollow Railroad wound its way through the miniature village and under the Racing Coasters. The locomotive was re-engineered by the park's shops to run on compressed air making it a one of a kind (Bush et al, 1977). *Author collection*

LUNA PARK 1905-1931

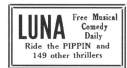

Luna Park located at East 110th Street and Woodland was dependent on the streetcar to bring its patrons and the sale of beer to bolster its profits. As more and more people acquired automobiles, Luna Park suffered from a lack of space for parking, and when prohibition was enacted, the park suffered even more. Finally with the Depression and competition from the more popular Euclid Beach, Luna Park was razed in 1931.

Figure 9-27a. This post card view of Luna Park in 1906 shows the many architectural styles that characterized the park. *Author collection*

119

Figure 9-27b. Luna Park was lit by thousands of incandescent bulbs in a time when electricity was still a thing of wonderment to many. *Author collection*

Lincoln Park (1906- ?)

Lincoln Park was built in 1906 on what was formerly known as Scenic Park. It boasted the only round dance hall in Ohio and a racecourse of wooden horses operated by electricity. It was built near the bottom of Sloane Avenue and despite being on the Clifton and Detroit streetcar Lines as well as the Lake Shore Electric Interurban, it never really became popular. The attractions were disassembled one by one until only the grounds and name remained. The name eventually reverted to Scenic Park, which today is the northern terminus of the Rocky River Reservation (Van Tassel and Grabowski, 1996).

Figure 9-28. Looking south from the Detroit Road Bridge at Lincoln Park, a "Flying Swing" and Roller Coaster are clearly visible in this photo. *Lakewood Historical Society*

Rockport Hamlet Driving Park

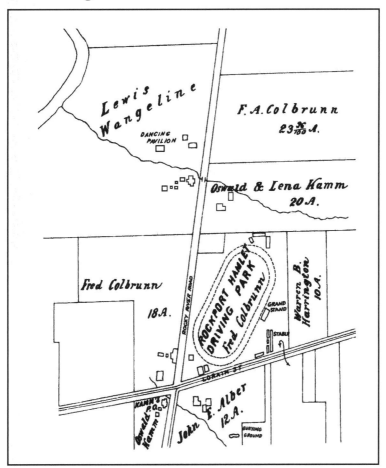

Figure 9-29. Plat map of Rockport Hamlet Driving Park in 1895.

Fred Colbrunn was one of the early settlers of Rockport arriving in 1830. He had been a successful linen mill operator in Germany and soon became one of the largest landowners in Rockport including several hundred acres on all four corners of Lorain and Rocky River Drive (Swinerton, 1986). His son Fred built the racetrack at Kamms Corners in 1890. This West Side landmark was a half-mile track for harness racing. The Colbrunns would organize harness racing for a two to three week period several times a year. By the turn of the century, top horses were attracted from all over the state, and the interurbans could bring fans right to the front gate.

Horseracing was one of the earliest forms of entertainment in the Western Reserve. As early as 1827, there were races on a quarter mile track on Water Street near the center of Cleveland. Later harness racing became popular at the Cuyahoga County Fair and throughout the area. Betting on races was, of course, an integral part of the event. This illegal gambling and association with crime gave a dubious reputation to the sport. By 1850, pacing and trotting events were being scheduled throughout the area. Horseback racing was considered vulgar in this era. This would not change until the 1920's when the betting public seemed to prefer the speed of the thoroughbreds to the moderately fast trotters. Glenville, which had been the horseracing center of the area, was annexed to Cleveland in 1905. Gambling was illegal in Cleveland so horse racers and players created the town of North Randall for racing, some of which survives to this day (Van Tassel and Grabowski, 1996).

Figure 9-30a. The Rockport Hamlet Driving Park was located between Lorain and Lucille facing West 159th Street (not there when the park was built). The stables were located on the south end along Lorain. A saloon and concession stand was on the West Side while the grandstands were on the east side of the track. *Kamms Corner Development Corporation Collection*

Figure 9-30-b. This view is taken from Kamm's Corners looking west on Lorain Street. The Cleveland and Southwestern interurban car is about even with Alger Cemetary. The buildings on the left are the stables for the Rockport Driving Park. *Cleveland Plain Dealer August 29, 1910*

Figure 9-30c. Looking at the Northeast corner of Kamm's in 1917. This site is known by most of us as the location of the Cleveland Trust/Key Bank Building. *Laverne Landphair-Buch Collection*

122

Perhaps these events are what led to the Colbrunns selling part of their track to the Cleveland Board of Education for $15,000 in 1923 when West Park was annexed to Cleveland. George Washington Elementary School was immediately built on the south end of the property and later, Newton D. Baker Junior High was opened on the north end of the property in 1955. The remainder of the field was used as a football stadium for John Marshall High School from 1923 until the new high school was opened in 1932.

Dance Halls

Dancing became popular in the "Gay 90's" with dance halls springing up everywhere. One of the earliest in this area was the Maple Cliff Villa Club (Fig. 9-31a) at the edge of the valley where Fairview Hospital is now located. The entrance to the club was just across the street from the Cleveland and Southwestern car house and power plant on Lorain Avenue. Another local dance hall was the Club/Beer Garden (Fig. 9-31e) at 15535 Lorain Avenue just east of the police station. Other local halls included Gilberts (Fig. 9-31d) on Detroit at St. Charles, McKasky's on Detroit at Belle, Rainbow Gardens (Fig. 12-14) on Rocky River Drive near Munn, Mahall's on Madison at West 132nd, Ragnatz's (Fig. 12-19) on Warren Road and the Homestead at West 118th and Detroit. And of course there were the dance halls at Puritas Springs, Lincoln Park, Euclid Beach (Fig. 9-31c), Chippewa Lake (Fig. 9-31b), and Cedar Point, all of which were frequented by West Parkers. A couple of other local favorites were at Springvale Country Club in North Olmsted (Fig. 9-31g) and the Columbia Ballroom in Columbia Station (Fig. 9-31h).

Figure 9-31a. Post card view (pre 1907) of the Maple Cliff Villa Club. *David Schafer Collection*

In 1937 an unknown band under the direction of Lawrence Welk was booked to play at Chippewa Lake for a week. At this same time the Musicians Union out of New York called a strike. This was at a time when big band music shows were very popular on the radio. In a very short time WHK radio in Cleveland called to see if a band was available at the park. Because Chippewa was out of the jurisdiction of the Cleveland and Akron area, the band was immediately pressed into service. Lawrence Welk had airtime three times a day on all three networks until the strike was settled. It was the only live band to be heard in this part of the country (Krynak, 1993).

Figure 9-31b. Dance Hall at Chippewa Lake in July, 1940. *Cleveland State University Library, Cleveland Press Collection*

Figure 9-31c. 1909 Postcard. "Interior of the largest and finest dancing pavilion in the world, Euclid Beach Park, Cleveland, Ohio". *Author collection*

Figure 9-31d. Gilbert Dance Hall, 14623 Detroit Avenue, November 1925. *Cleveland State University, Cleveland Press Collection*

West Park Beer Garden

Have you ever noticed, while walking westward out Lorain Avenue from the school, that deserted mansion-like house next to the Police Station?

If you have, did you realize that this musty old structure, built in the early part of this century, and the other crumbling buildings around it, once constituted the West Park's only real old-fashioned beer garden.

Yes, this was a real old-fashioned beer garden, where one could come and be served delicious chicken dinners, with a stein or two of sparkling, foaming beer. One could also enjoy dancing in that large circular building that now echoes with the blows of the mechanic's hammer as he repairs the modern carriages of this generation. It wasn't so very many years ago, that this same building, on many a warm summer evening, rang with the lilting strains of the popular hits of those by-gone days.

Under a canopy of glorious green trees one could also sip his beer, in one of those cozy little summer houses, in back of the dance hall. Pleasant indeed it was considered to linger over one's sandwich and a mug of ale, away from the crowd, with the music softly echoing through the trees, with a silvery moon sending down crystal beams, and a soft warm breeze gently fanning the trees. Alas! Those days are past, and the summer-houses are fast falling into ruin, but the moon, stars, and breeze still cast a spell of magic over the lonely scene, one of decadent solitude ("John Marshall High School Interpreter", April 24, 1931).

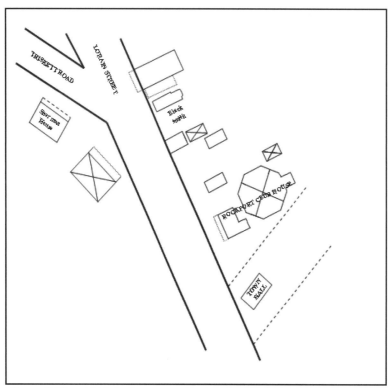

Figure 9-31e. 1913 Sanborn map showing the location of the Beer Garden/ Rockport Clubhouse.

Figure 9-31f. Banater Hall at 11934 Lorain as it appears today. *Author photo*

126

Figure 9-31g. Springvale Ballroom in North Olmsted is today the oldest operating ballroom in the Cleveland area. It was built by Fred Biddulph on his father's farm in 1923. Five years later a golf course was added. Both are now owned by the city of North Olmsted. *Author photo*

Figure 9-31h. In 1931, the Goodman family of Columbia Station converted their dairy barn into a ballroom. Although there is no longer regular dancing, the hall is still leased for wedding receptions. *Author photo*

Movie Theaters and Drive-ins

At the turn of the century a new form of entertainment, the motion picture, captured the fascination of the American Public. In Cleveland the first theatre house opened in 1903. West Parkers were no exception to the craze and soon began to patronize the area's earliest movie houses. The first, or one of the first, theatres in the area was the Pleasant View (Fig.9-32a) located on Warren Road behind what is now St. Mary's Hall. Shortly after World War I, Max Lefkowich built the West Park Theatre on farmland that he owned on the south of Lorain at West 170. When this early venture proved successful, he built the Riverside Theatre in 1939 at 16901 Lorain (Fig. 9-32b). His timing could not have been better as this was the year that Hollywood released two of its all time greatest films, "Gone With The Wind" and "The Wizard Of Oz." The theatre had 1200 seats and survived until 1978 when it was bought by the Lowes chain. It finally went dark for the final time in 1997 and was torn down to make room for a drugstore. Gone forever are Bank Nights, continuous running and the Saturday matinee with a double feature, serial and four cartoons for a dime! Also in the area were the Variety at West 118 and Lorain built in 1927 (Fig. 9-32c), and the Fairview in the shopping center at West 220 and Lorain built in 1954 (Fig. 9-32d). The Variety (on the National Register of Historic Places) was built without a parking lot, relying on moviegoers to use the streetcar lines of West 117 and Lorain Street.

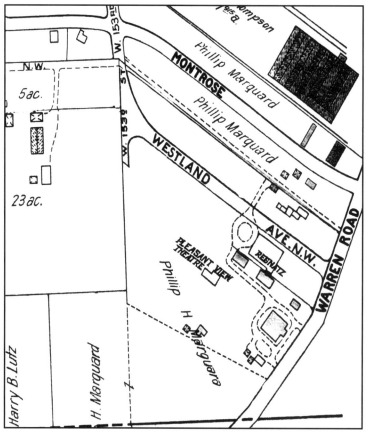

Figure 9-32a. Pleasant View Theater *Adapted from Sanborn Fire Insurance maps*

Figure 9-32b. Riverside Theater *Kamm's Corner Development Corporation Collection*

Figure 9-32c. Variety Theater *Author photo*

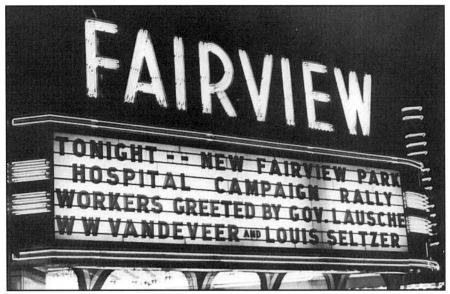

Figure 9-32d. Fairview Theater *Vollmer, 1969*

Finally, there were the Drive-In Theatres, which were a phenomenon born in Camden, New Jersey in the summer of 1933. By 1942 there were 95 drive-in theatres in 27 states. Ohio led the nation with 11. At its zenith in 1958 there were over 5,000 in the country (www.driveintheater.com). In Ohio there were 158 including the Memphis on Memphis Avenue (Figure 10-33a), the West Side Drive In at Brookpark and Riverside, (Figure 10-33b), the Auto on Brookpark Road (Figure 10-33c) and the Fairview Outdoor Theatre at West 210th and Center Ridge Road (Figure 10-33d). Today only the Memphis remains. The "passion pit" synonymous with the muscle car era of the 50's has all but disappeared from the American scene.

Figure 9-33a. Memphis Drive-In opened in 1950. Today, during warm weather, it does double duty as a flea market on Saturdays and Sundays. *Author photo*

Figure 9-33b. West Side Drive-In, 1953. *Cleveland State University Library, Bruce Young Collection*

Figure 9-33c. Auto Drive-In, 11395 Brookpark Road (at Tiedeman) June 19, 1947. *Cleveland State University Library, Cleveland Press Collection*

Figure 9-33d. September 7, 1947. The Fairview Herald proclaims the opening of the Fairview Outdoor Theatre.

****

132

CHAPTER 10
DISASTERS-WEATHER AND OTHER

The climate of Rockport, like most of the northeastern United States, is in the Temperate Continental Zone marked by warm summers and cool winters. The weather is highly changeable as the zone falls along one of the major storm tracks of North America. In Rockport, there are strong modifying influences from Lake Erie especially within a mile or two of the shoreline. Precipitation is moderate, about 38" per year, and is evenly distributed throughout the year.

Winter is somewhat ameliorated by the moderating effect of Lake Erie but this condition also produces an excessive amount of winter cloudiness and frequent snows. Snow cover rarely persists for long periods since above freezing temperatures are a regular occurrence. Spring is very brief, and some would say non-existent. It is usually just a short transition period from winter to summer. Summers are humid where thundershowers and storms are frequent visitors. Heat and humidity can be oppressive but are usually short lived. Along the shoreline, the lake breeze provides a moderating relief during hot days. Autumn is usually the most pleasant time with mild, sunny weather and low humidity continuing well into November (Ruffner and Bair, 1977). The growing season in Rockport, like most other lakeshore communities, varies from 195 days along the shoreline to 180 days inland.

Over the last two hundred or so years, climate and weather patterns have been very stable and predictable in the continental United States. In the long term, this predictable pattern is not the norm but is an exception. This weather pattern has been a contributing factor in the rapid rise of the United States as the breadbasket of the world. We simply have been fortunate to settle this country at the right time. It has been speculated that this stable era is ending, and we are returning to the more unpredictable norm. While average temperatures and precipitation remain relatively unchanged, the averages are arrived at by more extremes. This means longer warm, cold, dry and wet spells and more daily record highs and lows. The effect of this pattern on an agricultural society would be significant but within Rockport where agriculture no longer exists, the effects of the gradual change are insignificant and mostly unnoticeable. However, the climate, especially along the shoreline, played a major role in the development of Rockport as a major fruit supplier for the Metropolitan area. Nevertheless, with all the positive influence of climate and weather, Rockport like most communities has had its share of severe weather. The more significant weather events and their influence are noted below.

BLIZZARD: A dangerous winter storm lasting three hours or longer and including winds of 35 mph or more, considerable falling or blowing snow resulting in visibility of less that ¼ mile and temperatures of 20°F or less.

SEVERE BLIZZARD: has winds of 45 mph or more, falling or blowing snow producing visibility frequently near zero and temperatures of 10°F or lower.

November 9-11, 1913.

Cleveland was paralyzed with about two feet of snow and winds over 75 mph. The record at Cleveland up to that time for snowfall in a 24-hour period was 13 inches. The record was shattered with 17.4 inches and a three-day total of 22.2. It also set a low barometer record reading of 28.78 inches up to that time. High winds spread fires for seven hours. Overnight snows downed electric wires, which electrocuted horses, halted trolleys, and severed communication with other cities.

The worst part of the storm was experienced on Lake Huron where nineteen ships went down with all hands. A total of at least 244 lives was lost. The storm was best summed up in a report by the Lake Carriers Association.

"No lake master can recall in all his experience a storm of such unprecedented violence with such rapid changes in the direction of the wind and its gusts of such fearful speed! Storms ordinarily of that velocity do not last over four or five hours, but this storm raged for sixteen hours continuously at an average velocity of sixty miles per hour, with frequent spurts of seventy and over.

Obviously, with a wind of such long duration, the seas that were made were such that the lakes are not ordinarily acquainted with. The testimony of masters is that the waves were at least 35 feet high and followed each other in quick succession, three waves ordinarily coming one right after the other.

They were considerably shorter than the waves that are formed by an ordinary gale. Being of such height and hurled with such force and such rapid succession, the ships must have been subjected to incredible punishment." (www.crh.noaa.gov).

January 12, 1918.

Statewide blizzard. Temperatures were near freezing the day before the storm but as the cold air arrived, the thermometer plummeted 40 to 50 degrees. Winds averaged 48 miles per hour with gusts to 63 for fifteen hours. Train traffic was halted statewide as were most urban streetcars. Drifts of 10-15 feet covered homes, vehicles and trains.

The storm was just a part of the fourth coldest winter on record. Coal supplies were scarce in Ohio and throughout most of the east. Many businesses were closed for 10 Mondays beginning January 21 to conserve coal supplies. Several persons died outside, and several more died in their homes due to cold. Many cattle were frozen in rail cars. (Schmidlin and Schmidlin, 1996).

November 23-27, 1950.

The Thanksgiving blizzard. The Thanksgiving snowstorm of 1950 was the deepest in Ohio's history and is generally credited with providing the Ohio record for a 24-hour snowfall: 20.7 inches at Youngstown and the Ohio record snowstorm, 36.3 inches during three days at Steubenville. All of Ohio had more than 10 inches during the last week of November and the eastern half of Ohio measured 20-35 inches during the period. Strong winds and record cold made this one of the most disruptive Ohio snowstorms.

Thanksgiving temperatures were in the 40's across Ohio. Rain began during the afternoon in the northwest and changed to snow late on Thanksgiving. Snow started overnight in the eastern counties and became heavier statewide on the 24th. By Friday morning,

Figure 10-1 Daniel Weber, who took this photo said, "This picture of Kamm's Corners, looking southwest was taken on November 25, 1950. I went up to Kamm's to see if traffic was snarled. The bus on the left made a left turn to go south on Rocky River Drive just after I took the picture and promptly became stuck in the snow."

134

Toledo was at three above zero, the coldest ever recorded so early in winter. Winds intensified and reached 40-60 mph on Saturday when the worst storm conditions occurred.

The storm continued into Sunday, and by Monday morning, the 27th, Cleveland had totaled 29 inches and drifts to 10 feet. Throughout eastern Ohio, roads and rails were blocked; schools, stores, and industries were closed, and communities were isolated. Governor Laushe declared Monday a legal holiday so banks and courthouses could remain closed. Virtually all businesses and schools were closed until Thursday. In Cleveland, the National Guard was called out to clear streets, and snow was loaded into empty railroad cars on the lakefront. However, a week after the storm, drifting again closed many roads. Steubenville schools did not reopen until December 4.

The press reported that up to seventy persons were killed mostly from overexertion and heart attacks. Damage was extensive. Wires and trees were blown down by the wind, and there was no travel in eastern Ohio for five days. The nursery belt of Lake County lost virtually all their stock, and hundreds of roofs collapsed statewide under the weight of the snow. The snow did not last long, however, as temperatures reached the 50s and 60s in early December. (Schmidlin and Schmidlin, 1998).

January 26, 1978.
The "Great Blizzard of '78" was the worst winter storm in Ohio's history. It hit the Cleveland area just about dawn on January 26. It continued for two days and shut down transportation, schools, and businesses all across the state for up to a week. Rain and fog the previous evening gave little indication of the impending blizzard, but forecasters saw the signs and issued a blizzard warning the previous evening. The barometer reading at Cleveland reached a low of 28.28 which was the lowest ever recorded in the continental U.S. outside of a hurricane and was indeed lower than most hurricanes. An ore carrier stranded in Lake Erie off Sandusky reported sustained winds of 86 mph and gusts to 111 mph. Winds blew down thousands of trees and miles of electric and telephone lines. Barns and signs toppled, and windows were smashed by the winds. Hurricane-force winds drifted the snow to the peaks of houses, totally covering some in drifts 20 feet high. Cars and semis disappeared under the drifts. All air, rail and highway transportation came to an absolute halt. Major airports were closed for two days. The turnpike was closed its entire length for the first time in history, and I-75 was closed for three days.

Temperatures fell to near zero and remained near 10 degrees all day. The death toll rose as motorists were stranded and home heating failed. Twenty-two people died outside while struggling through the blizzard. Another 13 were found dead in stuck cars, and 13 died in unheated homes.

Agricultural losses were staggering. Dead livestock, lost production, and property and equipment totaled $73 million. More than 12 million pounds of milk were dumped when storage and transportation was not available. Forty-five Ohio National Guard helicopters flew 2,700 missions across Ohio, working around the clock for three days. They rescued thousands of stranded persons many in dire medical emergencies. Three hundred troops from Fort Bragg with arctic gear, bulldozers and fuel tankers were sent to Toledo to rescue persons in northwest Ohio. (Schmidlin and Schmidlin, 1998).

COLD WAVE: Mass of cold air covering a large area and moving relatively slowly.

February 10, 1899.
Weeklong cold spell in the eastern U.S. with hundreds of low records established that remain today. Cleveland set a record of 16°F below zero.

January 24,1963
One of the greatest cold waves of the 20th century. January was a cold month nationally as

temperatures fell below zero in every state except Louisiana and Florida. The last week of the month was the worst as temperatures fell to -15°F at all Ohio reporting stations. (Schmidlin and Schmidlin, 1998)

January 1977.

Coldest month and winter on record. Below freezing for the entire month for most of Ohio. Ohio River frozen. No coal barges move. Deep snows.

January 19, 1994.

Cleveland established a new record of -20°F. The temperature remained below zero for 50 consecutive hours.

HEAT WAVE: Mass of warm air covering a large area and moving relatively slowly.

July 21, 1934.

This was the hottest day in state history and the hottest summer. It was 113°F in Gallipolis. The summer was accompanied by severe drought, and Ohio was part of the "dust bowl" of the 30s. Hundreds died from the heat.

July 8-15, 1936.

Hottest week on record. Statewide many cities set all time record highs

1953.

The longest and most intense late summer heat wave in Ohio lasted for 10 days in late August and early September. Cleveland had three consecutive days of 101°F heat, and it was the first time the city had recorded consecutive 100° days.

DROUGHT: An abnormally long period of insufficient rainfall. Droughts are slow disasters, which come gradually over several weeks and occur about every 10 years. They generally affect a very large area. Any droughts that affected Rockport were most likely affecting the rest of Ohio and other parts of the nation.

The most obvious effects are on crops and livestock. By the twentieth century, most of Rockport was virtually unaffected by droughts as municipal water supply systems were being built with water from Lake Erie.

Notable droughts occurred in 1841, 1856, 1863, 1870-72, 1893-96, 1953, 1963-64, and 1988. The dust bowl years included 1930, 1934, 1936, 1939 and 1940. During the winter of 1935-36, an area from New York to California covering 50 million acres was affected.

FLOODS:

February 11, 1881

Toledo was hardest hit when ice jams broke loose on the Maumee River flooding large areas of the city. In Cleveland, disaster was averted when 30 cannon shells were fired into ice jams at the mouth of the Cuyahoga River to break up the ice.

136

February 3, 1883

        Flooding occurred statewide but in Cleveland, fires broke out in the flats burning 50,000 barrels of oil and many factories. Spectators lined the top of the valley to view the spectacle. (Schmidlin and Schmidlin, 1996). On the Rocky River, all bridges from Strongsville on the East Branch and from Liverpool on the West Branch all the way to Lake Erie were washed away (Holzworth, 1970).

The Great Flood of 1913 (March 25-28)

        This was Ohio's greatest weather disaster. Four hundred sixty-seven people were killed. Record water levels were reached on every major stream. The greatest damage was in Dayton and Columbus. In Cleveland, the Cuyahoga River flooded all lowlands causing great damage to docks, lumberyards, freight houses, trains and rail yards (Schmidlin and Schmidlin, 1996). The canal system in Ohio had been teetering on the brink of closing for a number of years. The flood caused destruction at locks and dams throughout the state and brought an immediate end to the canal system.

Figure 10-2. Even though the most severe damage occurred in southern Ohio, the Cuyahoga and Rocky rivers did not escape the devistation. The steamer William H. Mack was torn from its moorings in Cleveland and crashed into the West 3rd Street Bridge. *LaVerne Landphair-Buch Collection*

Figure 10-3. Scenic Park near the mouth of Rocky River was completely flooded as was the entire valley. *Cleveland Public Library Collection*

Lakewood Post July 3, 1924

Havoc Wrought By River Rise After Tornado

Rocky River Rises Fifteen Feet Driving Trees Before Its Rush

YACHTS DAMAGED

Anderson's Dockage Ruined By Shifting of Sand Bar in River

By Jack B. Clowser

The effect of last Saturday's terrific storm in Rocky River were clearly discernable in the damage done to the river valley by the flood waters which came sweeping down in the wake of the near cloudburst.

When one starts up the valley from the Yacht Club Island, the first evidences of the force of the torrent is shown by the wrecked condition of some of the summer cottages on the west bank. The water rose so suddenly that people on the west island had to leave suddenly and some, who waited too long, had to be rescued when in danger of being swept down the river.

Under the Nickel Plate railroad bridge is a huge pile of debris and trees, which were washed out by the rising waters. Tangled in the mass are about six small boats which the owners will probably never see again.

A thirty-foot power cruiser moored at the foot of the new Miramar Hotel was crushed by a tree which swirled down the stream and was so badly damaged that it sank. Its mooring ropes held however, and preparations are being made to raise it.

A trick played by the torrent has robbed Nels Anderson, proprietor of the boat house in the shadow of the bridge, of a place to launch his craft.

Just north of his establishment was a huge amount of dirt which has been dumped over the bank during the past year. The water cut away a great deal of this and deposited it in front of Andersen's place, so that instead of a waterfront he now has a coast-line.

In the lower parts of the valley crops were ruined by the rise of the water and debris was deposited all over the flats, leaving them in a condition much worse than before the Metropolitan Park Board completed its recent clean-up of the valley.

In some places particularly above the Lorain street bridge, the river was whirling down Sunday morning with a width of over half a mile, which resulted when the flats were flooded. Several bridges were badly damaged and the cottages in the valley by Puritas Springs were inundated.

Figure 10-4. July 1924. There was a string of cottages below Puritas Springs. It is clear from the photo that most of them had been washed away. *Cleveland Metroparks Collection*

June 3, 1947

Figure 10-5. By 1947, there was no privately owned land in Rocky River south of Detroit Avenue so flooding could no longer destroy any farms or homes. However, this photo shows that there was no one teeing off at Big Met following this storm. *Cleveland Metroparks Collection*

Figure 10-6. Ice jams often occur with the late winter or early spring thaw. This one in February 1958 was fairly typical and caused considerable damage to boats and docks at the Cleveland Yachting Club. *Cleveland State University Library, Cleveland Press Collection*

January 21, 1959

The temperature was 60 degrees at 9:00 AM on Wednesday, January 21. The snow on the ground was melting rapidly, but the frozen ground couldn't hold it. Then the cold front hit and the thermometer plummeted in a driving rain with winds up to 80 mph. By midday, streets and basements were flooded. At the Cleveland Yacht Club, 20 Island residents and 20 from the Clifton Lagoons on the Lakewood side had to be rescued. Damage to boats was estimated at $1 million. The floods had struck all of Ohio forcing nearly 50,000 people from their homes and destroying 31 bridges. It was the worst flood in Ohio since 1913. There were 16 deaths statewide with 7 in the Cleveland area.

Figure 10-7. Damage was extensive at Captain Eddie's Boat House. *Cleveland State University Library, Cleveland Press Collection*

TORNADOES: Dark, funnel-shaped cloud containing violently rotating air that develops below a thunderstorm and extends toward the earth. The diameter varies from a few feet to a mile; the rotating winds attain velocities of 200 to 300 mph and the updraft at the center may reach 200 mph. Ohio averages 13 tornadoes per year. The intensity of a tornado is measured on the Fujita Scale: F0 has winds 40-72 mph; F1 73-112 mph; F2 113-157mph; F3 158-206; F4 207-260 mph; F5 261-318.

April 21, 1909.

"Cyclone" damage occurred throughout Cleveland and surrounding area. "In Berea Township hundreds of trees and outbuildings were blown over, and between Middleburg and Rockport Townships the barns of E.J. Bradshaw, L. Hosfeld, Wesley Spafford, Thomas Campbell and a score of others were completely destroyed" (Cleveland Plain Dealer, April 22, 1909).

Figure 10-8. A thirty foot section of this B&O trestle was demolished just south of Berea. *Cleveland Metroparks Collection*

June 28, 1924.

The deadliest tornado in Ohio History hit Sandusky, Lorain, Sheffield and Avon. The number of fatalities is not known for certain, but, there were at least 85 killed, 72 of them in Lorain. The tornado was first observed just north of Sandusky where it struck the northern edge of the city at 4:35 PM. The U.S. Weather Bureau had an office in downtown Sandusky in 1924. The barometer had been falling rapidly all afternoon, but plunged 0.2 inch in five minutes and then rose 0.2 inch again as the tornado passed one thousand feet north of the Weather Bureau Office. It is possible that the tornado that came ashore in Lorain at 5:05 PM was not the same funnel that left Sandusky twenty-five minutes earlier. Large waves damaged cottages along the shore at Vermilion. The massive funnel came ashore at the Lorain Municipal bathhouse in Lakeview Park and tore a three-mile path through downtown Lorain in about three minutes. Its width varied from four thousand to five hundred feet, apparently becoming narrower at it progressed eastward.

The tornado lifted east of the city and set down again at Sheffield and Avon. In Lorain, more than a thousand homes were damaged and five hundred destroyed. All downtown businesses sustained some damage, and two hundred businesses were destroyed. At least two hundred automobiles were buried under bricks and other debris (Schmidlin and Schmidlin, 1998).

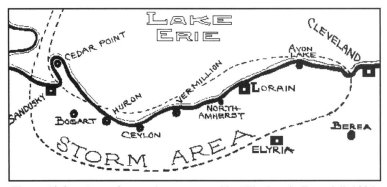

Figure 10-9a. Area of storm damage caused by "The Lorain Tornado", 1924. *Cleveland State University, Cleveland Press Collection*

Figure 10-9b. Looking north on Broadway in downtown Lorain. *Cleveland State University Library, Cleveland Press Collection*

Figure 10-9c. The Colorado Street district was reduced to matchsticks. *Cleveland State University Library, Cleveland Press Collection*

June 8, 1953

      At 8:55 PM, the Weather Bureau's new tornado watch system alerted radio and television stations of the impending storm. At 9:45, the tornado was spotted crossing the northwest corner of Hopkins Airport. It cut a swath to the lakefront at East 40th. The worst hit areas were between West 117th and West 130th south of Lorain Avenue and around Franklin Circle. Downed trees made streets impassable to fire engines and ambulances. Church steeples were toppled. Fallen trees and utility poles trapped streetcars and buses. Some streetcars were stranded on the lower level of the High Level Bridge when power went off. Morning traffic in the area was hopelessly snarled. Thirteen schools had to close. It

Figure 10-10a. Tornado damage between West 130th Street and West 117th Street. *Andy Mathews Collection*

took a week to clear all the streets and months to repair structural damage estimated at $50 million dollars. It was officially classified as an F4 tornado killing six in Cleveland, injuring 300 and leaving 200 homeless. It was one of the deadliest outbreaks in U.S. history as 155 were killed that same day in Flint, Michigan, and 90 the next day in Worcester, Massachusetts.

Figure 10-10b. Tornado damage between West 130th Street and West 117th Street. *Andy Mathews Collection*

143

Figure 10-10c. This house at 12112 Brooklawn was damaged beyond repair and condemned. *Cleveland State University Library, Cleveland Press Collection*

August 20, 1962

Violent thunderstorms with winds of 75 miles per hour for 5 minutes at the airport knocked down power lines and thousands of trees in North Olmsted and Lakewood. There were also tornadoes aloft.

April 11, 1965 "The Palm Sunday Tornadoes"

An outbreak of 37 tornadoes in Ohio, Michigan and Indiana killed 256 people. One of the more powerful ones wiped out the town of Pittsfield in Lorain County and ended just south of Rockport at the Ohio Turnpike in Strongsville. Several people were killed in the area.

Figure 10-11. At the junction of state roads 58 and 303, the town of Pittsfield was completely wiped out. *Cleveland State University Library, Cleveland Press Collection*

144

April 3-4, 1974

The April 3-4, 1974 (Super Outbreak) produced 148 tornadoes in 13 states and Canada in a 24 hour

Figure 10-(12a-f). Homer G. Ramby was a fireman with the Wayne Township Fire Department in Greene County, Ohio. On April 3, 1974, he and his wife were taking their son around on his paper route in Waynesville. At 4:20 p.m. he heard on his fire radio that a tornado had touched down in nearby southern Montgomery County. He went home, picked up his camera and headed toward Centerville. As he was driving, he noticed a dark cloud hanging from the stormcloud. Then all of a sudden to the east of his location (14.3 miles from Wilberforce) he saw a tornado form at ground level and build upward. It soon disappeared only to be replaced by another. Next two formed side by side and merged to from one massive tornado that eventually hit Zenia. At 4:42 p.m. the fully mature F5 tornado slammed through Zenia and continued to nearly completely destroy Central State University. *a-e Homer G. Ramby photos, f Homer G. Ramby Collection (photographer unknown)*

period. This was the largest outbreak ever. 315 people were killed and over 5,000 were injured. Immediately after the outbreak, aerial surveys were made of all damaged areas. Experts were surprised to find continuous damage paths on steep slopes, mountain tops and gorges. There were 12 in Ohio that day; the worst was in Zenia.

The Xenia tornado stayed on the ground for 32 miles, killing 33 and injuring 1150. Cancelled checks from banks in Xenia were strewn over 200 miles, many of them falling in the Cleveland area. Because the damage was so extensive and complete officials considered ranking this storm as an F6 tornado. No storm has ever been assigned this ranking and this was the first and only time it was ever considered (The Weather Channel, 2004). This disaster led the State to create the tornado awareness/ preparedness day each April. On that day all schools review their procedures and have tornado drills.

July 12, 1992

F0. Greatest outbreak of tornadoes in Ohio history, 28 in one day. This also contributed to setting a new state record of sixty-one for any single year. In Rockport, a tornado over the NASA Glenn (formerly Lewis) Research Center was visible from the control tower at Cleveland Hopkins Airport as it destroyed a mobile home, antennas, and trees.

OTHER SIGNIFICANT WEATHER EVENTS:

1816 "The Year Without Summer".

There are several local history anecdotal references to the year without a summer. However, there does not seem to be any record of a direct influence in our area. Throughout New England, Canada, and Europe, the years from 1812-1816 saw depression of summer temperatures that was the most severe on record. In 1816 frost was reported in every summer month in New England killing crops and forcing farmers to replant only to lose to the next month's frost. There were virtually no crops to be harvested the entire year, and the sudden cold spells killed thousands of newly shorn sheep and thousands of birds. In England, it was almost as cold as the United States, and 1816 was a famine year there as well as in France and Germany. The effect in the U.S. was felt mostly in northern New England where a few degrees drop in summer can result in killing frosts.

The cause we now know was from the eruption of volcanoes in 1812, 1814, and 1815. These eruptions spread ash into the atmosphere and depressed global temperatures with some areas more affected than others.

The effect on our area is more indirect. A great exodus of farmers from northern New England left for the Midwest. (Patrick Hughes, wchs.csc.noaa.gov/1816). However, Godard (1998) cited an Urbana Ohio newspaper that reported heavy snow on July 4.

Figure 10-13. These two houses at 15617 and 15621 Chatfield Avenue both had their roofs taken off as if surgically removed. The storm was on May 17, 1956 and was not offically listed as a tornado. It is hard to imagine such pinpoint damage being caused by something other than a tornado. *Cleveland State University Library, Cleveland Press Collection*

146

July 4, 1969 "The July Fourth Storm"

    Severe thunderstorms moved from Lake Erie into North Coast communities between 7:30 PM and 8:00 PM. This line of storms became nearly stationary for more than eight hours, aligned from Toledo southeastward through Fremont, Norwalk, Ashland and Wooster. Flooding, microburst winds up to 100 miles an hour, tornadoes, and lightning caused 44 deaths and injured 559 persons.

    More than 300 mobile homes and 180 farm buildings were destroyed or damaged. In addition 104 small businesses were destroyed. 700 boats and 7,000 cars were destroyed or damaged. Among floods, only those of March, 1913, and January, 1959, caused more damage in Ohio than this storm. Thousands of persons were outdoors on this holiday, and boats lined the lakeshore from Toledo to Cleveland. Parks were jammed with spectators awaiting the annual fireworks displays. At 7:45 PM, a large ship in Lake Erie reported winds of one hundred miles an hour. The storms struck the shore between 7:40 and 8:00 PM with winds of more than 80 mph, heavy rain, and intense lightning. Wind caused extensive damage to trees, wires, and homes along the shore in Lakewood. The Illuminating Company reported 175,000 homes without power after the storm.

    Most of the damage and deaths came as extreme rainfall developed inland late on the 4th and into the 5th. Thunderstorms continued to form all night along the line from Toledo to Wheeling, and rainfall rates exceeded two inches per hour. Total rainfall during the night was ten to fourteen inches in a band one hundred miles long from Ottawa County to Wayne County. Most of this fell in less than 12 hours. Farmers watched as crops were destroyed. Many of the floods were the greatest on record. In Fremont, cars were covered and water stood four feet deep in homes along the Sandusky River. High water or fallen trees blocked all roads leading into Huron County. Water was seven feet deep in Norwalk, and Greenwich was under six feet of water after a dam broke. The Huron River reached record levels, and more than 4,800 people were evacuated in Erie County. The Black River in Elyria and the Killbuck in Holmes also reached record levels. Ashland was isolated and without power for two days, and 30 bridges were damaged in the county. All sections of Wayne County were flooded, and 100 destroyed or damaged bridges blocked transportation throughout the county (Schmidlin and Schmidlin, 1998).

September 24, 1950 "Dark Sunday"

    "Smoke from extensive forest fires in northwestern Canada was channeled into Ohio, causing almost midnight blackness through the entire state, according to the Cleveland Plain Dealer. It became so dark from noon until 3:00 PM that thousands of people jammed phone circuits, calling to find the cause of the eerie phenomenon. Weather Bureau Forecaster C. George Andrus made several radio broadcasts to assure Cleveland that the midday darkness was perfectly natural and not related to war or the supernatural.

    During the height of the darkness, automobile headlights were on, landing lights came on at Cleveland Airport, and the afternoon game between the Indians and Detroit tigers was played under the lights at Cleveland Stadium. Even birds were fooled. Thousands went to roost as though night had come. Temperatures responded, cooling from 50° at 9:30 AM to 44° by 2:00 PM. The ocher sky raised fearful memories for some Ohioans as it reminded them of the sky before the Lorain Tornado of 1924 (Schmidlin and Schmidlin, 1998).

    I can remember sitting on the front steps of our house about 1:00 PM thinking how chilly it felt and how really weird the yellow green sky looked.

147

Figure 10-14a. West 117th Street and Madison Avenue following the explosion. *Cleveland State University Library, Bruce Young Collection*

OTHER DISASATERS:

Just three months after the deadly tornado on September 11, 1953, at 5:15 PM a series of explosions believed to be caused by sewer gasses ripped up a one-mile stretch of West 117th Street. The explosions left one woman dead and over 60 others injured. Water mains broke, flooding the area.Sidewalks disappeared and manhole covers sailed into the air to become havoc-wreaking missiles. "One manhole cover flew 150 feet and crashed through the roof of our one-story pet hospital on West 117th," remembers Dr. Wallace Wendt, Lakewood veterinarian. "The cover landed in an aisle between two rows of cages that housed 18 dogs, all of which were miraculously unhurt." Another came crashing through a fourth floor flat, and a third sailed through the roof of a two-story house and landed in the kitchen, just missing a woman preparing dinner.

Afterwards, toppled utility poles, twisted pipes and wires, smashed glass and paving rubble littered the torn street. Damage totaled at least $1,500,000. The pavement was alternately lifted and sunken five or six feet. A deep trench was blasted out from just south of Berea Road to Madison. Concrete chunks 20 feet long and 10 feet wide were scattered everywhere.

The cause was the subject of a running debate for many years. Some form of volatile gas in the sewer was the culprit. However, a negotiated $205,000 settlement of 91 lawsuits with total claims of

Figure 10-14b. Lake Avenue and West 117th Street. *Cleveland State University Library, Cleveland Press Collection*

Figure 10-14c. West 117th Street at Berea Road. *Cleveland State University Library, Cleveland Press Collection*

$2,500,000 ended in 1957 without any legal pinpointing of liability. Sharing in the restitution were Cleveland, Lakewood and five area firms—Sun Oil, Shell Oil, Union Carbide, White Sewing Machine, and Ferbert-Schorndorfer Division of Marietta Co.

****

CHAPTER 11
1900-1919 WEST PARK EMERGES

Figure 11-1. In the 1830's, John M. West owned a stock farm of over 700 acres in the Lorain Avenue-West 140th Street area. His home, built in 1842, was set well back from the south side of Lorain. He created a lake and picnic grounds near Lorain where the public was invited to spend the day. People began calling the grounds West's Park and eventually the name West Park was applied to the community. Several authors, including Barrett (1958), Swinerton(1986), and Van Tassel and Grabowski (1996) claim Benjamin West as the towns' namesake, but, Gary Swilik correctly pointed out that there was no Benjamin living in the area and the honor does indeed belong to John M. West *(personal communication, 2004)*. The home seems a little out of place today, as the surrounding area crowds the 13 room house onto a little lot on West 138th Street. *Author photo*

1900-1919 Rockport to West Park

In 1893, the U.S. Census Bureau declared that there was no more "open" land in the American West. This date is now widely held as "the end of the frontier" (Turner, 1921). With all land accounted for, the full energy of the country could be devoted to the industrial revolution. The next 25 years would be a truly exciting time with all the marvels that electricity would bring including lighting, machinery, streetcars, the birth of the automobile, paved roads, and central heating and plumbing.

Transitions within Rockport would also be dramatic. There would be the birth of new communities, the decline of agriculture, an increase in allotments, and the move towards a suburban way of life.

In this chapter, we will concentrate our efforts on the West Park area. The area does not change but the name does. West Park Township had its beginnings in 1900, thereby ending the last of Rockport

Township. In 1902 West Park Township is ended in favor of Rockport Village, and, in 1913, the name is changed to West Park Village.

By the turn of the century, Lakewood was well established and independent. Rocky River was not far behind, and Fairview Park was still a generation from its growth spurt. Nevertheless, these communities had gone their separate ways and established their own governments and identities. Today each community also has its own historical society leaving West Park as the orphan in this regard. Consequently, each has some published material on its respective community, and it is not necessary to reiterate that information here.

Perhaps it seems a little odd that we now turn our attention to a place that existed as a political entity for only 22 years. Had it remained independent, it would be among the larger cities in the state. According to the 2000 census, the population of West Park is just under 60,000. By comparison, Lakewood, which also has a population near 60,000, is Ohio's 14th largest city.

Mayors of Rockport Village/West Park	
1903-1907	John Seager
1908-1910	W.L. Nichols
1911-1912	Fred Feuchter
1912-1919	William Dahm
1920-1922	Henry Reitz

Figure 11-2a. The West Park community (Rockport Village within West Park Township) had grown to the point that it now had its own high school on Lorain Avenue at West 152nd Street. Henry Reitz was the first graduate in 1899 as a class of one. He would later become the last mayor of West Park serving from 1920-1922. The first additon, visible in rear, was let for bids in June of 1910. *John Marshall High School Alumni Association Archives*

School Notices--Ohio Correspondent Newspaper

"The commencement exercises of West Park high school were held at the Congregational Church June 2nd. The graduating class consisting of eight members rendered a very interesting program. Congratulations and best wishes for success in the future to the class and the superintendent." *Ohio Correspondent, June 10, 1910.*

"The Board of Education of Rockport Village will erect an addition to the village high school and also an addition to settlement school. The plans have been prepared by architects Bohnard and Parsson and bids will be received until early in July." *Ohio Correspondent, June 18, 1910.*

Figure 11-2b. The second addition was built on the front of the original building. *John Marashall High School Alumni Association Archives*

The Evolution of Rockport Township

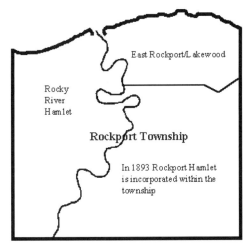

Figure 11-3a. In 1871 East Rockport was formed in the northeast part of the township and on 01/31/1889 it became the hamlet of Lakewood. On 12/19/1891 all the land west of the river became Rocky River Hamlet.

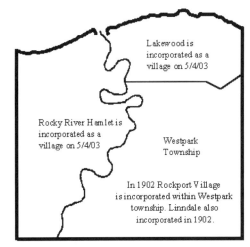

Figure 11-3. On 3/05/1900 the county commissioners granted the formation of Westpark Township. Rocky River became a township on 02/17/1904. This meant that there was no longer any form of Rockport Township government.

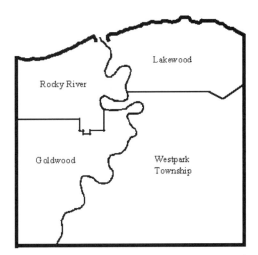

Figure 11-3c. On 04/20/1910 the south part of Rocky River became Goldwood Township.

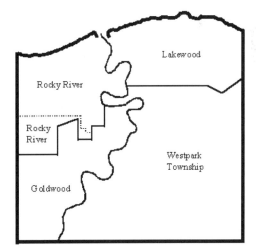

Figure 11-3d. On 07/14/1910 part of Goldwood was annexed to Rocky River and the next day Goodwood Village was incorporated.

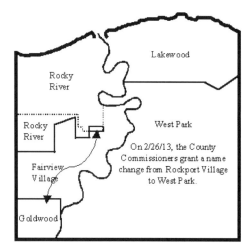

Figure 11-3e. Fairview Village was established out of Goldwood in September, 1910. Only Section 5 in the southwest corner and land along Center Ridge Road remained as Goldwood.

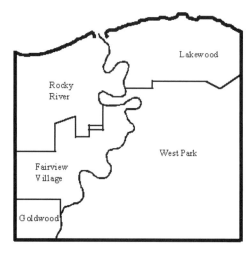

Figure 11-3f. The northwest corner of West Park was annexed to Lakewood in 1919.

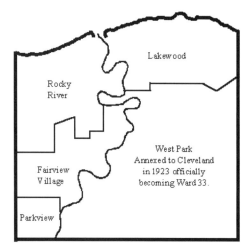

Figure 11-3g. The southern part of Goldwood became Parkview Village on 04/28/1925. The last remaining part of Goldwood along Center Ridge Road was annexed to Rocky River on 02/06/1926.

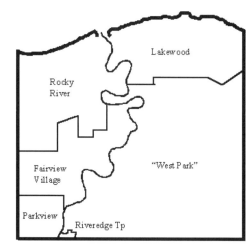

Figure 11-3h. In 1932 a part of Riveredge township was added to West Park. (See chapter 7 for the complicated evolution of Riveredge Township.)

154

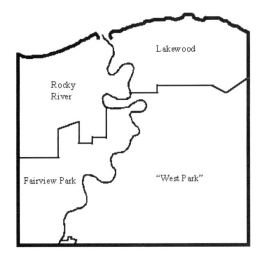

Figure 11-3i. Parkview was annexed to Fairview Park on 01/01/1967.

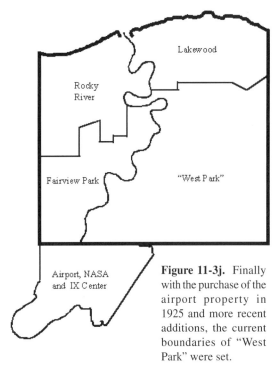

Figure 11-3j. Finally with the purchase of the airport property in 1925 and more recent additions, the current boundaries of "West Park" were set.

As you look at the maps showing the evolution of Rockport Township, it is curious to note the following: (1) the establishment of a township is/was originally a function of the state. (2) there were guidelines as to minimum size. The Cuyahoga County Commissioners, however, ignored those guidelines by allowing three other townships to be established within Rockport Township: West Park Township, Rocky River Township and Riveredge Township. I cannot explain this behavior, other than to say it does not seem to have occurred anywhere else in the state.

In their "Encyclopedia of Cleveland History", Van Tassel and Grabowski summarized West Park. "WEST PARK, the west side neighborhood and the last large suburb to merge with Cleveland, occupies a 12.5 square mile area between West 117th Street to the Rocky River Valley and from Lakewood's southern boundaries to Brookpark Road. Originally part of Rockport Township, West Park was named for Benjamin West, (actually John M. West) an early settler. During the mid 19th century, the area was a community of isolated homes and rutted wagon paths. Lorain Avenue, the only major thoroughfare, was a wooden plank toll road that ran past the Sherman House and Old Lorain Street House, rest stops for travelers. Oswald Kamm opened his grocery ca 1875 and later a post office on the southwest corner of Lorain and Rocky River Drive, thus inaugurating a commercial intersection thereafter known as Kamm's Corners. In 1900, the county approved the formation of the Township of West Park. With unimproved roads covered by snow in the winter and lost in a sea of mud in the spring, isolated West Park was often referred to as the "lost city."

Figure 11-4. Typical Rockport "Street" at the turn of the 20th century. This is Rocky River Drive near Munn Road. *James Foos Collection*

Figure 11-5. Village of Rockport in 1905. The first urban developments are beginning to appear. *Adapted from U.S. Geologic Survey Map , 1905 series*

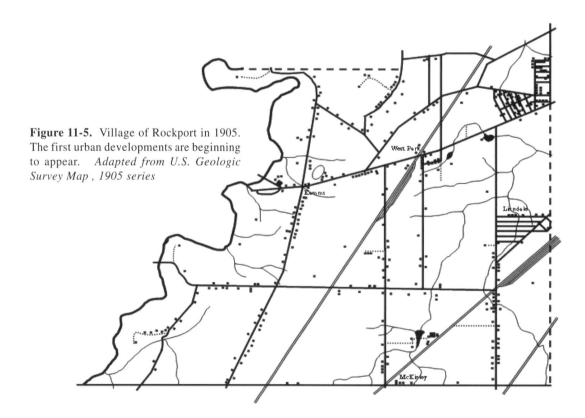

156

SELECTED ORDINANCES OF THE CITY OF WEST PARK AND ITS PREDECESSORS

Date   **Subject**

01/28/1895   Authorizing State Street (Lorain) high-level bridge over Rocky River for the Cleveland
                       and Berea Street Railway.
03/03/1900   Petition to make Rockport Hamlet a township.
04/05/1904   Sale of bonds for erection of water works and supply.
07/18/1905   Construction of sidewalks on Lorain between Settlement (W. 130) and Highland (W. 117).
                       Construction of sidewalks on Lorain from Settlement to Rocky River Bridge.
10/17/1905   Authorizing Short Line to build 4 tracks and underpasses on Settlement and Harrington (W. 150).
12/31/1906   Salaries: Mayor $75.00. Total for council $175
04/06/1907   Accepted streets: Clayton from Lorain to Midland Ave.
                              Midland Ave. from Ellis Place to Highland Ave.
                              Ellis Place from Leland Ave. to Midland Ave.
                              Belden St. from Raymond Ave. to intersection of Triskett Rd. and Highland Terr.
03/18/1908   Appropriation for a village engineer.
06/09/1908   Crosswalks for many intersections-sandstone 6" thick, 12" wide so that the crosswalks be 2 ½' wide.
04/19/1910   Providing for village solicitor.
03/06/1911   Set rates for water usage.
05/02/1911   Cleveland, Southwestern and Columbus Railway abandoned its stop near the residence of Henry
                       Peterjohn on Linndale Road. Therefore directed the railway to re-establish this stop.
07/05/1911   Change name of Post Office from West Park to Rockport.
09/19/1911   Establishment of a ditch (Peterjohn Creek).
10/1911   Permission to CEI to erect poles etc. on Lorain, Highland and Triskett to provide electricity to
                       residences and businesses.
11/08/1911   West Park Avenue dedicated.
05/07/1912   Regulations governing public dance halls and ballrooms, providing for $25.00 fine.
01/21/1913   Special assessments for construction of sidewalks on Lorain, Triskett, Settlement and others.
05/06/1913   Prohibit running at large, chickens, turkeys, geese, ducks.
05/24/1913   To number houses and provide street signs.
05/25/1913   Construction of city hall. (Fig. 11-6a)
06/15/1913   Authorize bonds for town hall, $15,000.
09/02/1913   Approval for construction of sewers on Puritas Springs and other roads.
10/27/1913   Land exchange with Anna Fischer for new city hall, city hall built in 1914.
12/18/1913   Granting permission to East Ohio Gas to lay gas lines.
01/15/1915   Traffic regulations.
07/15/1916   Ok to build firehouse; built in 1917.
09/06/1916   Bonds of $9,000 for fire engine and furnishings.
04/18/1917   First police car- $2,000.
12/1917   Garbage collection.
02/15/1918   Establish fire department.
04/02/1918   North-south named streets become numbered.
03/16/1918   Establish town marshal.
08/07/1918   Emission standards.
09/11/1918   Granted annexation of part of West Park to Lakewood, land adjacent to Lakewood with no legal
                       voters inhabiting the area.
11/14/1918   Recognizing Joe Talzarana, 31, an employee of the New York Central who saved Mary Kasper from
                       a train at the Lorain Road Crossing.
02/14/1922   Ok to build firehouse #2. (Fig. 11-6c)
12/29/1922   Last ordinance, naming Charles Hahn as Cleveland City Councilman for ward 33.

Ordinance Changing name of Rockport to West Park

"Whereas, by an order and decree of the Court of Common Pleas of Cuyahoga County,Ohio, the name of the Village of Rockport has been changed to West Park."

Signed February 4, 1913 by Fred Feuchter, Clerk of theVillage of West Park, State of Ohio.

Figure 11-6a. The West Park Town Hall was built in 1914 on Lorain Avenue near Triskett. *Cleveland State University Library, Cleveland Press Collection*

Figure 11-6b. West Park firehouse and town hall as they appeared in February of 1922. *Cleveland State University Library, Cleveland Press Collection*

Figure 11-6c. The second fire house in West Park at West 122nd Street and Lorain Avenue. *Author photo*

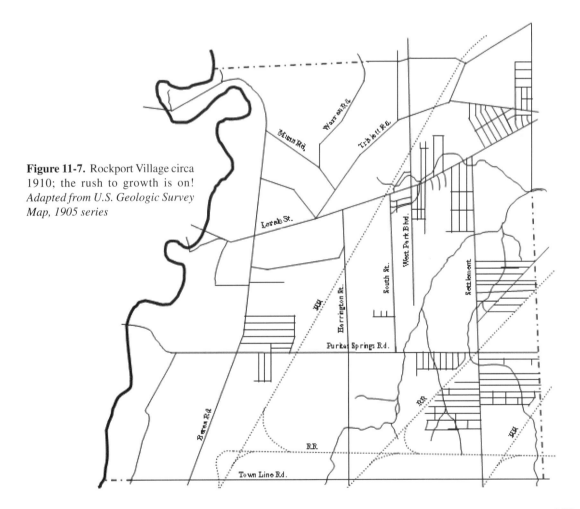

Figure 11-7. Rockport Village circa 1910; the rush to growth is on! *Adapted from U.S. Geologic Survey Map, 1905 series*

159

The Rayner Murder

It was close to midnight on Saturday August 27, 1910, and the Rayner family of Stop 27, the Elyria Line, was returning to their North Olmsted home from a day at their stand at the Westside Market. The Rayners were driving their high wagon, like a prairie schooner, second in a caravan of four that was strung out over 500 feet. Leading the way was Irving Dunford, florist, behind the Rayners were Miss Mabel Dunford and friend and last was Merrill Snyder, his wife and two children.

Figure 11-8a. The Rayner Wagon, X marks the fatal bullet hole.

The procession moved past the West Park Town Hall on Lorain Street. As the first wagon approached the racetrack at Kamm's, two young men ran from the roadside and ordered Dunford to "Halt." Dunford whipped up his horse and it broke free. The captors then fired shots that pierced his wagon as it passed by. The highwaymen then crossed the road waiting for the Rayners. Having heard the commotion, Walter Rayner began to make a u-turn with his wagon. When they saw him turning his rig, they fired at his wagon. One bullet pierced the heart of his wife Clara who died almost instantly. A second bullet lodged in the foot of his eight year-old daughter Blanche. Rayner continued to race back along Lorain until he reached Harrington's where a doctor was called as well as Marshal Stocker, Mayor Nichols and Sheriff Hirstius.

As the countryside got the alarm, a posse of 100 men was formed within 30 minutes. Armed men combed the fields, ransacked abandoned houses and sheds.

The groves and meadows were dotted with lanterns and occasionally a shot was fired as a signal. Automobile headlights penetrated the darkness . Horses that had worked all day pulled buggies holding three and four men. Down Lorain Road and Riverside Road, around the racetrack oval, down Berea Road and Madison; every thoroughfare in the township was alive with deputies. The highwaymen were traced through the racetrack to Riverside Road. At Henry Pilgrims house on Riverside Road, a horse was stolen. It was found three hours later at Minnot's saloon on Lorain at West 105th.

On the 29th there was talk of a vigilance committee and an addition to the one man police force of Marshal Stockard. The town had no protection from tramps that flocked in on the railroad or from those dumped in by the Cleveland Police.

Figure 11-8b. A. Hole made by bullet that killed Mrs. Rayner. B. Hole made by bullet that struck the child's ankle. C. Position of the assailants. D. Rockport track stables.

By August 30, County Commissioners had posted a $500 reward for the murderers, and Cleveland Police Detectives had joined the investigation at the request of Sheriff Hirstius. During the next several days, the Marshal and his deputies arrested several tramps and homeless men who were seen wandering in the village. On this same day, the funeral for Clara Rayner was held.

On September 8, Sheriff Hirstius arrested 19-year-old William Van Gelder who confessed after a "rigid sweatbox examination lasting more than two hours." Van

Gelder AKA William Grummitt implicated a companion, Earl Pender, in their two night spree of drinking and terror in Rockport, in wanton shooting, attempted hold-ups, barn burning and theft of two horses and buggies. By the time of Van Gelders arrest, Pender had left town.

Newspapers interviewed the mothers of both boys. Pender's mother, Mrs. Susie Zmich gave the standard response "I don't understand it at all. Earl was always a good boy and I know he hasn't done anything wrong." Van Gelders mother, Lillian Grummitt, took a different approach when she said "congenital insanity" would probably be the defense of William. "William's father and myself were cousins, and I believe the relationship resulted in William having a weak mind."

When the trial of Van Gelder began on October 10, there was considerable difficulty in securing a jury. Since this was a first-degree murder trial, capital punishment was a possibility. Potential jurists who were opposed to the death penalty were automatically excluded from duty. The actual trial was relatively short, and on October 21 Van Gelder was convicted of Manslaughter. Because he was under 21, he was sentenced to the Mansfield Reformatory.

On November 22, Earl Pender was brought back to Cleveland following his arrest in San Francisco two weeks prior. He had been turned in by two men who later submitted a claim for the $500 reward. Pender admitted his guilt at his mid December trial and was sentenced to life imprisonment in the Ohio Penitentiary. *Cleveland Plain Dealer*

At the turn of the century, over one hundred trains a day were passing through Rockport. As trains got to Cleveland a choke point developed at the single track drawbridge at the mouth of the Cuyahoga River. Faced with this rail traffic congestion, The New York Central Built a rail bypass around the southern and eastern sides of the City. The Cleveland Shortline Railroad (or simply, The Short Line) opened in part in 1910 and was completed in 1912. It was mostly a double track route without any grade crossings with streets. The western terminus was the yard at Rockport and the eastern terminus was at Collinwood.

Figure 11-9. The Short Line Bridge over West 130th street circa 1920. *Dr. Harlan Peterjohn Collection*

In the spring of 1894, John Alber and his wife Emma Colbrunn Alber moved to the "old red house" on the southeast corner of Kamm's Junction. The parcel included all the land from the corner to Alger Cemetery. The enterprising Albers wasted no time in taking advantage of the race track located directly across the street. Emma and her staff (Fig. 11-10) began preparing meals for workers and patrons of the track. This would probably qualify as the first restaurant in the area. With Kamm's as a major junction on the interurban line, and the race track as an anchor, the area would soon become the commercial center of West Park.

Around 1913-1915, John Alber would build a series of small buildings on the south side of Lorain which would become his own grocery store, (Fig. 11-12), Phillips Drug Store and Lanphairs Dry Goods.

Figure 11-10. The Alber family moved into this house on the southeast corner of Kamm's in 1894. It soon became the first restaurant in the Kamm's area. The home was torn down in 1928 to make way for new developments. *LaVerne Landphair-Buch Collection*

Figure 11-11. Lining up for a race on July 1, 1913. *James Foos Collection*

163

Figure 11-12. Alber Grocery Store 1913-1947. The man with the suitcase is probably waiting for the Interurban. *LaVerne Landphair-Buch Collection*

Figure 11-13. The Madison Avenue streetcar line was opened in 1893 with service from West 117 to downtown. It was not until September 16, 1917 that the line was extended to Riverside Drive (Christiansen, 1975). Developers then jumped at the opportunity to build in the last "open space" of western Lakewood. *ad from Lakewood Post October 4, 1917*

164

Lakewood Post August 14, 1919

FIFTY ACRES ON WARREN ROAD SOLD; TO BE CUT UP

INTO 300 LOTS

"The passing to the allotment stage of the last large farm in the garden truck district that lies between Madison avenue and Lorain avenue in Lakewood and West Park was noted yesterday in a fifty-acre deal between Joseph Laronge and Herman Klein.

The land changing hands is a fifty-acre farm that was purchased two years ago by Mr. Laronge from Frank Stahl. The consideration was said to be in the neighborhood of $125,000.

The property lies on the west side of Warren Road at Fisher road and extends westward more than one half mile to Carabell road. A part of it lies in the municipality of Lakewood and the other part in West Park. The tract is said to be the largest in that district of small farms that has been rapidly giving way to the builder of city homes.

Sewer and water put in by the city of Lakewood run to the edge of the property on several streets, which parallel Warren road. According to plans reported the farm is to be cut up into about 300 lots after new streets are cut through and improvements put in. When put on the market the lot, it is said, will represent a selling value of $400,000."

Figure 11-14. Gas well being drilled at Avalon Drive and Wager Road in Rocky River, property of L.E. Butzman, 21127 Avalon Drive in October, 1941. *Cleveland State University Library, Cleveland Press Collection*

165

Figure 11-15. Location of gas wells drilled in Rockport Township. The total appears to be 616 wells. *Adapted from Ohio Geological Survey Map*

Gas Booms

Drilling for gas and oil in Ohio is not as complicated or risky as it is in many areas. Most of the subsurface rock layers in Ohio are fairly even and horizontal. The major gas bearing rock is known as the Clinton Sandstone. Find the Clinton and you find the gas, and sometimes oil. In southeastern Ohio, it is found at a depth of about 8,000 feet. In north central Ohio, it is found at about 2,500 feet.

The first discovery of natural gas in the area was reported by the Cleveland Leader in 1885. Henry Mastick developed a well at Rocky River, and J.M. Gasser put one into production for lighting and heating his greenhouse near Phinney's Corners. However, because of the sparse settlement of the area, there was no market to justify exploring the resource. By 1913, however, things had changed. Gas was widely sought after, and the first of the Lakewood wells was drilled in January. So successful was the venture that within a year 34 wells had been drilled in Lakewood (Lindstrom, 1936). By 1915, the boom had spread to West Park. Figure 11-15 shows that 616 wells were eventually drilled in Rockport, and in the

166

1913-1915 period, it was one of the top producing areas in the Midwest.

Because of a lack of any regulation on drilling, wells sprang up everywhere, and the field was exhausted in a very few years. We now know that taking a little gas from a well on a regular basis will produce a lot more gas over the life of the well than pumping as much out as fast as you can. It was not until the 1960's during the Mt. Gilead, Ohio, oil boom that the state finally stepped in to regulate the industry in Ohio. The main street at that time had oil wells in everyone's front yard. It was probably very similar to that in Rockport, because citizens of Lakewood were outraged over the noise and pollution caused by the drilling. Just about the time Lakewood was starting to regulate the industry, most of the wells went dry. However, there are still a few wells productive to this day.

Most of the wells were simply abandoned when they stopped producing, and unless they are properly sealed (with 300 feet of concrete), they can leak small amounts of gas and oil for years. During the construction of John Marshall High School in 1930-31 an abandoned well was discovered in the middle of the foundation and had to be sealed.

Figure 11-16. It's Friday November 1, 1996 at the 40-yard line of John Marshall Football Field. The "Lawyers" are scheduled to play the Rhodes "Rams." For years, groundskeepers had a difficult task of trying to grow grass in an area of the field behind the snow fence. Someone discovered that an abandoned leaking gas well was the culprit. All games for the season had to be moved to alternate sites until the well could be capped. Because many schools used the field, it was a scheduling nightmare. *Author photo*

A Tisket A Tasket

In the early 1900's, baskets were as common as paper bags and plastic containers are today. They came in all shapes and sizes and were used to carry or store just about anything. The most common use was for transporting fruits and vegetables. It should not be too surprising to learn that with all the fruit and vegetable farms in Rockport, there was a basket factory right in the middle of town.

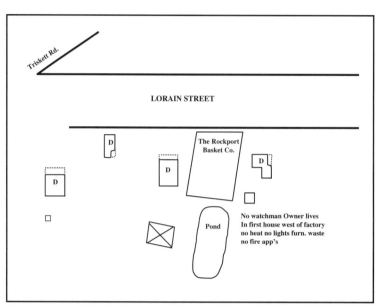

Figure 11-17a. The Rockport Basket Factory is shown on the Sandborn Fire Insurance maps of 1903. The map also indicates that "The Village of Rockport is 7.4 miles SW of Cleveland City Hall. No fire department or apparatus, water supply from wells and cisterns". *Adapted from Sanborn Fire Insurance Maps*

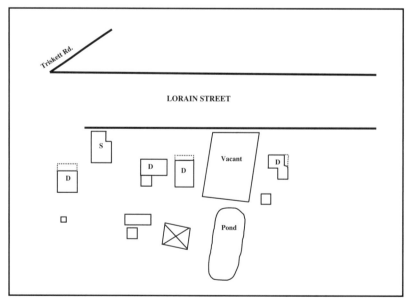

Figure 11-17b. In 1913, there were a few changes in the area including a store, but the factory is listed as vacant. *Adapted from Sanborn Fire Insurance Maps*

168

In 1917, William E. Asplin bought the land on West 150th at Lorain Avenue and built his basket company. In 1924, he built a second plant in Chardon, and, in 1927, a third plant in Hartville. A fourth plant was purchased from a grower's co-op in Garrettsville. The Asplin's had three daughters, Pauline, Merle and Wilma. In 1968, the Hartville plant was sold to Wilma and her husband Charles Kimberly. The Garrettsville plant was managed by J.D. Hart, Pauline Asplin's husband. After a number of years, this plant burned and was not rebuilt. The Chardon plant was also burned to the ground and was rebuilt. A few years later when the lease ran out, the plant was closed. In the 40's Asplin built another plant in South Carolina.

Meanwhile, in 1972, in Dresden, Ohio, David Longaberger had revived his father's basket business. In 1974, he approached Charles Kimberly and asked if he could bring employees from Dresden to Hartville on weekends to produce veneer for his handmade baskets. In 1980, Longaberger began to lease the plant on a month-to-month basis. In 1983, he agreed to buy the plant. However, before official paperwork could be prepared, the plant was destroyed by fire. Nevertheless, Longaberger honored the agreement and rebuilt the plant the next year. The plant is still in operation today.

In the 70's when boxes and plastic had replaced baskets, Asplin converted the South Carolina plant to a pallet manufacturing facility. He was 85 at the time. *(personal communication Merle Asplin Wearstler)*

Figure 11-17c. It would appear that a basket plant is a fire waiting to happen. There was also a basket factory in Rocky River. Built in 1920, it was located at 19537 Lake Road. This picture was taken on July 25, 1941 the day after fire destroyed much of the plant. Since the plant was located next to the Nickel Plate Railroad tracks, it was speculated that sparks from a passing locomotive may have ignited the fire. The plant was rebuilt. *Cleveland State University Library, Cleveland Press Collection.*

Many people remember buying their Christmas tree from the basket factory on West 150th. One of the major reasons for this was that Asplin owned 3,000 acres in the Adirondacks and was able to ship in his own trees. Another thing that many people remember was the association of many Japanese-American workers at the basket factory. This was clarified by information from the partial autobiography of William Tabata.

Bill Tabata was born in 1936 in Long Beach California. In 1942, along with his family and 18,000 other Japanese-Americans, he was sent to an "assembly center" at Santa Anita Race Track. After several

169

months, his family was "relocated" to a camp in Jerome Arkansas. In 1943, after a security check, his family was given permission to leave the relocation camp. They could go anywhere except back to the West Coast. His dad went to St. Louis, Chicago, Detroit and Cleveland. In Cleveland, he got a job with the Asplin Basket Company and then moved his family to Cleveland. Bill remembered that his father was a good worker and a good organizer, and Mr. Asplin soon made him a foreman. His dad got jobs at the Basket Company for other friends who were still in the relocation camps and had them move to Cleveland. "At one time there must have been over a dozen Japanese living there". (Tabata, 2003)

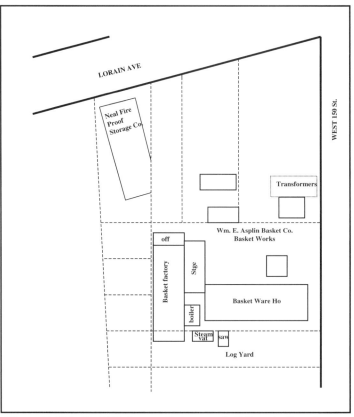

Figure 11-17d. By 1929 the new factory was in full production. It was finally torn down in the late 1960's. *Adapted from Sanborn Fire Insurance*

Figure 11-18. 3776 West 150th Street, The Asplin Factory in the 1950's. *Gary Brookins Collection*

170

THE CLEVELAND LEADER
MONDAY EVENING, OCTOBER 6, 1873
LINNDALE
CUYAHOGA Co.
FOUR & ONE HALF MILES
FROM PUBLIC SQUARE
CLEVELAND, O.
OFFICE 236 SUPERIOR
STREET
ROB'T LINN SUP'T
The New Suburban Village!
20 minutes ride by rail from the city.
Secure and Profitable Investment!
Now is the time to invest in Linndale Lots, which are
indestructible and cannot be affected
by runs upon Banks.
AN ADMIRABLE OPPORTUNITY
Is now afforded to insure positive safety with a sure
increase of 100 percent upon all money
invested in Linndale property.
LOTS TO SUIT PURCHASERS!
From $6 to $30 a foot—one-fifth cash, balance in
seven years.
To meet the convenience of all customers orders
on Savings Banks, Certificates of deposits, &e., will
be accepted as cash payments.
The location of Linndale is acknowledged to be
most desirable and with its Manufacturing Establishments now in operation and contemplated, the success
of Linndale is assured.
Every possible advantage conceded to purchasers
who for further information are referred to the
**Office 236 Superior Street,
CLEVELAND, OHIO.**

In 1873, real-estate developer Robert Linn was promoting the virtues of his new town of Linn-dale. There has always been considerable confusion as to where the exact boundaries of the community are located. Perhaps, more important, is the question, is it a political entity as much as it is an area? There are the original boundaries, the present boundaries, the Linndale railroad complex and the Linndale "Area." The interchangeable use of these terms has not helped to clarify the confusion.

Robert Linn's original town centered on the Big Four Railroad yard and station just east of West 117th Street. The original plans for the village extended from West 130th Street on the west to near the junction of present day Memphis and Tiedeman Roads. Most of the planned community was in Brooklyn Township.

Figure 11-19a. The old Linndale Station on March 18, 1930. This photo was probably taken shortly before the station was torn down and replaced with a large modern station built in conjunction with the opening of the Cleveland Union Terminal (Terminal Tower) complex. The new station can be seen in the lower right of figure 11-19b. *Cleveland State University Library, Cleveland Press Collection*

Towards the end of the 19th century, George Linn (probably Roberts's son) sought to make Linndale independent of Brooklyn and so the Village was incorporated in 1902. In 1904, all but six blocks of the Village was annexed to Cleveland. Linndale retained the small area because a fireworks factory was located there and Cleveland had an ordinance against such factories within their limits (Brady, 1990).

The railroad station, called Linndale, was located within the village of Linndale, but the giant railroad maintenance facility including the roundhouse was in adjacent Cleveland. Even so, the entire area was referred to as Linndale.

Figure 11-19b. The Linndale Roundhouse and station complex in 1951. *Cleveland State University Library, Bruce Young Collection*

172

In 1930 when the Terminal Tower (Cleveland Union Terminal) was opened, Linndale took on an even more significant role. $100,000 was spent on a new station. The Van Sweringen Brothers, who built the Terminal, did not want the dirt and soot from the steam engines in the new Union Terminal. Consequently, they built the Cleveland Union Terminal Railroad, which covered 17 miles between Linndale and Collinwood. At these two points, the steam engines would be replaced by one of 22 electric locomotives for their trip through the terminal and to the other side of town where another steam engine would replace the electric and continue the journey.

Figure 11-20. Electric locomotive 219 has just uncoupled from the train it brought from the Terminal Tower to Linndale. The steam engine is already hooked up to the train and ready to roll west out of town. The electrics lasted until November 1953 when they were replaced by diesel locomotives. The electrics went to New York City where they continued to work in commuter service until 1974. *J. William Vigrass photo*

It was around this Linndale area railroad facility and the triangular grid of streets between Bellaire Road and West 130th Street that the west side enclave of African Americans would develop. As has already been mentioned, George Peake was the first African American to settle in Rockport in 1809, and there were some African Americans living and working at the farms of Dr. Jared Kirtland into the 1850's. However, there seems to be a period of about 50 years after that when apparently no African Americans lived in the Rockport Area.

During the 1910-20 era, there was a tremendous migration of African Americans from the rural South to the major metropolitan areas of the North. There were several reasons for this migration. Many southern Blacks were dissatisfied with race relations in the South or were tired of sharecropping and tenant farming. Boll Weevil infestations and a series of floods in the Gulf States at the beginning of the 20th century had hit Black farmers especially hard. More importantly, with the onset of World War 1, immigration from Europe fell dramatically creating a need for northern manufacturers to acquire a new source of labor. It did not take long for manufacturers to begin recruiting African Americans to move north with the promise of good jobs. It was the jobs at the roundhouse that attracted these African American

Figure 11-21. March, 1942, the day shift crew at the Linndale Roundhouse poses for their photograph. The names of many of the Black workers shown here can be recognized as leaders in the West Park African American Community. Top row left to right: Norman Edwards, unidentified, Carl Green, unidentified, Henry Henderson, Jack Rhodes, Walter Love, Oliver Walker, unidentified, unidentified, Mr. Wood, Wilmer Clark, Jessie Edwards, William Latimore, Ellie Mapson Sr., Paul Peak, (no relation to George Peake) seated at right of second row is Coleman Edwards. *Ellie Mapson Collection*

workers to settle in the Linndale area. And for the first time, skilled as well as unskilled jobs were offered to African American workman (Brady, 1990). The New York Central employed most men from the African American Community in the 30's and 40's. With the closing of the roundhouse in 1956 and the Linndale station in 1957, the end of an era passed in the African American Communtiy. But the opening of the Ford and Chevy Plants in the early 50's provided the opportunity for even better jobs.

Figure 11-22. The Ford Plant in November of 1955 three years after it opened. *Cleveland State University Library, Cleveland Press Collection.*

In the fall of 2003, there was a dedication ceremony for an Ohio Historical Marker commemorating the West Park African American Community. The text of the marker summarizes the early development of the community.

THE WEST PARK AFRICAN AMERICAN COMMUNITY

"The West Park African American Community began in 1809 with the first black settler and one of the earliest residents of the area, inventor and farmer George Peake. With the growth of the railroad industry, African Americans were encouraged to move into the area to work at the New York Central Round House and Train station located in Linndale. First among these, in 1912, were Beary Frierson and Henry Sharp. As more and more African Americans came, African American institutions followed. In 1919, Reverend Thomas Evans and the families of Herndon Anderson and Joseph Williams founded St. Paul A.M.E. Church, the first black congregation on Cleveland's West Side. Reverend D.R. Shaw, the Ebb Strowder family, and Iler Burrow established the Second Calvary Baptist Church in 1923. Both became pillars of the community."

Figure 11-23. Ellie Mapson, area historian, poses next to the Ohio Historical marker commemorating the West Park African American Community. Ellie played a major role in helping to obtain the marker for the community. *Author photo*

April 18, 1988
Dear Sir:

     I thought you might have space in your historical archives for a bit of ancient history which I found when clearing my house in possible preparation for moving into a nursing home.

     Seventy years ago, the First World War was at its height as we three girls, the entire graduating class, gave this performance as our class night effort. Because the cast of characters was more than three we had to call on members of the lower classes to fill the other spots while we three had the starring roles. Patriotism was high and the citizenry was filled with the fervor of the war effort which was thought of as a crusade to rid the world of the scourge of war for all times.

     So this pageant depicted the spirit of the times and is reflected in the note to the audience. I hope you will find it interesting.

Most Sincerely,
Sara C. Harmon

West Park Public Schools

West Park, Ohio

GREETINGS

The Class of Nineteen Hundred Eighteen, assisted by the High School, presents the Patriotic Pageant

"Columbia Draws The Sword"

CHARACTERS

AMERICA .... Minnie Peterjohn

Great Britain .... Helen Peterjohn

France .... Sara Harmon

England—Jeanette Bartter

Scotland—Hazel Golder; Ireland—Marion Harmon
Wales—Irene Demaline; Canada—Alice Kuehn
Italy—Doris Basil.

Charity—Esther Wagner   Faith—Leah Schuster
Hope—Marie Foster   Mercy—Alice Kennedy
Soldiers and Sailors.

The audience are asked not to applaud. This pageant is so full of intense feeling that silence is the greatest approbation you can show the characters.

At the close the audience are asked to join in singing:

"Oh, thus be it ever, when freemen shall stand
Between their loved homes and the war's desolation,
Blessed with victory and peace, may the heaven-rescued land
Praised the power that hath made and preserved us a nation
Then conquer we must, for our cause it is just,
And this be our motto: "In God is our trust,"
And the star spangled banner in triumph shall wave
O'er the land of the free and the home of the brave."

GOOD NIGHT

J. E. Johnson Ptg. Co.   8516 Lorain Ave.

Figure 11-24. Program from the 1918 Senior Class presentation of West Park High School. *Sara Harmon Collection*

****

CHAPTER 12
1920-1929

Figure 12-1. It's recess at Settlement School in the early 1920's. The school was located on West 143rd Street near Puritas Road. It remained in use until 1951 when Artemus Ward Elementary School was opened. The building was used by the Cleveland Board of Education for storage until it was torn down in about 1975. *(Dr. Harlan Peterjohn Collection).*

Everything happened in the 20's. It was the "Roaring Twenties", "The Jazz Age", and "The Age of Intolerance." The world was recovering from the greatest war in history, and many new states arose in the ashes of Europe. It was an era of new inventions, rapidly changing fashions, art deco, more efficient travel and communication, political upheaval and economic change.

The 18th amendment had passed, and alcohol was outlawed. One of the hoped for benefits of this social legislation was a reduction in crime associated with alcohol. The reverse became true as it gave rise to the greatest outbreak of organized crime in history. The 19th amendment was also passed giving women the right to vote, but early on most women had little interest in politics.

Compared to most of Europe, the U.S. had suffered very little in the Great War. With most of Europe now substantially weakened, the U.S. would rise in power economically and politically. Warren Harding won the 1920 presidential election but died in office in 1923. The nation would soon find out that although Harding was honest, most of his administration was among the most corrupt in history.

The decade was one of great prosperity for many individuals and the nation as a whole. However, textiles, coal and agriculture were extremely depressed. Despite these areas of depression, modern conveniences and cars were finding their way into more and more homes aided by increasing consumer credit. People had more time for leisure activity, and the leisure industry became very important. Women were beginning to enter the workforce in an ever-increasing variety of jobs.

Many people acquired a distrust of aliens engendered by the "Red Scourge" of communism and the Bolshevik revolution. This attitude carried all the way to Washington, and for the first time, the number of immigrants to this country was limited. Furthermore, racism was on the rise, and membership in the Ku Klux Klan exceeded five million members.

Throughout the decade, profits had been rising, but wages had not kept up, and by the end of the decade many families had reached their limit in spending and borrowing. Unemployment began to rise; production declined, and Stock Market prices were way beyond real values. By the end of 1929, it all came apart as the Market crashed, and the 30's were welcomed by the Great Depression.

Figure 12-2. Warren Harding passed away from what was officially listed as a stroke on August 2, 1923. *West Side News, August 9, 1923*

West Park may not have been a mirror of the nation, but things were certainly not standing still. The decade saw more population growth, and home and retail construction than any other period up to that time. The biggest problem at the beginning of the decade in West Park was transportation. Still more rural than urban and still with more horses than automobiles, residents were dependant on streetcars for their travel.

West Parkers looked longingly at Lakewood, which had car lines on Clifton and Detroit since the turn of the century. Lakewood also had the Madison line, which was extended from West 117th to Riverside Drive in 1917. Cleveland streetcar lines came only to West 117th and Lorain, and residents of West Park had to rely on The Cleveland and Southwestern Interurban, which was less reliable and more expensive.

In 1910, the city of Cleveland was beginning to lose its title as "6th City" to Detroit and was trying to increase its size through annexation. Lakewood voted 1456 to 977 to rebuff Cleveland's annexation effort. By the early 20's, Cleveland again tried to gobble up Lakewood and added West Park to its "hit list." For West Park, the promise of a "5 cent carfare" was a carrot the residents could not ignore, and in 1922 they voted 2-1 to join Cleveland. Lakewood Post editorials had warned West Park residents about trusting Cleveland, and in the same election Lakewood voted overwhelmingly to remain independent.

ORDINANCE No. 2700
By Mr. J. Albin Neubauer

AN ORDINANCE to submit to vote the question of annexation of the City of West Park to the City of Cleveland.

WHEREAS, pursuant to ordinances heretofore passed by this Council and by the Council of the City of Cleveland, respectively, the Commissioners thereunder appointed have arranged the terms and conditions for the annexation of the territory of the City of West Park to the City of Cleveland, and their reports embodying the conclusions of said Commissioners has been duly held with the Council, now therefore.

BE IT ORDAINED by the Council of the City of West Park, State of Ohio,

Section 1: That the question of the annexation of the territory of the City of West Park to the City of Cleveland be submitted to the qualified electors of the City of West Park at the regular election to be held on the 7th day of November, 1922.

Section 2: The question whether such annexation shall be made shall be put in the form of "Shall the City of West Park be annexed to the City of Cleveland," "Yes." "No." and printed on ballots, and those who are in favor of such annexation shall place a crossmark after the word "Yes." and those who are opposed to such annexation shall place a crossmark after the word "No."

Section 3: Ballot boxes shall be provided and votes counted and returned and the election conducted as regular municipal elections.

Section 4: The Clerk of Council is hereby directed to publish this ordinance in a newspaper of general circulation in this corporation at least twenty days prior to the election hereby authorized.

Said Clerk is further directed to mail to each voter of this corporation at least twenty days before said election a printed copy of the terms and conditions of annexation as agreed by the Commissioners.

Section 5: This ordinance shall take effect and be in force from and after the earliest period allowed by law.

Passed July 18, 1922

E. J. SHORT, President of Council

Attest:

STEPHEN HENDRICKSON Clerk of Council

Read 1st time-July 18, 1922
Rules suspended Read 2nd time-July 18, 1922
Rules suspended Read 3rd time- July 18, 1922
Filed with the Mayor-July 19, 1922
Approved by the Mayor-July 19, 1922

HENRY S. REITZ, Mayor

For years, West Park had stood with Lakewood in fighting annexation. After annexation was officially completed in West Park, everyone in Cleveland seemed to lose interest in the streetcar promise. The councilman of the ward insisted that the pledge be kept. So after conferences and discussions lasting for several months, the final settlement was reached giving a 7 ½-cent fare. The entire rest of the system, including lines that went through and past East Cleveland, was paying only five cents, but West Park was obviously getting the short end of the stick (Lakewood Post, May 10, 1923).

The final insult was reported by Goebelt (1978). "When West Park was annexed to Cleveland, they had a fine new fire truck. After joining the City, it was taken from them and an old piece of junk was sent out instead. On its very first run, as it went over West 105th Street, then unpaved, the engine fell out of the chassis!"

One of the very first items of housekeeping following annexation was to change the names of many of the streets in West Park to bring them in line with the system of naming used in the City of Cleveland.

WEST PARK STREET NAME CHANGES, 1923

An Ordinance to change the names of various streets, avenues and roads, in the territory formerly known as the Village of West Park, and now a part of the City of Cleveland

Sec 2. That all avenues, roads and drives north of Lorain Avenue shall have the suffix N.W., meaning northwest, and all the avenues, roads and drives south of Lorain Avenue shall have the suffix S.W. meaning southwest.

PRESENT NAME	FROM	TO	NEW NAME
Alger Avenue	W. 144th Street	Warren Road	Alger Road N.W.
Arthur Avenue	N. City Line	S. Line Arthur Hts. Sub. No. 2	W. 155th Street
Arlington Road	Puritas Avenue	W. 140th Street	Thornhope Road., S.W.
Albert Street	Wyman Street	N. Line, Hyde Pk. Allot.	W. 146th Street
Brunner Avenue	W. 130th Street	W. 138th Street	Crossburn Avenue S.W.
Banner Avenue	Bellaire Boulevard	W. 137th Street	Ellwood Avenue S.W.
Brookpark Avenue	Old City Limits	Grayton Road	Brookpark Road S.W.
Beech Street	W. 140th Street	W. 143rd Street	Beech Avenue S.W.
Clarence Avenue	Rocky River Drive	Barthelman Road	Fernshaw Avenue S.W.
Clark Avenue	W. 140th Street	W. 143rd Street	Lakota Avenue S.W.
Crestview Avenue	W. 162nd Street	Rocky River Drive	Woodbury Avenue S.W.
Crestview Avenue	Rocky River Drive	Rustic Drive S.W.	Woodbury Avenue S.W.
Chester Avenue	W. 117th Street	W. 122nd Street	Milan Avenue S.W.
Cross Avenue	W. 135th Street	W. 136th Street	Blase Avenue N.W.
Clifton Street	W. 143rd Street	W. 146th Street	Wyman Avenue S.W.
Clarion	Montrose Road	Montrose Road	Glencliffe Road N.W.
Chestnut Street	Beech Avenue	S. Line, Cook & Beavis West Park Allot.	W. 142nd Street
Delmar Avenue	Munn Road	W. 159th Street	Doris Road N.W.
Derby Avenue	N. of Laureldale Avenue	S. of Laureldale Avenue	Eastway Road S.W.
Ednadale Avenue	Pearldale Avenue	Rocky River Drive	Valleyview Avenue S.W.
Ernadale Avenue	Rocky River Drive	W. Line Ernadale Pk. Sub.	Ernadale Avenue S.W.
Edgewood Avenue	W. 117th Street	W. 119th Street	Highland Road S.W.
Ellis Place	E. Line Lennox Pk Allot.	W. 122nd Street	Geraldine Avenue N.W.
Edgewood Avenue	Birchwood Avenue	Triskett Road	W. 141st Street
Everton Road	Brooklawn Avenue	W. 130th Street	Brooklawn Avenue S.W.
Esther Avenue	Warren Road	Easterly End	Westland Avenue N.W.

PRESENT NAME	FROM	TO	NEW NAME
Floral Parkway	E. Line, Riverside Manor Sub.	W. Line, Riverside Manor Sub.	Melgrave Avenue S.W.
Ford Avenue	W. 130th Street	Brookside Boulevard	Berkley Drive S.W.
Ford Avenue	Victory Boulevard	W. 140th Street	Berkley Drive S.W.
Forestvale Avenue	E. Line, Riverside Manor Sub.	W. Line, Riverside Manor Sub.	Valleyview Avenue S.W.
Garfield Avenue	W. 130th Street	Brookside Boulevard	Highlandview Ave. S.W.
Garfield Avenue	Victory Boulevard	W. 143rd Street	Highlandview Ave. S.W.
Glendale Avenue	Rocky River Drive	W. 190th Street	Fairville Avenue S.W.
Gray Road	E. Line, S.H. Kleinman's Glenmore Gardens Allot.	W. 150th Street	Justin Avenue S.W.
Glenview Avenue	Rocky River Drive	W. 196th Street	Fairborne Avenue S.W.
George Street	Wyman Avenue	N. Line, Hyde Pk. Allot.	W. 145th Street
Gray Road	E. Line, Kleinman's Brookline Allot.	W. Line, Kleinman's Brookline Allot.	Justin Avenue S.W.
Holmewood Avenue	Birchwood Avenue	125 ft. Northerly	W. 144th Street
Herman Avenue	West Park Road	E. Line, Evelyn Wagner Allot.	Lydian Avenue N.W.
Haxel Avenue	W. 162nd Street	Barthelman Road	BradgateAvenue
S.W.Holmewood Avenue	Fischer Road	120 ft. S. of Tuland Avenue	W. 144th Street
Hillview Avenue	Rocky River Drive	Rustic Road S.W.	Sedalia Avenue S.W.
Hillview Avenue	W. 161st Street	Rocky River Drive	Sedalia Avenue S.W.
Harding Avenue	W. 117th Street	W. 122nd Street	Wayland Avenue S.W.
Holmes Avenue	W. 130th Street	Bellaire Boulevard	Gilmore Avenue S.W.
Ingleside Avenue	W. 138th Street	W. 140th Street	Lyric Avenue S.W.
John Street	Wyman Avenue	N. Line Hyde Pk. Allot.	W. 144th Street
Kensington Avenue	W. 117th Street	W. 125th Street	Kensington Road S.W.
Lawnview Avenue	W. 130th Street	Westerly End	Aster Avenue S.W.
Ledgewood Avenue	Silsby Road	W. Line, Westland Hts. Allot.	Drakefield Avenue S.W.
Luverne Street	W. 117th Street	W. 120th Street	Stratford Avenue N.W.
Lynn Street	W. 117th Street	W. 121st Street	Sector Avenue N.W.
Merton Avenue	W. 140th Street	W. 142nd Street	Arlis Avenue N.W.
Midland Avenue	W. 117th Street	W. Line Western Hts. Allot.	Geraldine Avenue N.W.
Miner Avenue	W. 140th Street	W. 143rd Street	Elsetta Avenue S.W.
Norton Avenue	W. 140th Street	Victory Boulevard	Wainstead Avenue S.W.
North Avenue	W. 130th Street	W. 134th Street	Wesley Avenue S.W.
Nichols Avenue	W. 150th Street	Rocky River Drive	Chatfield Avenue S.W.
Oak Street	W. 140th Street	W. 143rd Street	Berwyn Avenue S.W.
Olive Avenue	320 ft. N. of Fischer Road	Alden Avenue	W. 160th Street
Overbrook Road	Lorain Avenue	Larchwood Avenue	Barthelman Road S.W.
Overlook Drive	Brooklawn Avenue	Berkley Drive	W. 126th Street
Parkwood Avenue	Rocky River Drive	Westerly End	Bernice Avenue S.W.
Park Road	E. Line Kleinman's Glenmore Gardens Allot.	W. 150th Street	Coe Avenue S.W.
Roosevelt Avenue	W. 140th Street	W. 143rd Street	Berkley Drive S.W.
Rockwood Avenue	W. 162nd Street	Rocky River Drive	Westdale Avenue S.W.
Regent Avenue	W. 140th Street	W. 142nd Street	Bidwell Avenue N.W.
Rosewood Avenue	Rocky River Drive	W. Line, Riverside Park Sub.	Elsmere Avenue S.W.
Richland Avenue	Fischer Road	Tuland Avenue	W. 141st Street
Riverside Drive	Northerly City Limits	Lorain Avenue	Rocky River Drive N.W.
Riverside Drive	Lorain Avenue	Brookpark Road	Rocky River Drive S.W.
Stahl-Ridge Drive	Warren Road	Alger Road	Fernway Avenue N.W.
Silverdale Avenue	Eastway Road	Rocky River Drive	Riverdale Avenue S.W.
Spring Street	W. 117th Street	W. 119th Street	Belasco Avenue N.W.
Summerset Avenue	W. 140th Street	W. 143rd Street	St. James Avenue S.W.

PRESENT NAME	FROM	TO	NEW NAME
Summerset Avenue	W. 130th Street	Brookside Boulevard	St James Avenue S.W.
Swift Road	Kirton Avenue	Bennington Avenue	Giles Road S.W.
Swift Road	Sprecher Avenue	N and S	Giles Road S.W.
Spencer Street	E. Line, Conger Helper Riverside Manor Allot.	Rocky River Drive	Melgrave Avenue S.W.
Temple Avenue	W. 150th Street	W. 152nd Street	Schuyler Avenue S.W.
Tiedman Street	Worthington Avenue	150 ft. Southerly	W. 120th Street
Tiedman Avenue	121.69 ft. N. of Brooklawn Avenue	Berkley Drive	W. 120th Street
View Avenue	Rocky River Drive	Claire Avenue	Marquis Avenue N.W.
Westend Avenue	Brooklawn Avenue	Berkley Drive	W. 129th Street
Williams Avenue	W. 161st Street	Barthelman Road	Larchwood Avenue S.W.
Woodrow Avenue	W. 118th Street	W. 129th Street	Summerland Avenue S.W.
Wilton Avenue	Wainfleet Avenue	Northerly	W. 134th Street
Wagner Avenue	W. 157th Street	Drakefield Avenue	Silsby Road S.W.
Yale Avenue	Bellaire Road	W. 130th Street	Emery Avenue S.W.
W. 125th Street	Lena Avenue (formerly) Lark Street	Longmead Avenue	W. 121st Street
W. 125th Street	Milan Avenue	Worthington Avenue	W. 122nd Street
W. 125th Street	Linnett Avenue	Milan Avenue	Lloyd Road S.W.
First Street W. of Riverside Drive	N. Line, Cleveland Sales Co.'s Grand Court Allot.	Woodbury Avenue S.W.	Rustic Road S.W.

THE RISE OF GLASS

As the fruit and vegetable farms began to disappear, they were gradually replaced by the greenhouse industry. The area would become a greenhouse vegetable capitol of the world in the 50's and 60's. In 1920, a co-op was formed to serve all the greenhouse operators in West Park, Rocky River and Columbia. At its peak, there were 420 acres under glass in the area.

With the energy crunch of the 70's many of the operators went out of business. Today the area greenhouses concentrate on tomatoes and gourmet cucumbers.

Figure 12-3a. The greenhouses on Puritas Road in February 1957. *Cleveland Public Library Collection*

Greenhouses in West Park included "Apelts" on Grayton Road, "James" and "Kuhlfeld" Greenhouses at the west end of Puritas Avenue, "Lorain Avenue Greenhouse" across from George Washington Elementary School, "Petersons" on West 150th Street, "Riverside Florists" at 3363 Rocky River Drive, "Rockport" at Lorain and West 144th Street, "Steinbrick's" on Triskett near Orchard Park Avenue, "Thompson's" at Warren and Montrose, and finally "West Park" and "Riverside" Greenhouses between Larchwood and Bradgate. Peterson's went out of business in 1968 after a hailstorm broke most of the greenhouse glass. Today the Marriot Inn occupies that property.

12-3b. Lorain Avenue Greenhouse. *Ross Bassett Collection*

12-3c. Rockport Greenhouse in October of 1949. *Cleveland State University Library, Bruce Young Collection*

A number of 20th century West Park landmarks were built during this decade. Most notable among these was the Central Trust Bank (Cleveland Trust), now Key Bank building on the Northeast corner of Kamm's. The building constructed in 1920 is made with Indiana Limestone quarried in south Central Indiana. The lobby of the building has high wainscoting made of Botticino Marble, a limestone quarried in northern Italy. The bases of the pillars are also made of Botticino. This combination of rock types coupled with the classical architecture is similar to that used for some downtown structures especially the Terminal Tower *(Joseph Hannibal, Cleveland Museum of Natural History, personal communication).*

Figure 12-4. Cleveland Trust Building under construction in 1920. *David Schafer Collection*

Other notable structures of the West Park area include the Neal Moving and Storage building at West 151st and Lorain, built in 1929, and the West Park Library at West 157th and Lorain, which opened in March 1928. The West Park Library was designed by the legendary Cleveland architectural firm of Walker and Weeks whose more notable designs include the Public Auditorium, the Board of Education Building, the Federal Reserve Building and the Hope Memorial Bridge.

Figure 12-5. In 1926-27 Walker and Weeks designed five Cleveland Public Library Branches. The West Park Branch was built with a steep gabled roof and tudor revival detail to harmonize with a residential section (Johannesen, 1999). *Ross Bassett Collection*

Figure 12-6a. The Neal Moving and Storage Building is under construction in the background of this February 7, 1929 photo. *Cleveland State University Library, Cleveland Press Collection*

Figure 12-6b. In March of 1930 the building was complete. At the time, the Neal Building was the tallest building in West Park. *Cleveland State University Library, Cleveland Press Collection*

185

In addition to public and commercial buildings, housing development continued at a breakneck pace.

Figure 12-7a. Warren Crest Allotment included Rosemary and Columbine Avenues between West 150th and West 151st Streets. *West Side News July 19, 1923*

12-7b. Rocky River Park Allotment included Ponciana, Flamingo and Puritas between Rocky River Drive and the West 186th block. *West Side News September 19, 1923*

12-7c. Metropolitan Golf Park Allotment included parts or all of Fairway Drive, Metropolitan Drive, Sunset Avenue, Puritas, West 185th, West 187th, West 189th, and West 191st Streets. *West Side News, January 21, 1926*

"Phillip Marquard is rapidly pushing the work on his summer residence "Pleasant View" on Warren Road. He expects to move out during the latter part of the month." *Ohio Correspondent, May 21, 1910*

Figure 12-8. The former Marquard Home at 3260 Warren Road. *Author photo*

The Marquard Estate

Phillip Marquard was a leader in the building field in Cleveland for 40 years. He was one of the pioneer developers of the old West Park district and built early homes in Lakewood. In 1912 he purchased a moderate-sized farmhouse, which became the nucleus of his amazing 52-room home. As his family grew to 12, more wings, rooms and floors were added to the home. The home was arranged into a half dozen complete suites for himself and some of his children who lived there at various times after they were married. (Cleveland Press, October 14, 1942)

Following his death in 1942, the home was purchased by William Bauer who leased the building to the War Housing Services Board who converted it to a 15-suite apartment house for war workers' families (Chandler, 1943). It is still an apartment building today.

Figure 12-9. Regnatz's *Barbara Unterzuber photo 1971*

Right next door to the Marquard Estate was perhaps the most famous restaurant of the 20th century in West Park. Regnatz's was a pioneer party center that catered banquets and wedding receptions. They always provided live music for dancing, and for a long time the music was carried over local radio. Both of the founders, Anton and Caroline Regnatz were hard workers, and decided to relocate on Warren Road "out in the country" after Phil Marquard made them an offer. He would not sell them the land but would allow them to build a dining hall if they would give him a percentage of the profits (Chabek, 1992).

From 1922 to 1941 regular menu features were their famous chicken, duck and T-bone steak dinners served family style. They grew most of their own vegetables, prepared their own pickles, dinner rolls, pastries, and noodles, and grew table flowers in their greenhouse. It was not unusual to serve up to 1,000 people at one time. At its peak, they used 50,000 chickens a year (Allyn, 1931).

After Caroline passed away in 1936 and Anton in 1939, the business was sold to a Chicago firm who operated it for a few years as the Show Boat Nite Club. In 1954 it was sold to St. Mary's Romanian Orthodox parish, and, unfortunately, it was destroyed by a fire on July 8, 1973 (Chabek, 1992).

As the decade of the 20's opened, most families did not own an automobile. Nevertheless, the nation was fascinated with an even more remarkable form of transportation, the aeroplane. The Post Office Department was once again at the forefront in experimenting with ways to speed delivery of the mail. Air Mail Service was instituted from Cleveland to Detroit in 1918. At that time, private airfields on the east side of Cleveland were used.

Coast to coast airmail flights were just a short time over the horizon, and airports where planes could take off and land at night would soon be a necessity. In 1925, The Cleveland City Council authorized a bond issue of 1.25 million for land acquisition and construction of a new airport. Land was purchased from Brookpark and cleared at a record pace. It officially opened in 1927 as the first municipally owned airport in the country and featured the world's first control tower.

THE FIRST RAILROAD
To Offer Through Service via
RAIL and AIR

Agents at Principal Stations
Can Now Sell You
A Through Ticket to Detroit
via SOUTHWESTERN and
Cleveland-Detroit Air Line

Fast - Comfortable - Safe
Cars and Planes

Let Us Tell You About It

SOUTHWESTERN

Figure 12-10. The country's first rail-air service. *Hays, 1988*

In 1928, the nations first rail to air service was initiated. In a final effort to increase ridership, The Cleveland and Southwestern Interurban line struck out on one last effort to gain publicity. By securing a deal with Stout Air Service, passengers could purchase tickets to Detroit at the Southwestern ticket office at Public Square. At first, two trips a day were offered and then expanded to include excursion tickets for a 50-mile aerial sight-seeing trip over Cleveland. Unfortunately, this partnership was about 30 years ahead of its time. When the stock market crashed a year later, it spelled the end for the Southwestern, which officially closed in 1931 (Hays, 1931).

The Southwestern legacy, however, would play an important role with the arrival of the air races at Municipal Airport. Their tracks ran down Rocky River Drive and right past the airport. Because the Southwestern owed so much money to Cleveland Railway, rather than tear everything up, the Southwestern turned their line over to the city to cover some of their debt. Cleveland streetcars then ferried a large portion of the crowd to the air shows.

In the early 20's there had been an Aeronautical Exposition held at various military air stations to showcase the latest aircraft and related technology. In 1928, the Exposition was moved to Los Angeles to afford more exposure to the public. In 1929, Cleveland hosted the Aeronautical Exposition and Air Races. Cleveland's new Municipal Airport had recently opened and was large enough to host the races at the west end without interrupting commercial traffic at the east end.

The event was a 10-day extravaganza in every aspect including attendance. The Exposition was held in the newly opened Public Hall with 250 exhibits. On the day before the opening of the races, 300,000 spectators from all over the country witnessed the Euclid Avenue parade of 200 floats, (most made of fresh flowers), 21 bands and an overhead armada of aircraft. On opening day of the races over 100,000 spectators were in attendance (Bill Meixner, 1999).

Figure 12-11. A rare double appearance at Kamm's. The Lindberg Parade heads from downtown to the airport to open the "Air Races" in 1929. It may also have been the only time a double-decker bus made an appearance at Kamm's. The double-deckers operated in Cleveland from 1925 to 1936 but only on the east and near west sides. *David Schafer Collection*

Following his historic transatlantic flight in 1927, Charles Lindbergh spent much of the rest of the year in a cross country tour with parades and banquets in his honor everywhere he went.

Marion Tourt Evans Recalled...
"I was 14 years old in August of 1927 when Colonel Lindbergh came to town. We lived just north of Kamm's Corners, off Rocky River Drive, and I had a great place to watch the triumphant parade as it came into view on its way from the airport – on the southeast corner. My Brownie 2A, loaded with film, was clutched in my hands. And I would have gotten a great picture of Lindbergh, seated in the open car with Ambassador Myron T. Herrick, had I not turned to stone at that moment. Luckily, a man standing next to me grabbed the camera and got a good picture for me. I hope I came out of my trance long enough to thank him." Unfortunately, the picture has been lost.

Figure 12-12. Ad from the West Side News, January, 14, 1926. The price of a radio was still not within the reach of most people. Since electricity had not come to many rural areas, radios were still battery operated.

Figure 12-13. A forty year tradition started in 1927, when Sterling-Linder-Davis Department Store put up the "World's Largest Indoor Christmas Tree." In the early 1960's the firm felt that they were in a prime downtown location (East 13th and Euclid) and decided not to establish suburban branch stores. By 1968, without outlying stores, the company was not profitable and was closed in September. *Author collection*

RIVERVIEW GARDENS

formerly known as the
RAINBOW GARDENS
RIVERSIDE DRIVE *and* MUNN RD.
WEST PARK

Cleveland's Most Attractive and
Convenient Garden Restaurant
(on the banks of Rocky River)
Opens Thursday, May 10th, 6:30 P. M.

Figure 12-14. "Riverview Gardens will seat a thousand people at a time." There was also a dance floor with live bands. *Lakewood Post May 10, 1923*

Part of the reason for the boom times of the 20's was the advance of the chain stores. Retailers who were successful due to the prosperity of the times felt the need to branch out. Woolworth, The Great Atlantic and Pacific Tea Company, and Kroger began in the 1880's. By 1929, there were over 500 A&P stores in the Cleveland area as well as 417 Kroger and 317 Fishers. For the first time these chain grocery stores became self-serve.

Figure 12-15a. A&P occupied the first floor of the Albers Building at Kamm's. In 1929, A&P had nearly 14,000 stores nationwide. *Cleveland Public Library*

Figure 12-15b. Kroger began in Cincinnati in 1883. By 1929, there were 5575 Kroger Stores around the country. This one at Kamm's Corner is adjacent to another popular chain store, Woolworth's "Dime Store." *Cleveland Public Library*

KIWANIS

"Kiwanis is a worldwide service organization of men and women who share the challenge of community and world improvement." (www.ohiokiwanis.org) It was originally founded in Detroit, Michigan in 1915. There are now over 8,200 clubs worldwide. Kiwanis clubs take on humanitarian and civic projects that public authorities are not prepared or able to perform. The second club ever formed was in Cleveland in 1915.

In 1927, The Cleveland Club sponsored the formation of the West Park Kiwanis, and in 1950, the West Park Club sponsored the formation of the Fairview Park Chapter.

The following is a partial list of some of the major projects the Kiwanis Club of West Park has undertaken:
* led campaign for construction of the railroad underpass at West 143rd Street and Lorain
* secured street lighting on Lorain Avenue from West 98th Street to the Rocky River Bridge
* organized early committees to spark the building of Fairview Park Hospital
* led campaign for construction of new John Marshall High School on West 143rd Street
* built, equipped and maintained the 2 cabins in Rocky River Reservation (Figure 8-20, 8-21)
* furnished funds and equipment for school for retarded children
* campaigned for flashing traffic lights in front of all schools
* sponsored the West Park-Fairview YMCA
* sponsored Key Clubs at John Marshall and St. Joseph's High Schools.

The list is far more extensive, but the amount of good that this organization has done for West Park can never be over estimated or be told often enough.

****

194

CHAPTER 13
1930-39

Figure 13-1. Looking west on Lorain Avenue at West 143rd Street in the early 1930's. *David Schafer Collection*

The photo shows the busiest railroad crossing in West Park. When this picture was taken in the early 30's, there were probably 100 trains a day passing here. In addition, there was also the switching activity at the West Park Yard as trains moved back and forth across Lorain Avenue (Figure 6-2). The importance of this crossing is evident by a number of factors. Quadrant gates (used only at the busiest crossings) prevented anyone from driving around the gates to "beat a train." Although there were no flashing lights, the watchman's tower was manned 24/7. The watchman controlled the gates and the bell (on the pole just below his tower). A streetcar can be seen approaching in the distance. Lorain Avenue had an east bound and a west bound track for street cars-except at this crossing where a single track was used by both east and westbound cars.

The workers appear to be cleaning out the flange-way between the road and the rail. If this becomes filled with packed snow and ice, a streetcar could easily "ride-up" off the rail. One would not like to see a streetcar derailed in the middle of such a busy railroad crossing.

When the West Park Kiwanis was formed in 1927, one of their first large civic projects was to get an underpass built at this dangerous crossing. This sort of project was a major undertaking involving the city of Cleveland, the County Engineer, Cleveland Transit System and the New York Central Railroad.

Figure 13-2. A streetcar in the loop just east of West 137 Street on Lorain Avenue. *David Schafer Collection*

Obviously their campaign was successful because in 1937, CTS built a streetcar turn around loop in a field on the south side of Lorain Street across from the Ohio Bell Building. The Lorain Avenue car line was cut back to this point on December 4, 1937 as work on the underpass began. In December 1938, service resumed to Kamm's Corners. However, it was now impossible to reach Brookpark because a huge sewer project was under way from Kamm's to Brookpark.

For the 1939 Air Races, a temporary track was laid over the sewer ditch. Labor Day, 1939 (September 3) was the date of the last run of the airport line. On October 1, 1942, streetcars again returned to Rocky River Drive and Puritas using a new loop built just north of St. Pat's. *(Christiansen, 1975)*

Figure 13-3. After the Cleveland and Southwestern Interurban ceased operation on February 28, 1931, North Olmsted obtained part of the franchise and set up a bus line to give North Olmsted and Fairview Village residents transportation to downtown Cleveland. *Fairview Park Historical Society Collection*

196

Another early project of the West Park Kiwanis was their campaign for a new public high school. Because of rapid growth in the community John Marshall had become severely over crowded. The PTA and Kiwanis were pressing the school board and when the newspapers showed the overcrowding on wooden stairways, the board set into motion plans for a new building.

Figure 13-4a. Two people to a locker. *Cleveland State University Library, Cleveland Press Collection*

Figure 13-4b. "Pupils at the crowded school jammed into narrow stairway when changing rooms between classes." *Cleveland State University Library, Cleveland Press Collection*

Figure 13-4c. Portables, extra classes hurriedly built to relieve the overcrowding. No running water and only a small coal stove for heat. *Cleveland State University Library, Cleveland Press Collection*

197

Figure 13-4d. "Exterior of the new high school which will be opened tomorrow. Built to care for approximately 1,800 pupils, the structure and equipment cost is slightly in excess of $1,000,000". *Cleveland Plain Dealer January 31, 1932, John Marshall Alumni Association Archives*

Figure 13-4e. The football stadium would be built behind the school on West 143rd Street but not until later in 1936. This March 11, 1936, photo shows that West 143rd Street is still nothing more than a mud lane. *Cleveland Public Library Collection*

Historical Sketch of the West Park-Fairview Branch YMCA and YWCA

(Prepared by Rev. J.H.L. Trout, D.D., for the Ground-Breaking service June 14, 1964)

This West Park-Fairview Branch of the Cleveland YMCA and YWCA has a history of 28 years as a Branch YMCA which was organized in the spring of 1936. Some YMCA work had been done prior to that date. More than 40 years ago, about 1921 or 1922, Oscar J. Fox, secretary of the Lakewood Y, organized HI-Y Clubs in the John Marshall High School of West Park and in the High School in Fairview Village. In the 1920's and 1930's, groups of boys assembled at Kamm's Corner to go on hikes and swims under the leadership of men like Don Carmichael and Kinsley Warfield. Some of these activities were discontinued when cuts in budget resulted in staff cuts during the Great Depression that followed the Wall Street crash in 1929.

Then came one of those incidents that give birth to institutions. An ideal place for YMCA work became available. As the John Marshall High School was moving into its new building, just prior to Feb. 1, 1932, I asked the principal, Ben Eggeman, what would be done with the old building. He replied,

"There is some talk about using it for a Junior High, but I hope they never use this building again as a school. It's a fire-trap with its wooden stairways and narrow corridors." Then, after a brief pause, he added. "The only part of the building that isn't obsolete and in need of repairs is the gymnasium in the rear, which is comparatively new."

"If the Board of Education sells it," I replied, "someone might buy it for the gym; but who would want to buy a gym?"

"It would make a dandy YMCA," he said.

"So it would," I replied, "and I know a man that might help us to start one. We need a YMCA in this community. I'm going to talk to Bill Landphair, who was helping to promote the work that the Lakewood Y used to do in West Park."

Bill Landphair was interested. We had lunch one day with Ben Eggeman in the teacher's lunchroom and decided that the next step was to get Oscar Fox's advice. Oscar met with the three of us at a second luncheon meeting, but said that, although a new branch in West Park would be fine, we couldn't start one because depression cuts in the Community Fund receipts made them forbid any Community Fund agency to start new branches or expand in any way. We decided to go ahead and organize anyhow, even though we would have to finance it ourselves. We did. Bill Landphair and I made a list of business and professional men in the community that should be interested--mostly Kiwanians-- and asked them to help. The response was heartening--almost unanimous. We met in the Assembly Hall of Bethany English Lutheran Church (on an unrecorded date) in the Spring of 1936, and organized the West Park YMCA with William Landphair as chairman and Guy Wheeler as secretary. Our next step was to find a someone to run it. Bill Landphair and I went to the office of the Metropolitan YMCA and announced that we had organized a YMCA and were looking for a man with experience in YMCA work to run it. You never saw such surprise and incredulity at the birth of a baby!

"You did what?" the YMCA official asked. "You can't organize a YMCA."

"But we did," I replied. "Can't any group of citizens organize a YMCA?"

"You certainly cannot," he almost shouted. "No one but the Metropolitan YMCA can start a new branch in the Greater Cleveland area, and we can't now on account of this depression. No new branches.

Community Fund says so, and they hold the purse strings."

We explained that we knew that, and that we were not asking for money--just information about where to find a secretary.

"But we forbid you to start a YMCA."

"All right," we replied, "we'll name it something else. We organized because the old John Marshall High gym is unoccupied, and we want to run some kind of community center there. We'll call it the West Park Community House. But we would still like a man with YMCA experience to run it for us. Will you help us find a man?"

It finally dawned upon the official that a baby had been born, and that a baby with a gymnasium as a home would be a nice baby to adopt. Why not adopt a baby--if they could--instead of murdering it?

"Who started this - this YMCA?" he asked.

"A group of leading business and professional men--mostly Kiwanians--in West Park and Fair-view Village."

"Well, I see you mean business," he said. "Let me explain this situation to the Board of the Metropolitan Y. After all, we didn't start it. You did. Perhaps if we take it to the Community Fund, they will believe us, and let us include you in next year's budget. Experience had taught us that you will need financial assistance."

The Community Fund said "no" to the request for funds, but agreed to permit this new organization to be included in their list of branches on one condition--that the Y would operate on the same budget. Absolutely no increase in budget.

There was only one way to do this. The other branches were informed of the situation and asked whether they would take a cut--voluntarily--so that this new branch could be opened. And they did. Every branch took a cut--$100.00 or $200.00 or $300.00, in spite of the fact that their work had already been curtailed and their budgets cut to the bone. They made heroic sacrifices to give us a start. The cuts totaled enough to pay a secretary's salary. As far as I know, this story has never been told publicly. I hope that telling it now will make us more grateful to these branches and more willing to come to their assistance if they need our help some day.

As for the rest of the story, it must be told in a few words. Steve Graves, our first secretary, began work on March 1, 1937, in the old John Marshall gym and the frame building, which had been the cafeteria.

Figure 13-5a. The first West Park YMCA. *Cleveland Public Library*

200

The Board of Education had permitted us to use it without charge. We eventually purchased the property when we had to buy or vacate the building.

From the citywide campaign in 1955, we were allotted enough money to erect our present building, but had to sell the gym in order to finish the basement and properly equip the building. When the building was dedicated in September, 1957, we invited the YWCA to share its use with us. Meanwhile, the name of the branch had been changed to the West Park-Fairview Branch.

From the 1963 Campaign we were allotted enough to justify letting the contract for the erection and equipment of a gymnasium, a swimming pool, and locker rooms.

Figure 13-5b. The West Park Fairview YMCA today. *Author photo*

FUELS

The number of automobiles continued to increase but at a slower and slower rate as the depression deepened. As the number of automobiles increased, so did the number of gasoline stations. The "service station" had not yet been discovered so most of the stations were very small buildings with two pumps.

a. 4557 West 130th Street 3-5-31

b. 15234 Triskett Road 4-13-37

c. 4871 Rocky River Drive 11-18-36

d. 4300 West 130th Street 3/12/38

e. 15515 Munn Road 5-20-36

f. 12827 Bellaire Road 5/21/31

g. 14120 Lorain Avenue 10-4-32

h. 13931 Lorain Avenue 10-18-31

i. 12931 Bellaire Road 9-20-32

j. 15201 Lorain Avenue 7-15-32

The other big fuel in this era was coal. Most homes were still heated with coal. Widespread use of natural gas did not come until after World War II.

Figure 13-7. Zone Coal and Supply at 14110 Lorain Avenue. 11-11-38. *Cleveland Public Library*

202

Figure 13-8. Penrose Coal Company ad from West Side News 11-23-39. *Cleveland Public Library*

Figure 13-9a. In 1933 these brick pillars guarded the entrance to Riverside Allotment on Montrose Road at Warren Road. It was planned as an exclusive community but the pillars were as far as they got. A large part of the tract became the site for Riverside Elementary School. *Cleveland Public Library*

Figure 13-9b. The mate to this pillar on the other side of Montrose was wiped out by an automobile accident in the mid 80's. This pillar was torn down in September 2004. *Laura Pfingsten photo*

Figure 13-10a. In 1931 another area landmark began its operation. The Winterhurst Skating Rink was the largest outdoor artificial rink in the country. *Cleveland State University, Cleveland Press Collection*

203

Figure 13-10b. In 1961 Winterhurst was purchased by the City of Lakewood who continued to operate the outdoor facility until 1975 when the indoor facility was built. *Cleveland State University Library, Cleveland Press Collection*

Figure 13-11a. Born in the 20's, art deco design was reaching the peak of its popularity in the early 30's. *Cleveland State University Library, Cleveland Press Collection*

In 1931, the National Air Races returned to Cleveland following a one year hiatus in Chicago. Cleveland would be the home of this extravaganza throughout the decade except for 1933 and 1936. It was a great diversion from the depression era economic woes. Crowds at the show were usually in excess of 100,000 people, and if you included viewers outside the airport, there were probably 200,000 to see parts of the show each day.

Figure 13-11b. Permanent grandstands built to hold 100,000 people were built along Grayton Road. At a spectacle like this today, vendors and participants would arrive and stay in their mobile homes. In 1931, they were most likely staying in the "Tent City" seen in the upper left of this photo. *Cleveland State University Library, Cleveland Press Collection*

204

Figure 13-11c. If you owned a farm in outlying areas anywhere near the race course, you could expect a lot of visiting friends and relatives. 8/29/32 *Cleveland State University Library, Cleveland Press Collection*

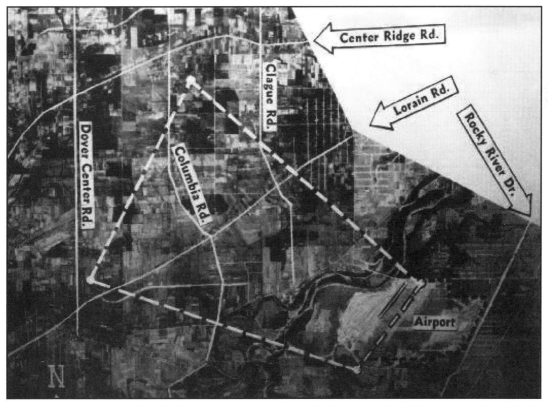

Figure 13-11d. This is the course for the 1938 Thompson Trophy Race. There would be another race in 1939, but no more until after the war in 1946. *Cleveland State University Library, Cleveland Press Collection*

Figure 13-11e. In 1935, Wiley Post and Amelia Earhart meet at the airport. *Cleveland State University Library, Cleveland Press Collection*

Figure 13-12. This photo taken in 1932 is looking north on Rocky River Drive at Midvale. Originally the track belonged to the Cleveland and Southwestern Interurban. However, they went out of business in February of 1931. In mid-August 1931, Cleveland streetcars began to run from Kamm's to Brookpark just for the air show until September 7. Regular streetcar service to Brookpark Road was started in late 1931 (Hays, 1988). *Cleveland Public Library*

Figure 13-13. This car is actually inside the airport compound for the air races circa 1933-34. *Northern Ohio Railway Museum*

Figure 13-14. September 9, 1939 heading north on Rocky River Drive. This could very well be the last run on this line. The line had been scheduled to be cut back to Brookpark after the air races had ended the previous week. *Northern Ohio Railway Museum*

Figure 13-15. In the winter of 1939-40, a CTS crew and crane are pulling up the track between the airport and Brookpark Road. *Northern Ohio Railway Museum*

Figure 13-16a. Kamm's Corners in the early 30's with Marshall's Drug Store on the corner. *David Schafer Collection.*

Figure 13-16b. Looking south on Rocky River Drive with Marshall's on the left, a barber shop and Mary's Lunch. *Cleveland Public Library*

Figure 13-17. Workers are already beginning to build Kamm's Recreation. This bowling alley is just getting started on July 20, 1938. Owned by Fred Alber who lived right next door, it became such an immediate success that the building would be expanded in 1940 (see Fig 14 - 19 a-d). *Cleveland State University Library, Cleveland Press Collection*

Figure 13-18. As the decade came to a close in November, 1939, ground had been cleared for the new NACA (NASA) Laboratory. *Cleveland State University Library, Cleveland Press Collection*

Figure 13-19a. In July of 1939, the sign in the window proclaims that Clark's Yorktown Restaurant will open soon. *Cleveland State University Library, Cleveland Press Collection*

Figure 13-19b. Clark's Sandwich Menu *Vern Rolland Collection*

****

CHAPTER 14
1940-49

As the decade opened, just about everything centered on the war in Europe. Although not yet directly involved, the United States and Cleveland were busy producing materials for the Allies. Factories were in full around the clock production and looking to expand as new war material contracts poured in every day.

Figure 14-1 . Construction is nearly complete at this new "service station" at the corner of Munn and Warren Roads. Up to this time most gas stations were small one-room buildings with two pumps. Around 1940 these were being replaced by the "service station". Each generally had two work bays and a lift. With gasoline rationing just over the horizon, it was probably not the best time to be entering this type of business. It seems that the pendulum has now swung back the other way as the service station has become an endangered species being replaced by the "pump your own/convenience stores."
Cleveland Public Library

The National Advisory Committee for Aeronautics (NACA), predecessor to NASA, opened its state of the art 8.4 million dollar research laboratory next to the airport in 1940. Later that year, President Roosevelt signed the Selective Service Act establishing the first peacetime draft, and men 18-64 were required to register.

Following the attack on Pearl Harbor in 1941, the nation and virtually every person was involved in or affected by the war. Everything was placed on a war time footing. Blackout regulations were established. Sale of Defense Bonds and Stamps soared, and voters passed levies for war relief. Eighty-six air-raid sirens were placed around the county. In neighborhoods, block clubs were formed to carry out blackout drills and conduct scrap drives. (My grandfather was a local air raid warden. His home on Tuttle Avenue had a full attic on the 3rd floor. I can remember asking him why he kept two buckets of sand in the attic. He told me that it was to smother small phosphorus bombs which were designed to pierce the roofs of homes and start fires).

Tire sales were halted to all but those in essential services. With tires unavailable, gasoline rationed, and buses jammed, people rode bicycles to work. The Plain Dealer business pages said that

Figure 14-2. There were no new cars to sell and the selection of used cars did not appear to be very large at West Park Chevrolet in August of 1945. *Cleveland Public Library*

Figure 14-3. Ad for Nash-not cars but planes. *Author collection*

Chevrolet dealers met to discuss, with no new cars to sell, how they could make their customers' old cars last through the war.

The Civil Service Commission started programs to train women for defense work. Business activity in Cleveland was almost 50 percent above prewar levels, and there was a shortage of workers and housing. The giant Bomber Plant (IX Center) opened attracting even more workers from out of state. The Office of Price Administration (OPA) controlled the price that farmers, factories, and merchants could charge for products. Coupon books were issued to every American. Coupons were needed to purchase sugar, coffee, soup, meat, butter, shoes, fuel oil and even whiskey. Home gardening and canning took on record proportions.

As the war continued, the black market began to thrive, and wartime controls were wearing thin with everyone. By 1944, meat rationing ended, and manufacturers were again permitted to make electric ranges and a few other appliances. Service men were returning to Cuyahoga County at the rate of 500 a month.

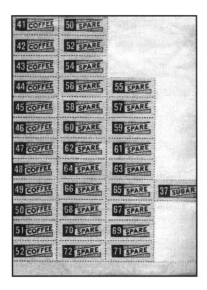

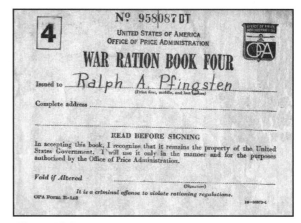

Figure 14-4. OPA War Ration Book. *Author collection*

A new set of problems loomed on the horizon as the end of the war was now in sight. More than half of the nations' production was for war goods, and in Cleveland the percent was no doubt higher. When the war ended, where would all the veterans work as well as the tens of thousands who migrated to Cleveland to work in the defense Plants?

And, through it all, young men died.

Cleveland Press Saturday February 17, 1940

"West Park fairly shouts of newness. Its hub is the bustling Lorain Avenue-Rocky River Drive intersection. There you find new storefronts, super-markets, a fine bank building, and a beautiful new theatre. These are attended by crowded sidewalks and heavy traffic.

West Park looks young, ever growing. Surrounding the business intersection are homes, new homes. They stretch out in every direction, blocks of them. Whole streets appear to have been built up solidly overnight with brown brick homes, white frame homes. Most of these homes are inhabited by couples 30-45 years of age. Their children are young, as shown by the overcrowded elementary schools.

Figure 14-5. "The row of new houses is on Southland Avenue, one of the newest developments in West Park".

But not everything is rosy in West Park, as Councilman Tom J. Gunning will testify. Sewers and transportation are the chief problems. When the first sewers were built by West Park, the officials figured the township's population would never go above 5,000 and thought that 6-inch sewers would be enough. But in the 14 square miles of West Park, there are some 50,000 residents. Gradually Mr. Gunning has had many of the sewers replaced." (Actual census figure for West Park in 1940 was 39,368).

"Out in the section off Rocky River Drive between Puritas Avenue and Brookpark Road, there are no sewers at all. That part of West Park is just like the country. But at present, with the aid of the WPA, a 72-inch storm and sanitary sewer is being built on Rocky River Drive to service this section. When it is completed, Mr. Gunning predicts 1,000 homes will be built between Puritas and Brookpark."

Figure 14-6. This was originally built as the West Park Town Hall in 1914 (see figure 11-6a). After West Park was annexed to Cleveland in 1923, it became the First District Police Station. It is shown here on September 9, 1940. *Cleveland Police Department Archives*

Figure 14-7. On April 3, 1947, the loop at West 137th Street was torn out and moved to the southwest corner of West 140th and Lorain. On June 17, 1950 this streetcar line was cut back from the Puritas loop (at St. Pats) to the West 140th loop. This photo, dated June 7, 1952, was taken one week before the Lorain Streetcar Line would be discontinued. Notice the single overhead wire for the streetcar but also the double wires for trackless trolleys that would take over the run to the square on June 15. The trolley buses would remain on the line until November 14, 1953 (Christiansen, 1975). *Jay Himes Collection*

But, this new sewer is helping to hamper the transportation problem. At present, some streetcars go out Lorain as far as Kamm's Corners; others go no farther than West 137th Street, and citizens must transfer to buses. Mr. Gunning finally has persuaded Council to order the carline extended out Rocky River Drive, but this has been postponed because of the sewer project" (McLaughlin, 1940).

A New Concept Born in West Park

Figure 14-8a. Alice and Gerald Brookins in 1963. *Gary Brookins Collection*

In 1936, Gerald and Alice Brookins began exploring the trailer/mobile home industry by selling and leasing trailers in Lakewood. However, it was not too long before Lakewood decided that it did not want trailer camps within their city limits. The image of trailer people and trailer camps was not a good one at that time.

Despite this image, the Brookins "envisioned a park for permanent residents that would be a beautiful place to live and an asset to the city." The booming defense industry of the early 40's began to create a larger market for trailers. In 1942, they purchased the old Harrington Farm at Lorain Avenue and West 150th Street. In 1943 "Trailer Gardens" opened with rigid standards and with rules and regulations that would make it a safe, peaceful and pleasant place to live. It became the first senior citizen park in the country.

As the industry grew, so did the size of trailers, from 8-foot wide legal limit to 14-foot wide legal limit. The park was laid out to 1943 standards, and new zoning regulations would not allow the wider trailers on narrow lots. So, in 1982, the decision was made to close the park. The six-acre parcel would become a small retail complex anchored by a K-Mart Store (Cleveland Press, January 15, 1982).

Figure 14-8b+c. Typical lots at "Trailer Gardens" in the 1950's. *Gary Brookins Collection*

214

Figure 14-9. April, 1947, looking east towards Kamm's Corners. *Daniel Weber photo*

Figure 14-10. At the east end of Kamm's at West 165th and Lorain there is a "Wet Paint" sign on the door and "Open for Business" signs in the windows of Gray Drugs. The Gables Restaurant sign is at the left and also recognizable is Western Auto and Burrows. *Cleveland State University Library, Cleveland Press Collection*

215

Figure 14-11. Howard Schreibman stands outside his Jewelry Shop at the grand opening in 1949. *Howard Schreibman Collection*

Figure 14-12. A mere shell of its former self, it is still recognizable to those who knew it as "The Gables Restaurant." *Author photo, 2001*

216

Figure 14-13. Birds eye view of Kamm's, August 5, 1949. *Cleveland State University Library, Bruce Young Collection*

217

Figure 14-14. The Old John Marshall High School would serve as the home to Leopold's Furniture from 1946 to 1986 *Cleveland Public Library*

Figure 14-15. One of the north-south bus lines in West Park is #86. Started in September 16, 1925, the line ran from Lakewood Park to Kamm's Corners by way of Warren Road, Munn Road and Rocky River Drive. Today the line has been extended all the way to the Brookpark Road Rapid Transit Station. In this April 25, 1944 photograph, the bus is stopped at Munn Road and Rocky River Drive. Shortly it will make a left turn and head south on Rocky River Drive to Kamm's Corners. *Cleveland Public Library*

Figure 14-16. In the 40's, Christmas Shopping meant a trip downtown for most West Parkers. In a scene that appears to be right out of the movie "Christmas Story" and before there were any suburban shopping malls, this was Higbees at Christmas just about any time in the 1940's. *Author collection*

The post war recession did not materialize even though defense contracts were cancelled overnight. There were a number of reasons why the economy continued to move forward. First of all, women were either forced or chose to leave their defense jobs in favor of returning servicemen. Secondly, there was a four-year back up demand for consumer goods, so manufacturers could turn their attention back to producing those goods. Finally, marriage rates skyrocketed as returning veterans were eager to start families. These facts caused a tremendous boom in the housing industry that lasted into the 50's.

Figure 14-17. In November 1949 this new development off West 143rd Street included all or part of Albrus, Courtland, Ledgewood, Viola, Lakota, Rockfern, Fairlawn, West 143rd and West 146th. *Cleveland State University Library, Cleveland Press Collection*

219

Figure 14-18. At the left of this photo is the newly completed development including the neatly laid out streets of Tuckahoe, Rainbow and Gramatan. Triskett Road is in the lower left and Lorain Street is in the lower right. *Cleveland State University Library, Bruce Young Collection*

Figure 14-19a. When Fred Alber wanted to expand his bowling alley (Kamm's Recreation-brick wall on left of photo) he moved his house from the corner of Albers Avenue and Rocky River Drive to a vacant lot he owned across the street. Earlier, he had donated land to the city to create Albers Avenue. In that era, moving houses was a fairly common occurrence, but today it is extremely rare. *Ruth Hyland Hall Collection*

Figure 14-19b. Getting ready for the move in June, 1941.

Figure 14-19c. The house is on its way across Albers Avenue on June 12, 1941.

Figure 14-19d. House sits on its new foundation at 17015 Albers Avenue.

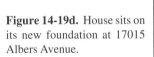

As was mentioned in the last chapter, coal was still the main fuel for home heating. Natural gas would not come into widespread use until after World War II. Not only did it become the fuel of choice in the post-war housing boom, but most people were converting their old coal furnaces to the new fuel. The result was that supply could not keep up with demand, and as a result, the Public Utilities Commission of Ohio issued the following order on September 16, 1947.

"Gas companies, including the East Ohio Gas Company, are prohibited from supplying natural gas to any new gas heating installation until April 1, 1948. This action was taken by the Commission because of its finding that the unprecedented demand for natural gas and the inability of the utilities and their suppliers to provide facilities to make sufficient additional gas available to consumers in the State of Ohio has created an emergency which will prevail at least during the coming winter 1947-1948" (Fairview Herald, September 25, 1947).

Fairview Herald, November 4, 1948

In April of 1948, the Village of Fairview Village asked the Postal Service to establish a post office in their community. Postal inspectors indicated that the village would have to officially change its name because there already was a Fairview Post Office in Ohio (Guernsey County). There was a vote in the November election from a list of 10 names previously selected by residents. The final results were: Fairview Park 1040, Fairview City 661, Fairpark 240, Fairhaven 224, Rockport 144, City of Fairview Village 123, Fairville 117, New Fairview (write in) 112, Riverview 110, Westbridge 56, Fairdale 55.

On December 20, 1940, Fairview officially became Fairview Park.

In 1946, the Air Races returned. After the war, people wanted the return of things that were normal prior to the war. The Aircraft Industrial Association brought back the National Air Races, and Cleveland once again obtained a five year lease on the event.

Figure 14-20. On August 30, 1946, Tony LeVier qualifies his P-38 at for the Thompson Trophy Race. *Cleveland Public Library.*

The planes developed during the war dwarfed older aircraft, and pilots could obtain used military fighters for as little as $1,000.

By 1949, urban sprawl had filled many of the open fields that the planes raced over. Then the inevitable happened when a plane crashed into a Berea home killing a mother and her infant son as well as pilot Bill Odom. Berea immediately passed an ordinance forbidding racers from flying over their community. Within a matter of weeks many other surrounding communities enacted similar legislation and the races, which had thrilled and excited hundreds of thousands of people, ended tragically.

Figure 14-21. September 5, 1949. The fatal crash which ended the air races. *Cleveland Public Library*

****

CHAPTER 15
1950-59

A sewer project, which began in December, 1952, left a sea of mud on Orchardhurst Avenue. Orchardhurst was the second street north of Brookpark Road in the southwest corner of West Park. Over a year later, residents were still trying to deal with the mess. The city would come out regularly with a load of cinders or slag. That simply made high spots out of low spots and in turn created new low spots. Residents parked their cars two streets away and walked home. Non residents trying to drive down the street usually ended up calling for a tow truck which, more often than not, also became stuck.

Final relief did not come for several more months. The memory becomes more faded with time as Orchardhurst was taken by the construction of I-480.

Figure 15-1. Mothers and children gather on Orchardhurst on February 3, 1954 to show what they have to put up with since construction started 14 months previous. *Cleveland State University Library, Cleveland Press Collection*

Figure 15-2a. In February of 1952 this temporary housing on Brookpark Road at West 135th Street was one of the last remnants of the war . Similar projects had been built on Rocky River Drive near the airport and at the north end of Berea. The projects on Rocky River Drive became part of the Cuyahoga Metropolitan Housing Authority and are today known as Riverside Park. *Cleveland Public Library*

Figure 15-2b. In the mid 50's Aunt Jemimah made a visit to the hall at Riverside Park "projects" on the occassion of the annual Kiwanis Club Pancake Breakfast. *West Park Kiwanis Collection*

The biggest story of the 50's in West Park and perhaps the city was the disappearance of Beverly Potts. The Plain Dealer called it the greatest search in the city's history.

The first report came to Cleveland Police at 10:30 PM on August 24, 1951. Ten year old Beverly Potts had left home after supper on that Friday with her next door neighbor friend to go to Halloran Park just a couple of blocks away. The "Showagon" sponsored by the Cleveland Press and the City Recreation Department, was bringing its performers to the park. Beverly had not returned home.

The search included police patrolmen, the mounted unit, detectives, railroad police, the Civil Air Patrol, Boy Scouts, Park Department personnel, waste collectors, and auxiliary police and firemen. Her picture was on all three television stations and on the front page of all three newspapers. Mayor Thomas Burke went on the radio twice with impassioned pleas for return of the little girl. Editorials proclaimed "Let's All Join the Hunt for Missing Child." Tips were coming in at the rate of 1,500 per day.

Figure 15-3. Beverly Potts. *Cleveland Plain Dealer*

Gradually the case disappeared from the headlines. And despite being the greatest search in the city's history, Beverly Potts was never found (Cleveland Plain Dealer, January 24, 1999).

Figure 15-4. Halloran Park today. *Author photo*

Post script: Years, even decades later, tips were still coming in, and police investigated them. One of the best leads occurred in 1988 when William Redmond, 69 was arrested in Grand Island Nebraska. He had confessed to killing an eight-year-old girl in Pennsylvania. Redmond was a carnival worker and truck driver with a history of child molestation who at one time lived in Conneaut, Ohio. Local authorities had been looking for an assembler and operator of Ferris wheels. There had been a carnival near Halloran Park at the time Beverly disappeared. Unfortunately, they never got a chance to talk to Redmond as he died of emphysema and heart disease before he could be brought to trial in Pennsylvania.

The Man In The Brown Suit and More....

Every Browns fan worth his salt knows the history of the early Browns, how the NFL Cleveland Rams left for the west coast in 1946, how Mickey McBride hired Paul Brown to put together a team for the new All American Conference, how the Browns won that conference championship all four years of its existence, going undefeated in 1948, and how in their first year back in the NFL in 1950 they beat the Rams for the title on a last minute field goal by Lou Groza.

Figure 15-5a. Celebration following the 1946 All-American Conference Championship Victory. Many familiar faces surround Coach Paul Brown and owner Mickey McBride. *Lou Abraham Collection*

Fans in the 50's recall that whenever Lou Groza kicked a field goal or extra point, there was always a guy at the back of the end zone to receive the kick and he always wore a brown suit. He soon became known simply as "the man in the brown suit." He was Abe Abraham who for many years owned a restaurant in West Park.

"It all started in 1946, Abe recalled, I operated a concession stand in the Leader Building. That's where Mickey McBride had his Browns' offices. Frosty Froberg was business manager of the team then and asked me if I wanted to see a Browns' game. I had never seen a pro game. He said come to the pass gate at 1:30 that Sunday.

Well, Frosty ran around and didn't have time to get me in until 2:15. I told him he needed an assistant. The next day McBride called me and said I was hired. I've been working at the pass gate ever since.

One game that season I was walking across the field to deliver a message when Lou Groza kicked a field goal. When he kicks field goals, they're line drives. His extra points had a high arc. I looked up, and there's this line drive coming right at me, so I stood there and caught it. The team doctor treated me after the game for bruised ribs.

He's been catching those line drives and high arcs ever since, but is avoiding the bruises. He takes the field to the accompaniment of thunderous cheers, as soon as the pass gate closed." (Cleveland Plain Dealer, January 13, 1965).

226

Figure 15-5b. Abe Abraham at the opening of "The Man In The Brown Suit Restaurant" on Puritas Avenue in 1966. *Lou Abraham Collection*

As an entrepreneur, Abe and his wife opened a corner deli at West 125th Street and Madison Avenue in 1953 called "JudyLou's" named after his two children. His best known venture however was "The Caboose Restaurant" at West 150th Street and Chatfield Avenue right at the railroad crossing.

His son Lou recalled that "it was a fun place to work. It was built in an old coal loading building for the railroad and was frequented mostly by truck drivers and railroad workers who always had interesting stories." Unfortunately, it was torn down about 1965 when the Rapid Transit was extended to the airport, and an overpass was built for West 150th Street. In 1966 he opened another restaurant called "The Man In The Brown Suit Restaurant" on Puritas Avenue at West 147th Street.

And Now, The Rest of the Story…

Figure 15-5c. Number one, Lou Abraham, was the Browns mascot in 1954 when the Browns thumped the Detroit Lions 56-10 for the championship. *Lou Abraham Collection*

As Lou grew up around the Browns it seemed only natural that he would play football in high school. For two years he spent a week at the Browns training camp in Hiram along with Pete Brown, son of the coach. They both participated in all the workouts, except the contact drills. The were also both kickers for their respective high school teams, Pete for University School and Lou for West Tech. Lou had been getting kicking lessons from his Godfather, Lou Groza, for years and was an accomplished punter and place kicker.

Figure 15-5d. Abe and Lou Abraham at Cleveland Stadium in 1963. *Lou Abraham Collection*

Lou graduated from West Tech in 1963 and joined the Navy. In 1967, at the start of training camp Paul Brown called the Commander of the Great Lakes Naval Training Center and requested Lou for a tryout as a kicker for the Browns. Lou was released from the Navy 8 days early to attend camp. He did get a tryout, but the Browns had committed a third round draft choice for a kicker named Don Cockroft. Lou did not make the team, but has always been grateful for the chance.

In 1998, the Pro football Hall of Fame in Canton established a Hall of Fans. Each team could select one fan from their city to be inducted each year. There would not have been a better choice in all of football than Abe, but he had passed away in 1982, and there was no provision for a posthumous award. When that provision was changed Abe became the Browns choice in 2001, and in 2002 it was Lou Abraham for the Browns. It is the only father son pair to be so honored (personal communication, Lou Abraham, 2003).

West Parks Largest Employer and How It Came To Be

On July 3 1892, friends from several congregations of the Reformed Church met to talk about founding a place where their sick could be taken care of in a kindly, sympathetic manner. The congregations of the Reformed Church at that time consisted almost exclusively of German-speaking people many of them recent immigrants. $4.73 was collected for the Society for the Christian Care of the Sick and Needy. What the founders planned was not to create a hospital but to educate Protestant Sisters of Mercy who would travel to homes of the sick.

In February 1894, the Society leased the first floor of a house on Scranton Avenue, which they named Bethesda Deaconess House. They issued circulars to the many German-speaking doctors on the West Side acquainting them with the Society. Within a short time, they were beginning to admit patients. In June of 1894, doctors conferred with Society Trustees about founding a hospital. By September 1894, the Society had leased a house at Franklin Circle and Hanover Street. It was quickly equipped with 20 beds and an operating room. The new institution was named German Hospital and Polyclinic of the City of Cleveland. The next year, the Society bought a large home on Franklin Boulevard and put up a brick addition for the Sisters. The new hospital was dedicated in September 1896 with 36 beds.

By 1899 private patients paid between $7-12 per week and ward patients $4-6 per week. About 1 in 5 patients were indigent and received free care. Balancing the books was a never-ending struggle. Despite financial problems, the need to expand was also clear. In 1909, a new fireproof wing was built bringing to 54 the number of patient beds. In that same year a nursing school was started. In 1914, they bought an adjoining property for the School of Nursing.

In April 1918, the Board bowing to strong public sentiment against Germany changed the name from German Hospital to Fairview Park Hospital naming it after a small nearby park.

Every year seemed to bring new improvements or additions. There was a new power plant, laundry, x-ray units, autoclaves, surgery lights, laboratory, pharmacy, the first full time anesthetist; interns and residents became regular additions to the staff.

Plans were made in 1929 to double the size of the hospital but the Depression intervened. In December of 1933 at the depth of the Depression, representatives from 14 Cleveland hospitals and the Academy of Medicine launched a group hospitalization plan. It provided for 21 days of care per year at a premium of 60 cents per month for a ward or 75 cents per month for semi private. The individual could select his hospital

By 1936, the Depression was easing so a campaign was begun to raise funds for the much-needed expansion. In 1937, West Park organizations were trying to encourage construction of a hospital near Kamm's. Both Lutheran and Fairview Hospitals gave some early consideration to this move to the southwest side of town. However, this only further delayed Fairviews' expansion plans.

Finally, in 1939 Fairview could wait no longer and broke ground for another addition, which opened in March 1940. In 1943 a new Joint Hospital Committee representing the Welfare Federation and the Cleveland Hospital Council was formed. It soon grew to include 15 hospitals and was designed to help hospitals plan for expansions and moves. They eventually helped relocate Fairview and Glenville Hospitals. In December 1945 The Fairview Board bought 13 ½ acres on Lorain near Kamm's in preparation for the contingency of moving.

Figure 15-6a. This is the property purchased as a contingency if Fairview Hospital decided to move to the Kamm's area. It is on the south side of Lorain right at the edge of the valley. *Vollmer, 1969*

In December 1949 a successful capital campaign was launched. With this and financial help from several sources, ground was broken for the new hospital on March 5, 1953. Even before the hospital opened, plans were being made for a residence hall for the school of nursing. On April 23, 1955, the new hospital was dedicated and the following day, 20,000 people came to the open house. At the opening ceremony it was pointed out that the original project started with $4.73, and the new building cost $4,730,000, exactly 1,000,000 times the original. There were 188 adult beds in the new facility, and when the school of nursing residence opened the following year another 93 beds became available on the fifth floor.

Figure 15-6b. This photo was taken April 6, 1955 just two weeks before the hospital opened. *Cleveland State University Library, Bruce Young Collection*

Fairview had barely moved into its new building when it leaders saw that community needs were twice the capacity of the new hospital. Of the eight communities that the hospital served, several still had their major population growth spurts ahead of them. For example in 1950, Fairview High School had 84 graduates, while North Olmsted had 43.

In 1963, a new expansion program started with construction scheduled for 1966. The Nursing Residence opened in December, 1956, and a research laboratory in 1961. Between 1956 and 1966, they purchased the apartment buildings across Lorain and well as apartment buildings and land on Groveland Avenue. In 1968, a 6th floor was added.

In 1965, a landmark disappeared. For more than a decade, a small white frame house had stood in the middle of the parking lot (Figure 15-6b). The property had been sold to the hospital with the provision

230

that the two Gollmar Sisters, Elizabeth and Katherine, who had owned it could remain in their house as long as they lived. The sisters and the hospital became the best of neighbors, and when they passed away, they bequeathed the property to the Hospital (Health Cleveland, 1992).

In 1966, Fairview again changed its name. When it became Fairview Park in 1942, no one expected that the hospital would be located on land adjacent to the city of Fairview Park. The coincidence led a great many people to assume that the hospital was located in Fairview Park or was a municipal facility. Therefore, the name was changed to Fairview General.

Figure 15-6c. In 1968 the cantilevered pavilion was ready for occupancy. It contained 5 new operating suites which were twice to three times larger than the old operating rooms (Vollmer, 1969). The building on the right is the Parkview Addition built after the nursing residence was torn down. *Author photo*

In 1976, the parking garage and doctors offices were added and in 1981, the apartment complex across Lorain Street was torn down and replaced with the Center for Family Medicine. In 1997, Fairview became affiliated with the Cleveland Clinic, and finally, in 1999 the nursing school was closed to make way for the Parkview Addition.

Fig 15-6d. The Center for Family Medicine was built in 1981. *Author photo*

231

Currently there are 2,562 full and part time employees at Fairview General Hospital, making it the largest employer in West Park. And there is little doubt that the size of the building and staff will continue to increase in the future.

The End and the Beginning

Figure 15-7a. On January 24, 1954 streetcars ran for the final time in Cleveland. 10,000 people waited patiently at Public Square to ride the Madison Avenue Line on that final day. These cars are shown at the west end of Madison Avenue at the Spring Garden wye. *Jay Himes Collection*

Figure 15-7b. A little more than a year after the last streetcar ran, the Rapid Transit brought its first patrons here to the West 117th Street Station. In 1969, the line was extended to the airport. *Jay Himes Collection*

Although few people realized it at the time, the end of downtown shopping was near. Small shopping centers were beginning to appear in suburbia and the first mall anchored by branches of the major department stores opened at Westgate. The Fairview Shopping Center opened in 1947 and The Fairwood and Warren Village Shopping Centers opened in 1951 in West Park.

Figure 15-8a. The Fairwood Shopping Center on Lorain Street between West 136th and West 138th Streets opened in late 1951. *Cleveland State University Library, Cleveland Press Collection*

Figure 15-8b. The Warren Village Shopping Center on Warren Road opened in September 1951. *Cleveland Public Library*

Figure 15-9. In 1955, construction was underway at the airport. It looks almost primitive by today's standards. *Cleveland State University Library, Bruce Young Collection*

Figure 15-10a. The Skyway Lounge on Brookpark Road at Rocky River Drive was a popular place in 1954. *Cleveland Public Library*

Figure 15-10b. After the Skyway, it became a "Brown Derby" Restaurant. Finally in 2002 it succumbed to airport expansion. *Author photo*

Figure 15-11a. In 1945, this was the only home located at the corner of Rocky River Drive and Brookpark Road. It would soon be transformed into another popular Airport watering hole called The La Conga Club. *Cleveland Public Library*

Figure 15-11b. The La Conga Club would eventually become "Nite Flights," and in 1998, it too would succumb to airport expansion. *Ross Bassett photo*

235

Figure 15-12. Royal Castle was one of the early hamburger chains. It was open 24 hours a day and specialized in silver dollar sized hamburgers smothered with grilled onions on square buns. A six pack of burgers was about one serving, and of course it would be washed down with a frosted mug of Birch Beer. The one at Kamm's featured a counter with 9 stools and three small booths. The chain went out of business in 1974. *Cleveland State University, Cleveland Press Collection*

Another landmark has taken its place. For the past 22 years Kathleen's Restaurant has occupied the same space. But when you walk in the door and look down at the terrazo floor, it still says Royal Castle. Kathleen's made news when President Bill Clinton stopped in on a swing through Kamm's in 1998.

Figure 15-13. Bearden's on Rocky River Drive just south of Kamm's was one of the early Drive-in Restaurants and synonymous with the muscle car era of the 50's. Although the one at Kamm's is long gone, there is still one in operation in Rocky River. *Cleveland State University Library, Cleveland Press Collection*

Figure 15-14. A restaurant noted for its home-cooked meals was Poshke's in the wedge shaped building at Triskett and Lorain. In this April 1957 photo, the new owners changed the name to Jerry's. By the 70's it would become an office building. Today the building has been razed and the lot is used by an automobile dealership. *Cleveland Public Library*

Figure 15-15. At 16505 Lorain Avenue, Babyland was a new concept in marketing-a store completely devoted to the needs of babies. *Cleveland Public Library*

Figure 15-16a. One of three great bakeries at Kamm's, Hermann's was at 17400 Lorain. This northwest corner of Kamm's is now the Kamm's Plaza Shopping Center. The other two bakeries were Kaase's and Wilke's. *West Park Kiwanis Collection*

Figure 15-16b. Though faded, the sign proclaiming Wilke's Bakery is still visible on the side of the building at West 159th and Lorain. *Author photo*

Figure 15-17. The corner of Albers Avenue and Rocky River Drive is once again a vacant lot in June 1956. A fire had completely destroyed Kamm's Recreation Bowling Alley. *Cleveland Public Library*

During the 50's construction of the interstate highway system through Cleveland began and was well under way by the end of the decade. It would be another ten years before the freeways were completed but the slicing and dicing of the city was quite apparent. In West Park, I-71 would cut diagonally through the heart of the community while I-90 and I-480 would crop off the northern and southern borders respectively. Homes were removed from the tax duplicate and families were displaced from those homes. It added to the plummeting population of the city and the population explosion of outlying areas.

I-90 removed West 141st, Braemer Dr., Stratford Ave., Tuland Ave., and parts of West 117th, West 118th, West 119th, West 120th, West 137th, West 138th, West 139th, West 140th, West 142nd, West 144th, West 153rd, West 155th, West 159th, West 160th, West 162nd, Alger Rd., Cloverdale Ave., Elmwood Ave. and Warren Rd.

I-480 and airport expansion removed, West 191st, West 196th, Bernice Ave., Elsmere Ave., Fairborne Ave., Forestwood Ave., Hillside Rd., Laureldale Ave., Maplewood Ave., Orchardhurst Ave., Riverdale Ave., SpringdaleAve. and West Lawn Rd. It also removed parts of West 185th, West 188th, West 190th, West 198th, West 200th, West 202nd, West 204th, West 205th, Bacon Ave., Grayhill Rd. and Midvale Ave.

I-71 removed parts of West 117th, West 120th, West 130th, West 140th, West 143rd, West 144th, West 145th, West 146th, West 150th, West 154th, West 167th, Brookside Blvd., Clifford Ave., Courtland Ave., Harwell Rd., Hirst Ave., Martha Rd., St. John Ave., Sally Ave., Victory Blvd., Woodbury Ave., and Wyman Ave.

However, all the arguments for and against the freeways get lost in the emotions when you look at one of the true classics of the 50's parked in front of J&L Appliances on West 117th Street.

Figure 15-18. A '57 Ford convertible and J&L Appliances, a couple of classics! *Cleveland State University Library, Cleveland Press Collection*

****

CHAPTER 16
1960-Today

As I start this final chapter, I realize that it is not the final chapter. The final chapter may never be written. West Park will continue to grow and change for a long time to come. The future will be tomorrow's history and will have to be chronicled then. For me, it has been an interesting journey into the past. The research becomes a near obsession as you finally find the answer to one question only to uncover four more questions. I would have liked to include some genealogy of some of the early township families and some of the influential families of West Park. For example, what ever happened to George Peake and his family? I would have liked to do more with some of the older homes especially the century homes. I would have liked to include information on the churches of West Park, and indeed, I did accumulate an enormous amount of information. However, there are at least 47 churches in West Park and that would fill yet another volume. In addition, I would have liked to include something on the long time businesses in the area. However, all of these things I will leave for someone else.

Although there are over 300 photographs in this work, there are a lot more that I could have included. I also know that there are hundreds of other interesting photographs hiding in attics around the area just waiting to be discovered. In fact, I suspect that this work will stimulate further interest in a West Park Historical Society.

West Park is very much alive and constantly changing, and these changes need to be continually documented. As I write this chapter, the very last "open" land is being developed. A six-acre plot between Chatfield and Larchwood Avenues is being developed into cluster homes on a street named Scullin Drive.

Figure 16-1. The most recent new homes in West Park are being built on Scullin Drive. Scullin is a double-ended cul-de-sac entered from Chatfield Avenue. *Author photo*

Moreover, in the area off Grayton Road and I-480, two large industrial/commercial parcels are being developed on land that has been idle for a long time (Figure 16-2,3,4). When these are completed, any future development must come by the replacement of something else. In fact, redevelopment has already taken place in many parts of the community. Some notable examples of this are the redevelopment of the Agrico Fertilizer Plant acreage into an industrial park (Figure 16-5), the Riverside Theatre site redevelopment into a viable commercial site (Figure 16-6), and the construction of about 20 town homes at the old Longmead School site (Figure 16-7).

Figure 16-2. The New Hilton Inn opened in 2000 at the intersection of I-480 and Grayton Road. *Author photo*

Figure 16-3. "One International Place" is the name of the first office building to have been built in the 77 acre Emerald Corporate Park off Grayton Road. *Author photo*

241

Figure 16-4. Looking east from the Hilton Inn. The Ford Plant is on the horizon in the upper right. On the left is the new 330,00 square foot SYSCO distribution facility under construction in the Cleveland Business Park between Grayton and Rocky River Drive. SYSCO will be one of the largest employers in West Park. *Author photo*

Figure 16-5. The finishing touches are being applied to this new warehouse that was built on the site of the old Agrico Fertilizer Plant (Figure 6-12). This area is a large industrial park south of Puritas Avenue at West 143rd Street. *Author photo*

Figure 16-6. The Riverside Theatre went the way of almost all local movie theatres. The giant multiplexes were favored by the public, leaving the old movie houses empty and broke. The area shown for redevelopment is outlined in white. The property now has a new drug store. *Kamm's Corner Development Corporation Collection*

Figure 16-7. New townhouses now grace the property formerly occupied by Longmead Elementary School. *Author photo*

243

Two organizations that are playing a major role in the redevelopment of West Park are the Kamm's Corner Development Corporation and the Bellaire-Puritas Development Corporation. Both are non-profit organizations dedicated to the development and redevelopment of their respective areas. When West Park first joined the city it was known as Ward 33. Over the years Ward boundaries have been redrawn several times so that today West Park includes all of Wards 20 and 21 as well as a portion of Ward 19.

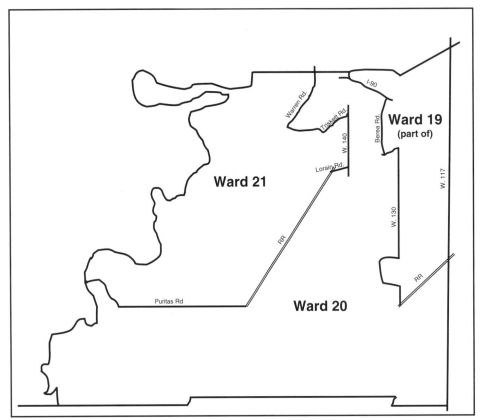

Figure 16-8. Ward 21 is served by the Kamm's Corners Development Corporation while Ward 20 is served by the Bellaire-Puritas Development Corporation.

THE HISTORY OF ONE PARCEL

Redevelopment of a parcel is simply part of the cyclic nature of things. In this country we tend to think that a person's property rights are sacred. That is true up to a point; after all, we all have a finite life span and what we hold sacred about our property may not be so sacred a hundred years from now. And we also have a basic responsibility to maintain that property so that it will have a useful value in the future. To somewhat illustrate this point, I have traced the history of one parcel of land in West Park from the time of settlement in the 1850's. Fortunately, there happens to be photographs of this parcel dating back to about 1900 showing all the uses up to the present.

The parcel in question is on the north side of Lorain Avenue at the edge of Rocky River Valley. In the original partitioning of the township in 1812, the area was part of a large tract purchased by Robbins and Calhoun. In 1854, A. Colburn owned the large tract. By 1895 the Cleveland and Elyria Railroad Company, (later merged into the Cleveland and Southwestern Interurban), had purchased a portion of the large tract. This is the parcel that we will examine. The parcel is nearly triangular and is approximately 7 acres in size. The Cleveland and Elyria built their car house and power generating station here, and these were the first structures to be built on the property. In 1900, a fire destroyed the car house, but it was quickly rebuilt. The first photograph in this series was taken shortly after the new car house was built.

244

Figure 16-9a. Cleveland and Elyria Railway Company car house at the turn of the 20th century. This would be the main piece in the merger of several interurban lines to form the Cleveland and Southwestern Interurban System. The tall stack is from the power generating plant. There were no public power producers because electricity was in its infancy. Throughout the country, the interurban companies were the first commercial producers of electricity, mostly for their own needs. However, in many cases, their production capacity was more than their own needs, and they actually supplied electricity to a few outside customers. *David Schafer Collection*

Figure 16-9b. An early aerial photograph taken on October 27, 1927. The Cleveland and Southwestern no longer produces its own electricity as indicated by the absence of the tall smoke stack. At this point in time The Illuminating Company was able to supply electricity more efficiently. *Cleveland State University Library, Cleveland Press Collection*

Figure 16-9c. The Interurban went out of business in 1931, but by March of 1934 the spacious car house was being used as a stable. *Cleveland Public Library*

Figure 16-9d. In April of 1938, a name change and probably a new owner, but it was still a stable. *Cleveland Public Library*

246

Figure 16-9e. In May of 1942, the stables have been torn down. *Cleveland Public Library*

Figure 16-9f. February, 1943 and more of the parcel has been cleared. *Cleveland Public Library*

Figure 16-9g. In December of 1943, these apartments are nearing completion just in time to help with the war-time housing shortage. *Cleveland Public Library*

Figure 16-9h. It's 1950 and the apartment buildings enjoy full occupancy. *Cleveland State University Library, Bruce Young Collection*

Figure 16-9i. In 1981, Fairview Hospital bought the apartment complex, tore it down and built the Center for Family Medicine (the building on the edge of the valley). Today the Cleveland Clinic Cancer Center has been added to the parcel. *Author photo February, 2004*

Figure 16-10. The Spang Bakery Delivery Truck. Julius Spang arrived in this country in 1882 with his wife and family. By 1889 he had opened a small bakery on Barber Avenue. They built their business specializing on home delivery of their baked goods. By 1950 they had a fleet of over 200 delivery trucks (www.fogas.org/history). Customers had a card measuring about 6" by 12" with a large red "S" on one side and a blue "S" on the other. If you wanted a delivery you simply placed the card in a front window where the driver could see it. One color indicated that you just wanted bread while the other indicated that the driver should also bring some baked goods to your door for selection. On March 1, 1957 this Spang truck ran into, of all things, a bakery. *Cleveland State University Library, Cleveland Press Collection.*

As the end of this historical journey approaches, I hope you have enjoyed it as much as I did in putting it together. I hope that it will stimulate some interest in a local historical society. I hope it will generate some discussions, questions, corrections and research. There is always room for improvement. The memories section in appendix C will touch on a few of the things I omitted. It is never too early nor is it too late to begin documenting the past!

Figure 16-11. In 1942 this Dairy Dell at 3875 West 130th Street was featuring five cent cones! *Cleveland Public Library*

Figure 16-12. In the 1950's, a new marketing concept came on the scene. Lawson's Milk Company of Cuyahoga Falls, Ohio, began opening convenience type stores around northeast Ohio. Their big selling point was that they sold milk in half gallons and gallons, which were not usually available in home delivery. They also sold milk with a butterfat content of 2%, which was nearly half of the 3.5% butterfat of whole milk sold by the home delivery dairies. All this obviously made the price of milk much cheaper. It did not take long before the home delivery dairies began to consolidate and eventually to disappear along with the milkman. *Cleveland State University Library, Cleveland Press Collection*

Figure 16-13. Olympic Recreation was built by Bob Barthelman in 1936 and operated by his family until 1975. At that time it was purchased by the Keegan family. In 1988 it was purchased by Fairview Hospital and torn down that same year. *Cleveland Public Library*

Figure 16-14. All traces of the bustling Linndale Station are gone except for the concrete platform next to the far track. *Author photo*

Figure 16-15a. On June 29, 1948, the sign covering part of "Ohio" proclaims that this spot at West 117th Street and Lorain Avenue will be the new home of Tony's Dining Car. This zoning board photograph even shows the outline of where the building will be located. *Cleveland Public Library*

Figure 16-15b. Tony's Diner shortly after it closed in 1998. *Author photo*

Figure 16-15c. The diner was purchased and moved to Port Clinton and was siting in a parking lot near the Port Clinton Airport in the fall of 1998. The sign in the window says "Tony's 1947 historic diner on the way to Port Clinton, OH opening June 1999". *Author photo*

251

Figure 16-16. Neisner's Dime Store, 12645 Lorain Avenue. *Cleveland Public Library*

Figure 16-17. It seems unimaginable today, but there was a time when you could walk out on the roof of the terminal at Hopkins and actually watch the airplanes take off and land. Part of the new terminal is under construction in 1953. *Cleveland Public Library.*

Figure 16-18. The name Rockport does not show up very often any more. However, the railroad yard just north of I-480 is still known as Rockport Yard. It was originally built by the New York Central, then part of Penn-Central, followed by Conrail and today it is part of the Norfolk Southern System. The view is looking west. *Cleveland StateUniversity Library, Bruce Young Collection*

Figure 16-19. And speaking of railroads! July 8, 1963. Police blamed juveniles who opened a switch to a spur track allowing the caboose to roll down onto Lorain Street. Traffic was slowed for four hours as trainmen worked to move the caboose off the street. *Cleveland State University Library, Cleveland Press Collection*

Figure 16-20. The Broken Wheel Junk Yard has been in business since 1949 helping to recycle automobile parts and saving money for the backyard mechanics of the area. *Author photo*

Figure 16-21. At 13630 Lorain Avenue, the Ohio Bell Building has had a name change but that's about all. *Cleveland Public Library*

Figure 16-22. West Park Gardens opened in the late 30' as Rose Lane Nursery, named after the lane that ran to the Impett Farm (see appendix B). In 1947, the name was changed to Warren Road Nursery when Rose Lane was eliminated. In 1986, the nursery was sold to St. Mary's Romanian Orthodox Church with the expectation that it remain a garden center. The center then operated as the Warren Road Garden Center until 1997 when the center was acquired by John and Diane Belko and now operates as the West Park Gardens and Gifts. *Author photo*

254

Figure 16-23. Over 60 years in business. *Ross Bassett photo*

Figure 16-24. White Wheel Alignment at the same location since the early 50's. *Author photo*

255

Figure 16-25a. Kamm's looks a little sleepy after the turn of the 20th century. *David Schaefer Collection*

Figure 16-25b. After the turn of the 21st Century, in April of 2004, Kamm's is anything but sleepy! *Author photo*

****

Bibliography

Allyn, Helen N. Uses 50,000 Chickens Each Year. Cleveland Press, January 13, 1931.

Atlas of Cuyahoga County and the City of Cleveland, Ohio. 1892. George F. Gram and Co. Publishers. Chicago, Illinois.

Atlas of Cuyahoga County. 1874. Titus, Simmons and Titus Publishers. Philadelphia, Pennsylvania.

Avery, Elroy McKendree. 1893. Cleveland in a Nutshell. Cleveland, Ohio. 160 p.

Avery, Elroy McKendree 1918. A History of Cleveland and its Environs, Vol. 1. Lewis Publishing Co., Chicago and New York. 727 p.

Barrett, Bill. 1958. Rapid to Begin New Chapter for West Park. Cleveland Press November 12, 1958.

Bennett, Dryck. 1996. On the Right Side of the Tracks and Between the Bridges. Founders Memorial Committee. Cleveland, Ohio. 85 p.

Brady, Dona Gallo. 1990. The History and Development of the West Park Black Community. Unpublished manuscript. Cleveland, Ohio. 49 p.

Brashares, Jeffrey R. 1982. The Cleveland, Southwestern and Columbus Railway Company. Privately printed. 102 p.

Bridges of Cleveland and Cuyahoga County. Privately printed, Cleveland. 1918. 40 p.

Brose, David S. 1971. The Early Historic Indians of Northern Ohio. Explorer, 13(1):21-29. The Cleveland Museum of Natural History. 1971.

Brose, David S. 1972. The Lake Prehistory Of The Lake Erie Drainage Basin: A 1972 Symposium Revised. Cleveland Museum of Natural History. Cleveland, Ohio. 355 p.

Brose, David S. 1994. The South Park Village Site and the Late Prehistoric Whittlesey Tradition of Northeast Ohio. Monographs in World Archaeology No. 20. Prehistory Press, Madison, Wisconsin. 226 p.

Bush, Lee O., Edward C. Chukayne, Russell Allon Hehr, Richard F. Hershey. 1977. Euclid Beach Park Is Closed For The Season. Amusement Park Books Inc. Fairview Park, Ohio. 331 p.

Butler, Margaret Manor. 1949. The Lakewood Story. Stratford House, New York, New York. 271 p.

Chabek, Dan 1992. Oldtime Party Center Had Real Country Atmosphere. Lakewood Sun Post March 12, 1992.

Chandler, James K. 1943. Marquard House to Make 15 Suites. Cleveland Press June 21, 1943.

Cherry, P. P. 1920. The Western Reserve and Early Ohio. Russell L. Fouse Pub. Akron, Ohio. 334 p.

Chevy Branch Restoration Underway. 1999. The Rap-Up. Publication of the Cuyahoga River Remedial Action Plan. Spring, 1999, vol. 10 No. 1.

Christiansen, Harry. 1963. Lake Shore Electric Railway. Cleveland, Ohio. 84 p.

Christiansen, Harry. 1973. Trolley Trails Through Greater Cleveland and Northern Ohio. Vol 3. Western Reserve Historical Society. Cleveland, Ohio. pp 327-512 .

Christiansen, Harry. 1975. Trolley Trails Through Greater Cleveland and Northern Ohio. Vol. 2. Western Reserve Historical Society. Cleveland, Ohio. pp 156-326 .

Cleveland Herald. November 16, 1827.

Cleveland Press. October 9, 1977.

Cleveland The Metropolis of Ohio. Compiled by the Mercantile Advancement Co., Cleveland, Ohio 1897.

Cleveland Yachting Club 1973. Published by and for members of Cleveland Yachting Club, Rocky River, Ohio.

Clingman, Harvey 1932. "Moving Day" Recalls History of Old John Marshall. John Marshall High School Interpreter. January 15, 1932.

Cuyahoga County Auditor. Record of Maps of Villages and Hamlets.

Dancey, William S., ed. 1994. The First Discovery of America. The Ohio Archaeological Council, Inc. Columbus, Ohio. 214 p.

Davis, Russell H. 1972. Black Americans in Cleveland. Associated Publishers, Washington, D.C. 525 p.

Fairview Park News, Fairview Park Chamber of Commerce, 1997.

Fisher, Daniel C. Bradley T. Lepper and Paul E. Hooge. 1994. Evidence for the Butchery of the Burning Tree Mastadon (43-61), in The Discovery of America, William S. Dancey ed.

Foos, James R. 1999. Florida? Hawaii? It's Kamm's Corners at the Turn of the Century. Kamm's Corners Magazine. 7(1):10.

Forsyth, Jane L. 1989. The Geologic Setting of Ohio Salamanders in Pfingsten, Ralph A. and Floyd L. Downs eds. The Salamanders of Ohio. Ohio Biol. Sur. Bull. New Series Vol 7. No. 2. 315 p.

Friedman, Tim. 199-. Across The Years with Lakewood Kiwanis. Excerpts from the 25th Anniversary Booklet of Lakewood Kiwanis 1946-1971.

Gallagher, John S. and Alan H. Patera. 1979. The Post Offices of Ohio. Published by The Depot. 318 p.

Gieck, Jack. 1988. A Photo Album of Ohio's Canal Era, 1825-1913. Kent State University Press, Kent, Ohio. 310 p.

Gobelt, Margaret Schaefer. 1978. Fairview Park In Historical Review. Fairview Park Historical Society. Fairview Park, Ohio. 364 p.

Goldthwait, Richard P. 1959. Scenes in Ohio During the Last Ice Age. Ohio J. Sci. 59(4): 193-216.

Goldthwait, Richard P., George W. White, and Jane L. Forsyth. 1961. Glacial map of Ohio. U.S. Geol. Sur. Miscell. Geol. Invest. Map. I-316.

Gottschang, Jack L. 1981. A Guide to the Mammals of Ohio. OSU Press. Columbus, Ohio 176 p.

Grazulis, Thomas P. 1993. Significant Tornadoes 1680-1991. Environmental Films, St. Johnsbury, Vermont. 1326 p.

Gregory, William M. and William B. Guitteau. 1929. History and Geography of Ohio. Ginn and Company. Boston, Massachusetts. 280 p.

Hatcher, Harlan. 1991. The Western Reserve. Kent State University Press. Kent, Ohio. 328 p.

Hays, Blaine. 1988. Airport Rapid-RTA Continues a Fine Transit Tradition. Published for the employees of the Greater Cleveland Regional Transit Authority. 20th Anniversary Edition November 15, 1988.

Hays, Blaine. 1999. Cleveland Union Terminals. Published for members of the Northern Ohio Railway Museum March-April, 1999.

Health Cleveland. 1992. The Centennial History of Fairview General Hospital. Health Cleveland, Cleveland, Ohio. 92 p.

Holzworth, Walter F. 1966. The Story of Cedar Point Valley. North Olmsted Historical Society. North Olmsted, Ohio. Mimeographed ms. 29 p.

Holzworth, Walter F. 1966. Township 6; Range 15. Private Printing. Olmsted Falls, Ohio. 332 p.

Holzworth, Walter F. 1970. Men of Grit and Greatness. Private Printing. Olmsted Falls, Ohio. 220 p.

Holzworth, Walter F. 1973. The Spirit of Independence, A History of the City of Brookpark. Olmsted Falls Printing. Olmsted Falls, Ohio. 185 p.

Hothem, Lar. 1990. First Hunters Ohio's Paleo-Indian Artifacts. Hothem House, Lancaster, Ohio. 163 p.

Insurance Maps of Cleveland, Ohio. Volume 17, 1929. Sanborn Company, New York.

James Ford Rhodes High School. 1946. South Brooklyn. Cleveland, Ohio. 113 p.

Johannesen, Eric. 1999. A Cleveland Legacy, the Architecture of Walker and Weeks. Kent State University Press. Kent, Ohio. 200 p.

Johnson, Crisfield, 1897. History of Cuyahoga County, Published by D.W. Ensign and Company, Leader Printing Company, Cleveland, Ohio.

Kamm's Corners Magazine, Kamm's Corners Development Corporation. 1996.

Klein, Daniel B. 1994. Private Highways in America 1792-1916. The Freeman, a publication of The Foundation for Economic Education, Inc. February 1994, Vol. 44. No. 2.

Knepper, George W. 1976. An Ohio Portrait. Ohio Historical Society. Columbus, Ohio. 282 p.

Knight, Thomas A. 1903. The Country Estates of Cleveland Men. Cleveland Britton Publ. Co. 142 p.

Kraynek, Sharon L.D. 1993. Chippewa Lake Park 1800-1978, Diary of an Amusement Park. 3rd printing. Pittsburgh, Pennsylvania. 156 p.

Kubasek, Ernest R. 1976. The History of Parma. Kubasek and Survoy Pub. 298 p.

Lerch, Walter. Was the Puritas Springs Cyclone Dangerous? Cleveland Plain Dealer, July 26, 1946.

Lindstrom, E. George. 1936. Story of Lakewood, Ohio. Lakewood, Ohio. 160 p.

Lupold, Harry F. and Gladys Haddad. 1988. Ohio's Western Reserve: A Regional Reader. Kent State University, Kent, Ohio. 277 p.

The May Dugan Center. 1993. Whatever Happened to the "Paper Rex" Man. 108 p.

McDonald, H. Gregory. 1994. The Late Pleistocene Vertebrate Fauna in Ohio: Coinhabitants with Ohio's Paleoindians, 23-42, in The Discovery of America, William S. Dancey ed.

Meixner, Bill. 1999. "50th Anniversary of the Berea Crash". A Talk from the Society of Air Racing Historians to the Berea Historical Society. September 23, 1999.

Memorial Record of the County of Cuyahoga and city of Cleveland, Ohio. 1894. Lewis Publishing Company, Chicago, Illinois. 924 p.

Morris, Ruth and Olga Boieru. 1973. Fairview Park Ohio. Cuyahoga County Public Library. Cleveland, Ohio. 18 p.

Naftzger, Duane M. and Andrew C. Neff. eds. 1962. Valley City and Liverpool Township Commemorative Book. Valley City Sesqui Inc. Valley City, Ohio. 72 p.

Neighbors, A Family Newspaper Serving The West Park Community. March, 1993.

Nesbitt, Burton J. 2002. Big Bands On The Lake Front, 1932-1950. Compiled by Burton J. Nesbitt, privately printed. Rim Shot Graphics, Amherst, Ohio. 144 p.

North Royalton Historical Society. 1992. The History of North Royalton 1811-1991. King Court Communications. Brunswick, Ohio. 230 p.

Northwest Territory Celebration Commission. 1937. History of the Ordinance of 1787 and the Old Northwest Territory. Marietta, Ohio. 95 p.

O'Bryant, Michael, Ed. 1997. The Ohio Almanac. Orange Frazer Press. Wilmington, Ohio. 712 p.

Ohio Correspondent. 1910. Cleveland Correspondent Publishing Company. Cleveland, Ohio.

Ohio Department of Natural Resources, Division of Geological Survey. Map of Well Locations in Rockport, Cuyahoga County. 1988.

Ohio Department of Natural Resouces, Division of Wildlife. Wild Ohio Magazine. Winter 1999-2000.

Ohio Historical Bridge Inventory Evaluation, and Preservation Plan. Pub. By ODOT in cooperation with The Federal Highway Administration. 1983. 270 p.

Ohio Historical Records Survey Project. December, 1939. Inventory of the Municipal Archives of Ohio. No. 18 Cuyahoga County. Volume 5, Cleveland. Columbus, Ohio. 538 p.

Pfingsten, Ralph A. and Floyd L. Downs, eds. 1989. Salamander of Ohio. Ohio Biol. Surv. Bull. New Series Vol. 7 No. 2 xx + 315 p. + 29 pls.

Plat Books of Cuyahoga County, Ohio Volume 6. 1927. G.M. Hopkins Co. Publishers. Philadelphia, Pennsylvania.

Poh Miller, Carol. 1992. Cleveland Metroparks Past and Present. Cleveland, Ohio. 42 p.

RAP-UP. Spring 1999. A publication of the Cuyahoga River Remedial Action Plan vol 10, No. 1.

Rehor, John A. 1965. The Nickel Plate Story. Kalmbch Publishing Co. Waukesha, Wisconsin. 483 p.

Rhoads, Roger R. 1999. Groundwork for Free Delivery. American Philatelist vol. 113, No. 11 (1073-77).

Richards, Ralph D. and Ron Gabel. City of Rocky River Golden Jubilee and Ohio Sesqui-Centennial Celebration, 1903-1953. 46 p.

Robishaw, William M. 1993. You've Come A Long Way Westlake. Westlake Historical Society. Westlake, Ohio. 503 p.

Rose, William Ganson. 1950. Cleveland: The Making Of A City. World Publishing Co., Cleveland, Ohio. 1272 p.

Roseboom, Eugene and Francis P. Weisenburger. 1954. A History of Ohio. The Ohio State Archaeological and Historical Society. Columbus, Ohio. 417 p.

Ruffner, James A. and Frank E. Blair (Eds.). 1977. The Weather Almanac, 2nd edition. Gale Research Co., Detroit, Michigan.

Rummel, Merle C. 1998. Brethren on the Ohio Frontier. Brethren Life, Church of the Brethren Network.

Schmidlin, Thomas W. and Jeanne Appelhans Schmidlin 1996. Thunder in the Heartland: A Chronicle of Outstanding Weather Events in Ohio. Kent State University Press, Kent, Ohio. 362 p.

Seeman, Mark F., Garry Summers, Elaine Dowd, and Larry Morris. 1994. Fluted Point Characteristics at Three Large Sites: The Implications for Modeling Early Paleoindian Settlement Patterns in Ohio, (77-92). in The Discovery of America, William S. Dancey ed.

Shaw, Willard H. 1936. Historical Facts Concerning Berea and Middleburg Township. Mohler Printing Co., Berea, Ohio. 52 p.

State Road Records. 1829-1841.

Strongsville Historical Society. 1967. History of Strongsville Cuyahoga County, Ohio. Book 1. 96 p.

Swinerton, Hal. 19(86). Old Rockport Township Historical Trail. mimeographed ms. Sponsored by West Park Watch. 26 p.

Tabata, William K. 2003. The Life of William K. Tabata. unpublished manuscript. 10 p.

This is Kamms Corners, a Publication of the Kamm's Area Development Corporation. April, 1982.

This is Kamms Corners, a Publication of the Kamm's Area Development Corporation. March, 1983.

Thomas, F.W. City Clerk. The City Record – Official Publication of the City of Cleveland – West Park Supplement. June 16, 1926. 1221 p.

Trautman, Milton B. 1977. The Ohio Country from 1750-1977 -A Naturalists View. Ohio Biol. Surv. Biol. Notes No. 10. 25 p.

Turner, Frederick Jackson. 1921. The Frontier in American History. Henry Holt and Co. New York, New York.

Van Tassel, David E. and John J. Grabowsi eds. 1996. The Encyclopedia of Cleveland History. 2nd ed. Indiana University Press. Bloomington, Indiana. 1165 p.

Vexler, Robert I. 1977. Cleveland: A Chronological & Documentary History. Oceana Publications, Inc. Dobbs Ferry, NY. 153 p.

Vittek, James G. 1981. Clyde McAllister's Steam Powered Dream. The Western Reserve Magazine, Vol. 8, no. 7 special supplement pp 62-66.

Vollmer, Rev. Philip B. 1969. The Vollmer Memorial History of Fairview General Hospital. Privately Printed. Cleveland, Ohio. 96 p.

Watson, Sara R. and John R. Wolfs. 1981. Bridges of Metropolitan Cleveland. N.p.: n.p.

West Park. Cleveland Transit System Souvenir Booklet. November 15, 1958.

White, George, Chairman. Northwest Territory Celebration Commission. 1937. History of the Ordinance of 1787 and the Old Northwest Territory. 95 p.

Wilcox, Max E. 195-. The Cleveland Southwestern and Columbus Rwy Story. Privately printed. 36 p.

Wild Ohio Magazine. Winter 1999-2000. Ohio Department of Natural Resources, Division of Wildlife, Columbus, Ohio.

Williams, Arthur B. 1940. The Geology of the Cleveland Region. Cleveland Ohio. Cleveland Museum of Natural History. Pocket Natural History, No. 9. Geological series, No. 1. 61 p.

Wilmer, Kathryn Gasior. 1979. Old Brooklyn. Commerical Press. Kent, Ohio. 82 p.

Wilmer, Kathryn Gasior. 198-. Old Brooklyn New, Book II. Old Brooklyn Community Development Council. Brooklyn, Ohio. 108 p.

262

Wittke, Carl. 1941a. The History of the State of Ohio, Volume I, The Foundations of Ohio. Ohio State Archaeological and Historical Society. Columbus, Ohio. 507 p.

Wittke, Carl. 1941b. The History of the State of Ohio, Volume II, The Frontier State, 1803-1825. Ohio State Archaeological and Historical Society. Columbus, Ohio. 454 p.

Wittke, Carl. 1941c. The History of the State of Ohio, Volume III, The Passing of the Frontier, 1825-1850. Ohio State Archaeological and Historical Society. Columbus, Ohio. 524 p.

WEBSITES

http://ech.cwru.edu/
http://homenyr.rr.com/johnmiller
http://home.neo.rr.com.camelot2/CLPnews.htm
http://keiper.dnsalias.com/Longaberger/
http://lkwdpl.org/kiwanis
http://serform.sos.state.oh.us
http://xroads.virginia.edu/~hyper/turner
http://wchs.csc.noaa.gov/1816.htm
http://wchs.csc.noaa.gov
http://www.coasterglobe.com/features/lostlegends
http://www.cycrr.org/hist
http://www.dnr.state.oh.us
http://www.fogas.org/history
http://www.history.amusement-parks.com
http://www.lakechamber.com/longaberger.htm
http://www.memphiskiddiepark.com
http://www.nhlink.net/spa/kammhist
http://www.ohiohistory.org
http://planning.city.cleveland
http://www.s363.com
http://www.sos.state.oh.us/sos/
http://www.tridentgum.com

www.airrace.com
www.archives.gov
www.clevelandairport.com
www.clevelandmemory/org/lakewood
www.cmnh.org
www.crh.noaa.gov/dtx/stm_1913htm
www.cr.nps.gov
www.driveintheatre.com
www.druglibrary.org
www.ecocitycleveland.org
www.lakewood.org/history
www.ohiokiwanis.org
www.rootsweb.com/-indacatu/history
www.rootsweb.com/~ohwcl/
www.universitycircle.org
www.usps.com/history

CHRONOLOGY OF EVENTS IN AND AFFECTING ROCKPORT

Under the charter of April, 1662, signed by King Charles II, Connecticut claimed all land lying between the 41st parallel and 42nd parallel west to the Mississippi River except that part granted to the Duke of York (New York). Pennsylvania disputed the claim between the Delaware River and its present boundary. A federal court sustained Pennsylvania, and thus the Connecticut claim was limited to Connecticut itself and the land west of Pennsylvania to the Mississippi River.

1780. Continental Congress suggested that Colonies owning wasteland cede them to the federal government. Thus Connecticut gave up lands east of the Mississippi River up to a line parallel to and 120 miles east of the western boundary of Pennsylvania. This 120 miles they kept or reserved for themselves (The Connecticut Western Reserve). Questions arose as to title to lands within the Reserve. Finally on May 30, 1800, the President was authorized to convey all rights within the Reserve to the state of Connecticut. During the Revolutionary War, the British sailed through Long Island Sound and entered several Connecticut harbors burning and plundering houses and public buildings. Those people suffering most were from the towns of New Haven, East Haven, Greenwich, Danbury, Ridgefield, Norwalk, New London and Groton. These people sought relief from the Connecticut legislature which set aside 500,000 acres at the West End of the Reserve for those who were burned out. This area became known as the Firelands, present Erie and Huron Counties, and many of the present township names within these counties were derived from the names of those burned out towns.

1786. General Arthur St. Clair became the first Governor of the Northwest Territory.

October 27, 1787. The Ordinance of 1787 was approved. (Legislation concerning formation of the Northwest Territory)

1788. First permanent settlement in the Northwest Territory was founded at Marietta, Ohio.

July 27, 1788. Governor St. Clair established Washington County (Marietta area). Washington County included almost half of what was to become Ohio.

1790. Cincinnati was regarded as the Capitol of the Northwest Territory.

May 1792. Connecticut set aside 500,000 acres of land at the West End of the Reserve as the Firelands.

May 1795. 3,000,000 acres of the Western Reserve (excluding the Firelands) was offered for sale by the Connecticut General Assembly. This was to provide proceeds for a permanent school fund for Connecticut. Forty-nine citizens organized as the Connecticut Land Company and purchased all 3,000,000 acres for $1,200,000 or about 40 cents per acre. The sale was on credit (Van Tassel and Grabowski, 1996)

August 5, 1795. General Anthony Wayne defeated Indians at the Battle of Fallen Timbers (west of Toledo), and established the Greenville Treaty Line.

1796. Moses Cleaveland arrived at the mouth of the Cuyahoga River to begin surveying the Western Reserve.

1799. The first gristmill in the Western Reserve was built at Newburgh.

July 10, 1800. Governor St. Clair named the Western Reserve as Trumbull County - a part of the Northwest Territory.

November 1800. Chillicothe became the Capitol of the "eastern part" of the Northwest Territory.

February 19, 1803. Congress declared the eastern portion of the Northwest Territory south of Lake Erie to be the State of Ohio, and Chillicothe became the Capitol.

1803. The last record of a bison being shot and killed in Ohio in Lawrence County, (Ironton area).

1805. A United States Post Office was established at Cleveland.

July 4, 1805. The Treaty of Fort Industry (near Toledo) moved the Greenville Treaty Line to the western boundary of the Western Reserve. Up to this time, land west of the Cuyahoga had been considered Indian Territory. When settlers began arriving shortly after this treaty, there were still 200 Indians living in the Cuyahoga Valley. (Today there are several thousand).

1806. Congress ordered the construction of the National Road. By 1815, it would extend from Cumberland, Maryland to Wheeling, West Virginia, but it would not reach Columbus, Ohio, for another 16 years.

1806. The first iron furnace in the Western Reserve is built in Niles, Ohio.

April 4, 1807. The draft for townships west of the Cuyahoga River takes place-Rockport's first owners.

1807. Zanesville becomes the temporary Capitol of Ohio.

1807 Late Winter. Columbia became the first settlement west of the Cuyahoga. By 1810 there were 100 people in the village at Columbia making it almost twice the size of Cleveland.

1808. The Cleveland to Erie mail route was established.

February 10, 1808. Cuyahoga County created by the state legislature.

April 10, 1808. Philo Taylor arrived at the mouth of Rocky River with his family and built a cabin where Clifton Park is today. He had to move because he did not have clear title to the land, and because Gideon Granger was planning the township's first subdivision called Granger City. Gideon Granger had purchased all of section 24 shortly after Township 7 (Rockport) was partitioned. Granger City included part of Clifton Park and land immediately west of Rocky River (Clifton Beach).

November 1809. First birth in Rockport, Egbert Taylor, son of Philo.

1809. Brooklyn Township was surveyed. The first settler was Samuel Lord who owned most of the Township. He arrived in 1818 with son and brother-in-law and settled near the mouth of the Cuyahoga River about the time the Township was organized.

1809. The State of Ohio appropriated money to build a road from Cleveland to the mouth of the Huron River, which was then a part of Cuyahoga County. George Peake and his family were the first to use the road when they moved into the area in 1809 and thereby became the first permanent settlers of the township.

1809. A mail route from Cleveland to Detroit was established. Three couriers on foot carried mail about once every two weeks. Horses were put into use in 1811.

1810. Alfred Kelley arrived to become the first lawyer in the Western Reserve.

1810. The population of Cleveland was 57, Cuyahoga County was 1,459 (smallest in Ohio) and Ohio was 231,000.

1810. Seba Bronson Jr. cleared land in Hardscrabble, Liverpool Township, Medina County. The salt springs at Hardscrabble would become important to settlers all over Northeastern Ohio.

ca 1811. Datus Kelley erected a sawmill next to a creek on Detroit Road near present Elmwood. This was the first industry in Rockport Township.

March 4, 1811. County Commissioners authorized a road to be built from Lake Road (from Dan Miner's property east of Rocky River) to the north line of Columbia at Hoadley's Mill (in southeast corner of Olmsted Township). (State Road Records). Since Riverside Drive was not extended north to Lake Road until 1832, it can be assumed the route of the road was mostly on the west side of Rocky River including what are now Wooster, Mastick and Columbia Roads.

1812. The Capitol of Ohio reverted back to Chillicothe.

June 1812. The Algers (Nathan, his wife and four sons) settled in sections 12 and 13 (Kamm's area). He would have received 640 acres (a full section) if he had lived there for a full year. Unfortunately, he died before the year was over, and his family received only 320 acres. Few settlers were attracted to the west side of the Cuyahoga River because of dense forest, swamps and too many streams. The high embankment (at Rocky River) precluded anchorage of sailing craft.

June 18, 1812. War began with Great Britain.

1812. Columbia blockhouse was built to protect nervous citizens during the war of 1812, and settlements were abandoned as settlers moved back to more secure and safer locations including this Blockhouse.

1812. Following the war of 1812, steamboats began to function on the Ohio and Mississippi Rivers.

September 10, 1813. Perry defeated the British in the Battle of Lake Erie thereby ending the War of 1812.

January 1814. The first marriage in Rockport. Chester Dean to Lucy Smith at the home of Datus Kelley.

December 23, 1814. Cleveland was chartered as a village.

1815. Alfred Kelley became the first President of Cleveland.

1816. The year without a summer.

1817. Construction began on the Erie Canal in New York connecting Lake Erie with the Hudson River and New York City. The commerce of the West now had access to the New York markets.

December 1, 1817. Columbus was finally chosen as the State Capitol.

June 1, 1818. Brooklyn Township was organized.

February 24, 1819. Rockport Township was formed out of Township 7 Range 14 of the Western Reserve consisting of 21 full sections and 4 fractional sections (due to the irregular shoreline of the lake). It consisted of level, good soil well adapted to growing fruit. There were 18 families in the township at the time of formation. The name was chosen because of the high rocky embankments on the lakefront and both sides of the Rocky River. This township form of government lasted for the next 70 years.

June 24, 1819. Charles Miles was elected first Justice of the Peace in Rockport.

1820. The population of Cleveland was 606, and Ohio was 581,000. Independence Road (State Route 21) was opened to Akron and stage lines were organized to Columbus, Norwalk and Pittsburgh.

1821. The first toll bridge connecting the east and west sides of Rocky River was completed on the Detroit Road (Rose, 1950).

1821. The Ohio General Assembly established the common school system.

1821. Gypsum (Plaster of Paris) was discovered on government lands near Sandusky Bay.

1822. Isaac Warren (an original stockholder in the Connecticut Land Company) settled in Rockport (near present Madison and Warren Roads). In 1824. Warren Road was laid out (Rose, 1950).

1823. The stage road to the southwest (U.S. Rt. 42) was converted to a turnpike by private interests and soon became one of the best highways in Ohio (Rose, 1950).

1824. A patent was issued for Portland Cement.

February 1825. Ohio and Erie Canal construction was authorized in the Ohio Legislature, and Cleveland was chosen as the northern terminus after much political fighting by Toledo and Sandusky.

March 3, 1825. Congress appropriated $5,000 to build a pier into the lake from the east shore of the river (Nutshell, 1893).

October 26, 1825. The Erie Canal was opened from New York.

1826. Joseph Triskett arrived in Rockport and bought 50 acres near the present West 117th and Triskett area (Rose, 1950).

July 4, 1827. First Erie Canal Boat arrived in Cleveland.

1827-1850. This period was the height of influence of the canals.

1828. Henry Newberry brought the first load of coal to Cleveland mined from his land on the banks of the Cuyahoga River in Tallmadge close to the Canal. It was widely disdained, as cleaner wood was still preferred.

1830. The population of Rockport was 368 of which 44 were "free colored."

July 10, 1830. Navigation began on The Ohio Canal to Newark.

1830. Jonathan Spencer bought 125 acres in southwestern corner of Rockport (Western part of Fairview).

1830. John M. West owned a 700-acre stock farm south of Lorain east of West 140. He built a lake with rowboats and had a picnic grounds known as West's Park. This eventually became the name for the West Park Community. In 1914, son Charles drained the lake and sold lots.

1831. A land boom occured on the West Bank of the Cuyahoga River, and a ship canal was excavated from the river near its mouth to the old riverbed to the west.

1832. Fischer Road was built (State Road Records).

1832. Riverside Drive was extended north to Lake Road (State Road Records).

December 1832. Spencer Road (West 220th) was built (State Road Records).

October 15, 1832. First boat to travel the entire Ohio and Erie Canal arrived in Cleveland.

April 22, 1833. Erie and Kalamazoo Railroad was chartered.

1833. Datus and Irad Kelley purchased the western half of Cunningham's Island in Lake Erie.

March 3 1834. Cleveland and Newburgh Railroad was incorporated.

1834. Population on both sides of the Cuyahoga River doubled in a year.

August 1835. The population of Cleveland was 5,080 and Ohio City was 1,150.

April 19, 1835. Puritas Road was extended from the West Bank of the river to intersect Wooster Road in the southwest corner of the township. (State Road Records).

1835-36. First settlers to Rockport on the west side of Rocky River are Jonathan Spencer in western part, Stephan Jordan in eastern part, Benjamin Mastick in Mastick Valley and Russell Hawkins in the center (Fairview Herald).

1836. Free schools were established in Cleveland.

March 3, 1836. The City of Ohio (Ohio City) was chartered becoming the first city in the county. Cleveland was not chartered until April 11, 1836.

March 14, 1836. Cleveland, Columbus and Cincinnati Railroad was chartered.

1836. The Cleveland and Pittsburgh Railroad was chartered (the final connection to Pittsburgh was not completed until 1852).

1837. The famous physician and naturalist Jared P. Kirtland moved to Rockport (West 140th and Detroit Road area).

1837. Joseph Hall cleared 100 acres of virgin forest in Rockport (Hall Ave., Lakewood) (Rose).

1837. First school board formed in Cleveland (Avery, 1893).

1837. Louis Daguerre produced first photograph.

1840. Cleveland Schools had 900 pupils and 16 instructors (Avery, 1893).

1840. The population of Rockport was 1,235 of which 46 were "free colored."

1841. (Approximate) paving (planking) of Superior Street.

1842. For days at a time, Cleveland skies were darkened as millions of passenger pigeons soared overhead. "The roar of their wings sounded at the distance of miles...one shot could bring down many birds and street peddlers sold them at less than a penny apiece. The last known passenger pigeon, "Martha" died in the Cincinnati Zoo in 1913.

1843. Indians still lived on a reservation in Seneca County (Tiffin area).

Late 30's and 40's. First schools appeared in the township at Cannon Avenue in Granger, Phinney's Corners (Center Ridge and Wooster) and Lorain near Triskett.

May 9, 1846. Lake Shore and Michigan Southern Railroad was chartered; this later became the New York to Chicago mainline of the New York Central Railroad.

1847. Letheon (ether) was first used as a general anesthetic at the Medical Department of Western Reserve College (Rose, 1950).

1847. The United States Postal Service began production and use of the first postage stamps (Rose).

1847. The first telegraph service in Cleveland was established with a connection to Pittsburgh (Avery, 1893).

1848. Lake Telegraph Company was chartered providing service from Cleveland to Buffalo.

November 3, 1849. First railroad service arrives in Cleveland (Cleveland, Columbus, and Cincinnati, The Big Four Railroad).

1849. Cleveland Gas and Coke Company was supplying gas for street illumination (Avery, 1893).

1849. The population of Cleveland hit 17,034.

1850. The population of Rockport was 1,441.

1850. Plank road company built a new toll bridge across Rocky River at Detroit Road.

1850's. Horse drawn street railways were in common use in Cleveland; these are the predecessors of the electric streetcars.

1850. Gas lights were in use on Superior Street. None were used on the West Side until 1867. Gas lighting continued only until 1879 when Charles Brush invented arc lighting.

1850. Ohio was the third most populous state in the nation.

1850. Ohio canal system suffered stiff competition from the railroads, which traveled more east-westrather than the north-south orientation of the canals.

August 8, 1850. The Big Four Railroad was completed to Wellington and the first train arrived in Cleveland.

1850. Rivalry between Cleveland and Ohio City escalated as more industries settled on the west side of the Cuyahoga River culminating in the bridge war.

1851. The first sewing machine was exhibited in Cleveland. This invention revolutionizes the boot and clothing industries (Rose, 1893).

February 18, 1851. First through train from Cleveland to Columbus on the Big Four. (New York Central).

February 1851. The first train of the Pennsylvania Railroad arrived in Hudson, Ohio. The line was completed to Pittsburgh the following year.

1852. The best wheat grown in Ohio this year was produced by Thomas Hern on his East Rockport (Lakewood) Farm (Rose, 1950).

1852. The New York Central Railroad from Buffalo to Toledo (through Cleveland) was opened.

1853. The first iron ore (1/2 dozen barrels) was shipped to Cleveland (Avery, 1893).

April 2, 1854. Cleveland annexed Ohio City.

1856. Central Viaduct opened.

1856. Central Market established.

1857 Approximate. Omnibus (stagecoach) routes within city and to outlying settlements increased.

1857. Erie Railroad line completed to Youngstown.

February 1858. Cuyahoga County Historical Society established.

1859. William Case constructed a building for the Kirtland Society of Natural History (predecessor to the Cleveland Museum of Natural History).

October 25, 1859. Kinsman Street Railroad Company received a 20-year charter to operate horse drawn streetcars in a part of Cleveland. Within 20 years several more companies would be chartered in the City.

1860. The population of Rockport was 1,794. 930 males and 864 females.

1860. Ohio led the nation in the value of agricultural products and also had more miles of railroad than any other state.

April 12, 1861. Fort Sumter was fired upon, thus beginning the Civil War. In all 340,000 Ohioans would serve with the Union forces. (Gregory and Guitteau, 1929).

1861. The canal system was leased to private operators.

1862.   Cleveland Volunteer Fire department gave way to paid firemen (Avery, 1893).

January 1, 1863. Emancipation Proclamation.

November 3, 1863. First train arrived directly from New York on what would later become the Erie Railroad.

1863.   Free city delivery of mail.

1865.   An amateur baseball team called the Forest City Baseball Club was formed in Cleveland as baseball was emerging as the national pastime.

1867.   Rockport Hamlet School was opened.

1869.   Dummy Railroad (Rocky River Railroad) was organized. Single track from West 58 and Bridge to the rear of the Cliff House. At the West End of Lakewood there was a roundhouse and machine shop at Nicholson Ave and passing sidings at Summit, Nicholson and Hird. There were three 12-ton locomotives and 12 coaches with seats along the sides. The Nickel Plate bought the Dummy on September 9, 1881 thus giving the Van Sweringen brothers railroad access to Cleveland from the west. Ironically, Cornelieus Vanderbilt could have bought this line very inexpensively and kept competition with his New York Central Line out of Cleveland.

1870.   African Americans gained the right to vote in Ohio.

1870.   Macadam pavement was used experimentally near Public Square.

1871.   Residents of East Rockport (Lakewood) voted to have a separate school district east of the Rocky River.

1872.   The first bowling alley opened on West 6th street in Cleveland.

1873.   The giant Collinwood shops of the New York Central Railroad opened.

1876.   The Cleveland and Berea Street Railway was organized.

1876.   In 1857, Thomas H. White (1836-1914) had invented a small, hand operated, single thread machine called the New England Sewing Machine. Seeking a central location near markets and materials, he moved his company to Cleveland. In 1876, the White Sewing Machine Company was formed and within 10 years, 2,000 units per week were being produced making Cleveland the center for the manufacturing of sewing machines. Today not a single machine is made in the U.S. (http://ech.cwru.edu/).

1877.   The state reclaimed the canal system but large sections had become inoperative or abandoned.

February 13, 1879. The last legal hanging took place in Cuyahoga County. Afterwards all executions were carried out at the State Penitentiary in Columbus.

Figure C-1. White Sewing Machine ad 1898.

271

1879. First telephone service in Cleveland.

1879. Brush Arc Lighting of city streets, made Cleveland the first city in the nation with electric street lighting.

1879. New York, Chicago, and St. Louis Railroad (Nickel Plate) is organized in New York.

January 1882. The Connotton Valley Railroad, predecessor of the Wheeling and Lake Erie, arrives in Cleveland.

September 4, 1882. Authorization of Berea Plank Road (West 143rd from Lorain to Puritas) (State Road Records).

October 23, 1882. The Nickel Plate line from Buffalo to Chicago (through Cleveland) opened.

July 26, 1884. The first electric streetcar in the country begins service in Cleveland.

1885. *Cleveland Leader*, July 14, 1885
"In addition to the gas development by Henry A. Mastick at Rocky River, J.M. Gasser, the florist near Phinney's Store, has struck gas, which he proposes to utilize for lighting and warming purposes in his greenhouse. W.H. Lawrence of Dover Bay has also succeeded in getting gas at a depth of 600 feet. The time is not far distant when natural gas will be used for all purposes thereabouts, and when the streets of this desirable suburb will be lighted by it."

1886. Kamm's Post Office opened. It closed in 1920.

1887. The first football game was played in the area when Central High School defeated Case School of Applied Science.

1888. 10,236 rail cars of stone are shipped from the Berea Quarries. The quarries closed in 1931.

May 1888. Famous wolf hunt (not Hinckley). Citizens from Berea, Middleburg, Strongsville, Royalton, Liverpool and Columbia joined in a great circle of the Lake Abram area. Only one gray wolf was killed (Holzworth, 1970)

August 31, 1889. East Rockport becomes the Hamlet of Lakewood.

October 11, 1889. Cleveland Railroad Company formed from the merger of three lines.

1889. Cleveland Spiders admitted to the National Baseball League.

Figure C-2. A section of the famous Berea quarry. *Gregory and Guitteau, 1929*

1890. Rockport Hamlet Driving Park opened at Kamm's Corners. Built by Fred Colbrunn, the popular racetrack remained open until 1920.

May 1, 1891. League Park opened.

September 9, 1891. Petition presented to county commissioners that all of Rockport west of the river become the hamlet of Rocky River—it took effect December 19, 1891 (Rose, 1950).

July 6, 1892. Petition was presented to the County Commissioners to establish Rockport Hamlet bounded by the Rockport Township line on the east and south, Rocky River on the west and Lakewood hamlet on the North. Granted on October 8, 1892. (Lindstrom, 1936).

1893. Rockport Hamlet was incorporated.

April 26, 1893. Cleveland and Buffalo Transit Company began steamship lake service. Passenger excursion business including trips to Cedar Point reached their peak of popularity in the 20's. The depression and competition from trucks forced the company's bankruptcy in 1939.

July 18, 1893. The Sandusky, Milan & Norwalk became the second electric interurban railway line to operate in the country, and it was also the longest electric railway in the world. This began the Interurban Era.

1894. Basketball was introduced to the area by the YMCA.

1894. The first concrete road in the U.S. was built at Bellefontaine, Ohio. Local officials are so skeptical that they insist on a five year guarantee from the builder.

Figure C-3. East Ninth Street Pier. Cleveland home to the C&B and the D&C. *Avery, 1918*

1894. The Baltimore & Ohio Railroad entered Cleveland.

1894. First class to graduate from Lakewood High School.

1894. City acquired 6,000 feet of shoreline creating Edgewater Beach and Park.

1894. The Puritas Springs Bottling Company opened on 10 acres at the West End of Puritas Road.

October 1894. Cleveland and Elyria Electric Railway chartered.

1895. Golf is introduced to the area by Samuel Mather.

1895.   Euclid Beach opened.

1895.   Cleveland and Southwestern Traction Company organized.

November, 1895. The first high level Lorain Road Bridge was completed over Rocky River.

December 15 1895.   The first interurban car of the Cleveland and Southwestern Traction Company travels the 17 miles from Cleveland to Elyria causing the stage line to go out of business overnight. Electric power was supplied from their own power plant built with the car barns on the north side of Lorain Road at the east end of the Lorain Road Bridge.

1897.   A class of 5 graduated from Rocky River High School.

1897.   The Cedar Point Resort Company was organized.

October 6, 1897. Lorain and Cleveland Railway opened from Rocky River to Lorain.

1898.   The Cleveland and Southwestern Railway opened Puritas Springs Amusement Park. This same year they built a branch line from the western boundary of Cleveland (West 98) up West 105 to Bellaire and out Puritas to the Park. This line was torn out in 1927, and the park closed in 1958.

1899.   Henry Reitz became the first graduate of West Park High School. A class of one.

January 1, 1900. Rockport Hamlet petitioned the County Commissioners to become West Park Township. The petition was granted on March 5, 1900.

1900.   The population of Fairview was approximately 150.

1900.   There were 8,000 cars in the U.S. By 1919 there would be 6 million.

1901.   Cleveland Automobile Club sponsored the first auto race in the area.

September 24, 1901. The Lake Shore Electric Railway was born from the consolidation of four lines.

1902.   Rural Free Delivery of mail began.

1902.   Linndale was incorporated.

1902.   Rockport Village was incorporated.

May 4, 1903. Lakewood and Rocky River were incorporated as villages.

1903.   A 20 horsepower Winton Touring Car completed the first cross-country automobile trip from San Francisco to New York in 46 days.

January 23, 1904. Flooding washed away the Nickel Plate Railroad Bridge over the Cuyahoga River.

February 17, 1904. County Commissioners granted permission to form Rocky River Township.

1905. Construction of the Belt Line Railroad began connecting Linndale to Collinwood by way of the southern edge of Cleveland.

1905. Detroit Road was paved

1905. Hotel Breakers opened at Cedar Point.

1905-1930. Luna Park in operation. The Roller Rink lasted until 1938 when it was destroyed by fire.

April 19, 1906. Over 1,000 people die in the San Francisco Earthquake.

March 4, 1907. Several lines merged into the Cleveland Southwestern & Columbus Interurban Line.

1907. Lakewood Hospital was incorporated.

1907. Zoo moved from Wade Park to Brookside Park.

March 4, 1908. Lakeview Elementary School in the Village of Collinwood catches fire and kills 172 of 396 pupils and 2 teachers making it the worst disaster in Cleveland area history. Contrary to popular belief, the doors did not open inward. (Van Tassel and Grabowski, 1996).

April 27 1908. Cleveland Railway Company consolidated the remaining city streetcar lines.

August 12, 1908. The first Ford "Model T" rolled off the assembly line.

1909. Rocky River High School was discontinued, and pupils were sent to Lakewood and Cleveland.

1909. One of the first brick roads in the U.S. was laid from Cleveland to East Liverpool.

1910. Census shows that for the first time in Ohio more people lived in cities than in rural areas.

1910. Taxicabs introduced in Cleveland.

1910. Harvard-Denison Bridge was completed.

February 8, 1910. The Boy Scouts of America were incorporated.

April 20, 1910. South part of Rocky River Village (south of Center Ridge Road) withdrew to form new Goldwood Village.

July 14, 1910. County Commissioners granted annexation of part of Goldwood to Rocky River Village.

July 15, 1910. Goldwood Village became incorporated.

September 1910. Some residents broke away from Goldwood and established Fairview Village leaving Goldwood Village as Section 5 (which would later become Parkview) and a strip along Center Ridge which would later be absorbed into Rocky River.

1910. Glen Curtis flew 65 miles over water from Euclid Beach to Cedar Point.

1910. Rocky River Bridge was completed and is the longest unreinforced concrete arch bridge in the world.

1910.   296 autos were owned by persons in Medina County.

1910.   Goodyear sent 18,000 employees on 15 trains of 10 cars each to Cedar Point for a company outing.

1910.   Boy Scouts of America chapter was organized in Cleveland area.

1910.   Cleveland Railway Company had 245 miles of track in the City of Cleveland.

1911.   Natural Gas was discovered in Lakewood.

February 3, 1911. The population of Rocky River was 1,861.

February 17, 1911. Lakewood was incorporated as a city.

1912.   Jane Edna Hunter established the Phyllis Wheatley Society to provide services similar to the YWCA for African American girls.

April 15, 1912. The Titanic sank.

January 24, 1913. The Lakewood Gas Company was formed. By 1914, it had 34 wells in production in Lakewood.

February 26, 1913. The County Commissioners granted the name change from Rockport to West Park.

1913.   The Great Flood wiped out the remains of the canal system. Rain started Easter Sunday (3/23/13) and continued for a week, 8 1/2" of rain fell in four days causing the greatest flooding in Ohio history. This later gave rise to Muskingum Watershed Conservancy District, and a series of flood control dams were built throughout eastern Ohio.

1913.   CEI furnished electricity to Fairview Village.

1914.   Cleveland installed the first traffic light in the nation.

1914.   A Girl Scouts of America chapter was organized in the Cleveland area.

May 7, 1915. A German U-Boat sank the Lusitania killing 1,256 passengers.

1915.   East Ohio Gas furnished gas to Fairview Village.

1915-1916. Brookpark was the scene of a short-lived gas well boom that started in Lakewood and Rockport and spread to Berea and Brookpark.

May 18, 1916. First Kiwanis national convention was held in Cleveland.

1917.   Lakewood and Cleveland schools were too crowded to accept any more pupils from Rocky River.

July 23, 1917. Cleveland Metropolitan Park Board was formed under the direction of William Stinchcomb. Two years later they acquired their first property.

December 24, 1917. Detroit-Superior Bridge with trolley deck was opened.

1918-1919. Great flu epidemic. 20,000,000 die worldwide and 600,000 in the United States.

January 1919. The 18th Amendment to the constitution was ratified, and shortly thereafter prohibition began.

March 29, 1919. New Rocky River High School was dedicated.

1920. Population of Cleveland was 796,841, making it the fifth largest city in the U.S. There were 92,000 autos registered in Cuyahoga County.

1920. The 19th Amendment to the U.S. Constitution gave women full voting rights.

December 13, 1920. Cleveland Museum of Natural History was chartered.

1922. WHK became the first radio station in Ohio.

November 1922. West Park voters approved annexation to Cleveland.

1923. By virtue of annexation, West Park became Ward 33 of the City of Cleveland adding 3,560 people and an area of 12.5 sq. mi., with assessed property valuation of $25,975,520.91. 1930 population of Cleveland hits 900,429.

1924. The Cleveland School Board bought the Rockport Hamlet Driving Park for $15,000 and built George Washington Elementary on the south end of the property.

1923. Water main from Cleveland extended to Fairview Village.

June 28, 1924. Lorain-Sandusky Tornado, 85 die. Water was 10 inches higher than the 1913 floods. Sixty cottage goers have to be rescued from the Rocky River Valley.

April 28, 1925. The southern part of Goldwood Village was incorporated as Parkview Village.

1924. Westlake Hotel was built.

July 1, 1925. Municipal Airport opened. Location chosen in part because Cleveland and Southwestern Interurban ran right past the main gate. On July 2nd, 200,000 people watched the arrival of the first air mail flight into Cleveland.

1925. A bus route was established on Rocky River Drive.

February 6, 1926. The last remaining (northern) part of Goldwood Village was annexed to Rocky River.

1926. Riveredge Township was created from Brookpark Village.

May 21, 1927. Charles Lindberg landed in Paris completing his solo trans-Atlantic flight.

July 5, 1928. The Cyclone Roller Coaster opened at Puritas Springs.

1928. Fairview High School opened. Prior to that, children went to West High, West Tech or later to Rocky River. In 1928 about 50 students from Fairview were attending Rocky River High School.

1929. The Cleveland National Air Races started at the airport.

1929. No Cuyahoga County Fair was held at the Berea Fairgrounds due to the depression.

1930. The population of Cleveland was 900,429.

1930. Rocky River achieved city status when population exceeded 5,000.

1931. Cleveland Municipal Stadium opened.

January 29, 1931. Cleveland Southwestern and Columbus interurban ceased operation.

September 7, 1931. Severance Hall dedicated.

1932. Additional land was added to Riveredge Township, but it was divided shortly thereafter when Cleveland annexed part for the airport.

1933. The 21st Amendment to the Constitution was ratified repealing the 18th Amendment, and Prohibition came to an end.

June 30, 1934. Brookpark Road Bridge was opened.

1934. Lorain Road became State Route 10.

1934. The old Lorain Road iron bridge over the Rocky River was dismantled.

June 28, 1936. The Great Lakes Exposition opened in Cleveland.

August 1936. The new Lorain Road Bridge over the Rocky River was opened.

1937. Cleveland Arena opened.

1938. The Lake Shore Electric Railway was abandoned, ending the era of interurbans in northeast Ohio.

March 30, 1938. WBOE-FM began broadcasting. (operated by Cleveland Board of Education)

June 27, 1939. Bob Feller pitched a one hit game against the Tigers in a 5-0 win in the first night game at the stadium.

April 16, 1940. Bob Feller pitches first opening day no-hitter.

1943. Postal zoning instituted.

December 16 1945. The Cleveland Rams won the football championship. Rams moved to Los Angeles in January 1946.

1946. Browns become the new team and win the Championship of the American Football Conference all four years of the league's existence.

1947. Fairview Shopping Center opened.

1947. City of Cleveland opened the Lakefront Airport.

1948. Tribe won the World Series.

December 20, 1948. Fairview Village established its own post office and changed its name to Fairview Park.

1949. Crash of race plane into a home in Berea killed three and brought an end to the National Air Races in Cleveland.

1950. Kiddie Land Opened.

May 1950. Lorain Streetcar Line was cut back from Puritas to the loop at West 140th and Lorain. The cutback section was taken over by trackless trolleys.

June 1950. Fairview High School graduated 84 while North Olmsted High School graduated 43.

1950. The population of Cleveland was 914,808.

June 8, 1950. The Lorain Streetcar Line ended.

1951. The Village of Fairview Park became the city of Fairview Park when the minimum population of 5,000 was exceeded (9,234).

June 8, 1953. West Park tornado.

January 24, 1954. The last streetcar line in Cleveland ended with the final run on Madison Avenue.

1954. Westgate Shopping Center Opened.

May 5, 1958. Puritas Springs Amusement Park Closed.

1963. Postal Zip Code began.

January 1, 1967. Parkview Village was annexed to Fairview Park.

1968. Peterson Greenhouse on West 150th closed due to a hail storm. The Marriott Hotel would eventually be built on the property.

September 28, 1969. Euclid Beach closed.

September 1979. Forced integregration by "busing" began between John Marshall High School and John F. Kennedy High School. The rest of Cleveland Schools would begin the plan in 1980.

1983. The Airport purchased the Riveredge Township trailer park; the township remains unoccupied.

1999. Few notice that Morse code officially fades into oblivion.

PROPOSED TERMS

for

ANNEXATION

of the

City of West Park

to the

City of Cleveland

◇

*To be voted upon at the
Regular Election, November 7, 1922*

REPORT OF COMMISSIONERS OF THE TERMS AND CONDITIONS OF ANNEXATION

To the councils of the City of Cleveland
and the city of West Park.

The Commissioners heretofore appointed pursuant to ordinances passed by the Councils of the Cities of Cleveland and West Park , respectively, have arranged the terms and conditions for the annexation of the territory of the City of West Park to the City of Cleveland, and said Commissioners herby respectfully report to their respective Councils the result of their action as follows:

TERMS AND CONDITIONS OF ANNEXATION

The question whether such annexation shall be made shall be submitted to the electors of the Cities of Cleveland and West Park at the General Election to be held on the 7th day of November, 1922, in the manner provided by law.

That in the event a majority of the electors of said cities, voting on the question so submitted, vote in favor of such annexation, shall be as follows:

I. HOW CORPORATIONS ARE TO BE GOVERNED

When the annexation is completed, the two former corporations shall be governed as one, embracing the territory of both, and the inhabitants of all such territory shall have equal rights and privileges, subject, however, to the terms and conditions of annexation. The annexation shall not affect any rights or liabilities existing at the time of annexation, either in favor of or against the corporations except such as are affected by the terms and conditions of annexation, and suits founded on such rights and privileges may be commenced and pending suits prosecuted to final judgment: and execution as though the annexation had not taken place. (G. C. 3574)

II. STREETS AND HIGHWAYS

All public streets and highways in the City of West Park shall become public highways of the City of Cleveland without being accepted and confirmed by ordinance adopted by the Council of the City of Cleveland. (O. S. 610.)

III. INDEBTEDNESS

All outstanding bonded indebtedness of the City of Cleveland and The City of West Park shall be merged and become the bonded indebtedness of the City of Cleveland.

IV. APPROPRIATION FOR THE FISCAL YEAR 1922

Monies heretofore respectively appropriated by the City of Cleveland and the City of West Park for the fiscal year 1922 shall be and remain appropriated to the respective area named in the respective appropriation ordinances.

(a) The Charter of the City of Cleveland shall apply to the two former corporations.
(b) All ordinances of the City of Cleveland of a general character shall, upon the consummation of annexation, be and become applicable to the entire territory of the City of Cleveland as then constituted.

(c) All legislation passed by the Council of the City of West Park relating to improvements to be made by the method of assessments according to benefits, and in effect upon the date when annexation shall take place, shall have the force and effect as though duly passed by the Council of the City of Cleveland.

VI. POLICE AND FIRE DEPARTMENTS

(a) *Police*. All members and officers of the Police Department of the City of West Park in active service on the effective date of annexation shall become active appointees in service of the Police Department of the City of Cleveland, and shall be placed in a grade not lower than their respective former positions in the Police Department of the City of West Park, drawing like salaries.

All such police shall, upon paying into the Pension Fund of the Cleveland Police Department a sum of money equivalent to one-half of 1 per cent of their total salaries earned while members of the Police Force of the City of West Park become eligible to the benefits of the Pension System of the Police Department of the City of Cleveland receiving the same benefits under said system as governs other patrolmen and officers of like grade. The length of past service in the Police Department of the City of West Park shall be credited in full to each patrolman and officer of the City of West Park automatically upon his having paid such sum of money into the Pension Fund of the Police Department of the City of Cleveland.

(b) The above provision shall not apply to any member of the Police Department of the City of West Park who may be receiving the benefit of a pension as a result of former service in the Police Department of the City of Cleveland.

(c) *Fire*. All members and officers of the Fire Department of the City of West Park in active service on the effective date of annexation shall become active appointees in service of the Fire Department of the City of Cleveland, and shall be placed in a grade not lower than their respective former positions in the Fire Department of the City of West Park, drawing like salaries.

All such firemen shall, upon paying into the Pension Fund of the Cleveland Fire Department a sum of money equivalent to one-half of 1 per cent of their total salaries earned while members of the Fire Department of the City of West Park become eligible to the benefits of the Pension System of the Fire Department of the City of Cleveland receiving the same benefits under said system as governs other firemen and officers of like grade. The length of past service in the Fire Department of the City of West Park shall be credited in full to each patrolman and officer of the City of West Park automatically upon his having paid such sum of money into the Pension Fund of the Fire Department of the City of Cleveland.

(d) The above provision shall not apply to any member of the Fire Department of the City of West Park who may be receiving the benefit of a pension as a result of former service in the Fire Department of the City of Cleveland.

VII. CIVIL SERVICE EMPLOYEES

(A) Any and all employees of the City of West Park in the service upon the effective date of annexation, not otherwise herein provided, who have qualified for their positions under the rules of the Civil Service Commission of the City of West Park, shall be certified to the Civil Service Commission of the City of Cleveland, shall continue to hold their respective positions, shall receive the same compensations governing such positions as provided by ordinance of the City of West Park as of July 15, 1922; shall become active appointees in the service of the various departments of the City of Cleveland and graded according to their respective positions and salaries, and shall hold their respective positions at least one year after the effective date of annexations, excepting thereto any overt act or transgression of Civil Service Rules, in which case Civil Service Rules and procedure shall govern; provided, however, that in the event any such Civil Service employee of the City of West Park shall have a classification title equivalent to the ranking officer provided for in any department of the City of Cleveland that irrespective of his salary, he shall become the subordinate officer to the like officer of the City of Cleveland.

VIII. REPRESENTATION

In the event of annexation, the territory formerly constituting the City of West Park shall become a separate ward of the City of Cleveland. There shall be deemed to be a vacancy in the office of the councilman representing such ward. The member of the Council of the City of West Park in office immediately prior to the effective date of annexation shall by majority vote, designate an elector of the territory now comprising West Park and in the event of annexation, the Council of the City of Cleveland shall duly elect such person so designated as the Councilman for such ward to serve until January 1, 1924.

IX. PUBLIC UTILITIES

(a) That when annexation is completed, the inhabitants of the West Park territory shall receive water from the Division of Water of the Public Utilities of the City of Cleveland at the same rates and upon the same terms as citizens of other parts of the City of Cleveland. Within one year from the date of annexation the Division of Water of the Public Utilities of the City of Cleveland shall install its water mains for all service rendered in the present territory of West Park and the Council of the City of Cleveland shall authorize and direct with the concurrence of the Board of Control of the City of Cleveland the reimbursement to all owners of meters in the City of West Park of the cost of said meters which has been determined to be Six Dollars ($6.00) per meter.

Adequate Water Supply. The Commissioners recommend that within one year from the effective date of annexation a twenty-four inch water main be placed on Lorain Avenue from West 117th Street to the westerly corporate limits of the territory now comprising West Park, as a means of affording proper and adequate water supply to the inhabitants of said territory.

X. SCHOOLS

When the West Park territory is annexed to the City of Cleveland, such territory which comprises the City School District of the City of West Park shall become a part of the City School District of the City of Cleveland and the legal title to school property in such territory for school purposes shall be vested in the Board of Education of the City School District of the City of Cleveland from and after the date of the completion of such annexation. Provided, however, if there be any indebtedness on the school property in the territory annexed, the Board of Education of the City School District of the City of Cleveland shall assume such indebtedness and shall levy a tax annually sufficient to pay such indebtedness. (G.C. 4690).

XI. CONTRACTS

All existing contracts entered into by the City of West Park shall be continued in full force and effect and shall be completed by the City of Cleveland in accordance with the terms of such contracts, and the money provided by the City of West Park for such contracts by bond issues or otherwise shall be used for such purpose only.

XII. BOND ISSUES

All money derived from the sale of bonds issued for a specific purpose by the City of West Park shall be used only for such purpose.

XIII. GAS FRANCHISE

That the contract now existing between the City of West Park and the East Ohio Gas Company for gas service is to be continued in full force and effect during its entire term or until such time as the Council of the City of Cleveland are able to negotiate a contract which is more advantageous to the inhabitants of the City of West Park than present exists.

XIV. STREET LIGHTING AND ILLUMINATING FRANCHISE

(a) That the contract now existing between the City of West Park and the Cleveland Electric Illuminating Company or the street lighting be continued in full force and effect during its entire term or until such time as the Council of the City of Cleveland are able to negotiate a contract which is more advantageous to the inhabitants of the West Park territory.

(b) That the franchise now existing between the City of West Park and the Cleveland Electric Illuminating Company for house lighting service shall be continued in full force and effect during its entire term or until such time as the Council of the City of Cleveland shall be able to negotiate a contract which is more advantageous to the inhabitants of the West Park territory.

XV. PUBLIC SERVICE EXTENSIONS

Upon annexation the City of Cleveland as rapidly as possible shall extend over the territory theretofore constituting the City of West Park its systems of garbage collection and disposal, its system of ash and refuse collections, and its system of street cleaning.

XVI. STREET RAILWAY SERVICeS

In the event of annexation we recommend that the Traction Commissioner of the City of Cleveland make an immediate investigation of street railroad transportation facilities in the territory now constituting the City of West Park and use diligent effort to secure proper and needed use of street car service for that territory.

IN WITNESS WHEREOF the Commissioners have duly added their signatures to duplicates hereof this 12th day of July A.D. 1922, at the City of Cleveland Ohio.

J. P. LAMB
G. A. GESELL
COMMISSIONERS FOR THE CITY OF CLEVELAND

LEROY S. MILLS
CHARLES P. VANEK
R. C. HUBER
COMMISSIONERS FOR THE CITY OF WEST PARK

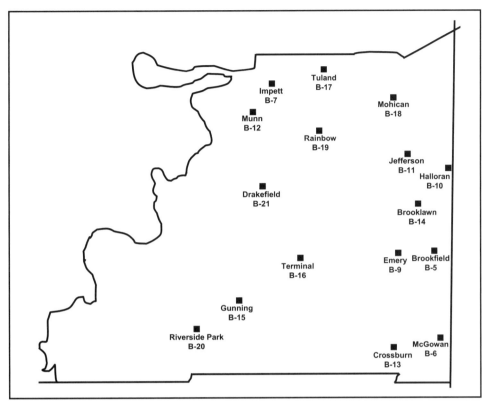

Figure B-1. Index and location of the parks and playgrounds in West Park. Numbers indicate photo in this section.

APPENDIX B: THE STREAMS PARKS AND PLAYGROUNDS OF WEST PARK

Figure B-2. At the time Rockport was first settled, streams drained into three different watersheds. Those along the north shore drained directly into Lake Erie, those in the southeast corner of the township drained into the Cuyahoga River and the remainder drained into the Rocky River.

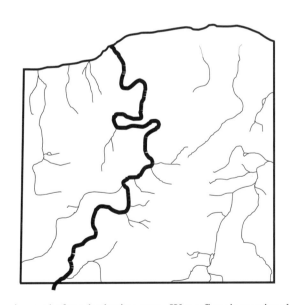

Most of the streams in West Park that are still exposed at the surface are in the eastern part of the community and drain into the Cuyahoga River. Most have been abused and are in need of tender loving care. Water flow is restricted in many places due to channelization, illegally dumped yard waste, and desperate attempts at stream stabilization resulting in putrid smelling water and increased flooding in certain areas (RAP-UP, Spring, 1999).

285

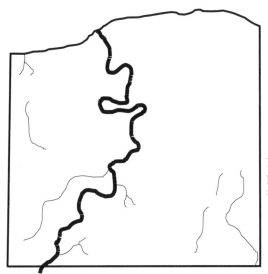

Figure B-3. Today there are very few streams left exposed at the surface. Almost all rainwater now enters sewers and underground culverts.

Figure B-4. About the only time anyone notices an urban stream is following a heavy downpour when the sewer system cannot carry the water away fast enough. Basements fill with water and the few exposed portions of streams spill out onto the streets. Such is the case on May 14, 1956, on Gilmore Avenue and West 131st Street. *Cleveland State University Library, Cleveland Press Collection*

Figure B-5. Although this stream has no official name, the city of West Park referred to it as Peterjohn Creek in 1911 when they passed legislation to "ditch" this stream. Presently it is part of the retention basin for the Industrial Park south of West 143rd Street and Puritas. The Bellaire-Puritas Development Corporation is exploring the possibility of turning this into a managed wetland. In the meantime, a pair of mallards swims up stream not caring one way or another. *Author photo*

286

Figure B-6. A stream restoration demonstration project has been completed on this small stream in Brookfield Park between Brookfield and Guardian Avenues. Funded by the Cuyahoga River Remedial Action Plan, Northeast Ohio Regional Sewer District and the City of Cleveland, the goals are to increase the stream's capacity to store water, and to demonstrate the use of soil bioengineering and vegetation for stream bank restoration (RAP-UP, Spring, 1999). *Author photo*

Figure B-7. Another part of this stream is exposed at McGowan Park at West 123rd Street and McGowan Avenue. *Author photo*

Figure B-8. Looking south from Brooklawn Avenue, this looks like a clean woodland stream. From this point north, however, it disappears into a culvert never to be seen again. *Author Photo*

Cleveland Press May 2, 1941
Aged Couple Still Farming 6 Miles From Downtown

"Spring, sweet maid the poets write about, comes tripping back again, picking her way across cropped city lawns to the shaggy Impett farm, one of the few farms left within the city limits of Cleveland. Spring and the elderly man who cultivates the farm remember when those lawns were woodland, and the farmer, then a youth gunned for ducks in marshes now a part of Lakewood. Fred Impett, the farmer, and his sister, Miss Bessie Impett, have lived there nearly all their lives. Now they approach 80.

Their father had the farm before them. Nearby was the farm of their grandfather, John Impett. It's just a one-horse farm the brother and sister work. They rent a second horse to make a team for plowing or other heavy tasks. Two cows graze in the lush grass of an ancient orchard now blossoming white and pink. One cow is named Cherry; the other Spot.

Miss Impett has four or five cats, and three kittens for which she would like to find a home. She thinks half a dozen cats are enough. A barking terrier is tied in the dooryard to keep him from running away. Another dog tags at Miss Impett's heels. He's a mongrel that showed up one day and wouldn't leave.

There's a garden of daffodils and tulips, a flock of hens, some ducks and several guinea hens. A great lilac bush in the front yard, to blossom soon, annually attracts admiring members of the Garden Club of Cleveland. There are no electric lights in the house, no plumbing, no running water. In summer a cistern serves as a refrigerator. Life on this farm goes on much as it always has, leisurely and old-fashioned. The farm is on Rose Lane, off the end of Arthur Avenue, near Lakewood. Thirty-two acres aren't many, but they make a big farm to be six miles from Public Square and within the city limits of Cleveland."

Figure B-9a. In Impett Park, part of the old farm has been allowed to grow into this stand of Pin Oaks. *Author photo*

Cleveland Press January 21, 1948
City Moves to Force Woman to Sell Farm

"The City of Cleveland moved today to appropriate the last remaining farm of any size within its limits, the 34-acre property of Miss Bessie Impett that lies along Rose Lane to the west of Warren Road.

But Miss Impett, who has lived all but seven of her 85 years on that land, will not give it up without the best struggle that her remaining health and vigor will permit. The city wants the land for a playground. Miss Impett was offered $1000 an acre for the property, but she turned it down. The price in any case is not important, for she does not want to sell.

Tomorrow, Assistant City Law Director, Ernest J. Halambeck, will go into Common Pleas Court to ask that a jury be impaneled to set a "fair price" for her holdings. If and when that jury names a price, Miss

288

Impett, according to the law, must sell and leave. Miss Impett, bedridden, says she will not leave. She came to the land when she was seven, has lived there ever since. For years, she and her brother, Fred, farmed it alone. Then when the brother died three years ago, Mr. and Mrs. Harry Jones came to run it for her. They raise vegetables and flowers, have two horses, two cows, ducks, chickens and geese.

Jones, an experienced truck farmer, scoffs at the price the city offers. "Why the topsoil on this land alone is worth $3000 an acre," he says. He also notes that Miss Impett recently was offered $50,000 for the acreage by a real estate firm.

For seven decades, Miss Impett has watched the city grow out to meet her, then spread around her. She has been in such fights as these before and has always won. Once a nearby property owner tried to have Rose Lane, that leads down to her farm, closed off. She fought the case to Appellate Court and won.

Figure B-9b. Swimming pool at Impett Park. That stand of Pin Oaks is in the background. *Author photo*

Figure B-10. Emery Park on West 130th Street just south of I-71. *Author photo*

289

Figure B-11. Halloran Park at West 117th and Linnet Avenue. Although there are the usual baseball diamonds and swing sets, the main feature is the outdoor skating rink used in the winter. *Author photo*

Figure B-12. Jefferson Park at West 132 and Lorain. At one time, the city would flood a low spot in winter for skating. *Author photo*

Figure B-13. Munn Park on Munn Road near Rocky River Drive is a former greenhouse site. *Author photo*

290

Figure B-14. Crossburn Park on Crossburn Avenue just west of West 130th Street. *Author photo*

Figure B-15. Brooklawn Park on Brooklawn Avenue just east of West 130th Street. On this day, April 5, 2004, a crew from the city of Cleveland was installing the backstop on the new baseball diamond. The First District Police Station is on the distant left of the picture. *Author photo*

Figure B-16. It's 10 a.m. on April 7, 2004, and the lot is nearly full at the Gunning Recreation Center on Puritas at West 168th. This facility opened in 1995. *Author photo*

Figure B-17. Terminal Park at St. James Avenue and West 146th Street. *Author photo*

Figure B-18. Tuland Park At West 144th Street and I-90. Tuland Avenue was taken by the construction of I-90 but the name was not lost. *Author photo*

Figure B-19. Mohican Park at Triskett and Berea Roads. There is a soccer field on the far left and three ball diamonds in this view. *Author photo*

Figure B-20. Rainbow Park on Rainbow Road. *Author photo*

Figure B-21. Riverside Park on Parkmount Avenue. *Author photo*

Figure B-22. Drakefield Park at Drakefield Avenue and Silsby Road. *Author photo*

WEST PARK MEMORIES

In 1998, a brief article appeared in the Newsletter of the John Marshall High School Alumni Association inviting people to share their fondest memories of the West Park Community. More than 50 responses were sent in which provided an interesting ride down memory lane. There are many common threads that wind their way through these reminiscences, but there are also many things mentioned that just could not be included in the text of this book. The responses are listed in alphabetical order by author and include the year of graduation.

My special memory of Puritas Springs Park is of my Aunt Lil (Gustin '41) taking my brother Larry ('51) and myself roller skating, and then many years later on July 4, 1956 watching fireworks with my husband and younger sister, Cindy, and leaving early because of labor pains. Our daughter Doreen was born on July 5.

On the day of the great tornado, I was working downtown and attended a street fair after work; the wind was so strong I decided to head for home. Minutes after I got home using the 85 bus from downtown, the tornado struck the exact route my bus took. My father brought baseball size hailstones in from the outside. Luckily, the garages on our street were moved but our homes were untouched.

I will never forget when John F. Kennedy made his trip from the airport to downtown using Rocky River Drive en route. I stood for hours with son Paul, then in a stroller, and got a curbside spot taking wonderful close up pictures when the president was going downtown and also on his return. I was so excited to have gotten those wonderful close ups, only to find out later when my husband came home from work that he had given me a camera with no film in it!

The early air races were very exciting as the planes came over the homes on the west side and in Berea.

One favorite memory is of the Riverside Theater. When we were very young, my grandfather would take Larry and me there on Friday night bingo. He won once, thought we were his lucky charms, and continued to take us for a long time.

Connie Gustin Abend (6/52)

Let's test the memories of the 1960 graduating class and the associated Marshall/Baker era. Do you remember when...

- Puritas Road was only paved to in front of Puritas Elementary
- Those attending Puritas had to walk home for lunch because the school had no cafeteria. The city buses ran only to the turn around in front of Puritas Springs.
- Grayton Road was pothole city and not paved
- You drove down a deep valley and back up the other side on the way to Brookpark Road
- The unpaved trip down Puritas into the valley was a single lane winding dirt road.
- JMH homerooms G1, G2, and G3 were in the balconies of the boy's gym.
- Parking permits were needed to park your cars on the side streets around JMH as you could not park on school grounds
- Picking up your girl friend every day on the way to school.
- Army and Navy tests in PE with those jump rope and sit up tests that made it tough to get out of bed the next day.
- Artemas Ward Annex, the four room school at W. 140 and Puritas that was home to Puritas Elementary graduates for one semester because Newton D. Baker was not completed on schedule.

- The air races when a plane crashed in Berea and killed people in the house. (This was the last race at Cleveland Hopkins.)
- The four-hour marathon horror shows at the Variety Theater on Halloween.
- The no booze beatnik bar at W. 117 and Lorain that served apple cider with cinna mon sticks.
- The Skyline Bar where you got beer as soon as you were eighteen or sooner with your fake ID.
- My 1929 Model A with a rumble seat that would backfire at football games (got suspended from driving to school for two weeks for that).
- Receiving a JMH letter sweater for stage management
- We told everyone the "S" stood for swimming.
- Having to run two miles in less than fifteen minutes on the JMH track before you could graduate.
- Vehicle safety checks and having to crank my '28 Model A car by hand to start it. The police laughed so hard they passed it without even knowing only half the brakes worked.
- Going to the Roxy Theater on 9th St. before we were old enough, to watch the tassels "bump and grind"
- Wing tip shoes with a snap down tongue instead of shoelaces. Belts that were only 1/4 inch thick, tight leg pants, collars up on the back of your neck, and school rules that said no Levi's.
- Catching the bus from Baker at Kamm's where the gangs from the projects on Rocky River Drive hung out and laid for you, dumping your books, tripping you, and beating you up.
- Getting a seating assignment in study hall across from Lucy Garzone and thinking you had died and gone to heaven.
- Getting jumped in the boys rest room outside the cafeteria, beaten up to the point you had to wear glasses the rest of your life.
- Getting a ticket at Lorain and Triskett for "impersonating an ambulance". I had red lights on the front of my '56 Ford convertible in the grill (real cool).
- My first date was in the seventh grade with the prettiest girl at Newton D. Baker, Carolyn Bell. Her mother drove us in the '56 two passenger Thunderbird. She had to sit on my lap...WOW!

Jim Baker (6/60)

I remember that I always enjoyed the Dairy Dell at Kamm's Corners for ice cream. Across the street at the Riverside Theatre, we got a double feature, news, a short subject and a cartoon. We did not care what the movie was; we went to meet friends.

Mildred Swegle Betcher (1/48)

Much of my life after school was spent at the old Puritas Park and Puritas skating rink. It was one of the last of the little community permanent amusement parks in the city. I can only picture this park in its heyday, full of kids and families with their picnic baskets filled to over-flowing with goodies to tide them through the day. I imagine the picnic pavilion with ladies in their long gowns and horse drawn carriages tied up near by. The tables would be busy, and eager riders would be lined up for the thrills of the roller coaster, the merry-go-round, the fun house and the Ferris wheel.

By the time I began roller skating at the rink beyond the park, the buildings, and rides were in a state of disrepair and people didn't frequent the grounds much anymore, but — there was still enough fun and excitement for some of us teenagers.

The bus would drop us off up in front of the park, and we'd work our way through and across a small bridge and down a lane over to the rink.

It was the skating rink, where most of my time was spent. The flooring was good, the organ music and organist were terrific, and the music and tempos accommodated most anything you'd wish to skate to. The rink had a snack bar and repair area and everyone compared their skates. I still have my skates; they haven't been used in years. But I will again sometime!!

My friend, Gloria (Ermer) Lefevre, and myself would go several times each week. There were always friends there from John Marshall and other area schools, and everyone got to know each other pretty well. The rink even had parties on special occasions, and I think I remember a couple getting married there. Try as I might, over the 4 to 5 years of high school skating, I never did become very good at it. It always amazed me at the little kids who could skate circles around me.

One of the saddest times was when they told us the rink would close to make way for a new housing development. We skated for the last time there, I believe in 1957. I went inside one time to look around. It still looked basically the same. Had I had my skates, I would have put them on and skated around, even though some windows were broken out and debris was scattered.

The rink came down along with the amusement park buildings and rides. There are homes there now with nothing to remind you of the music, the thrill on the roller coaster turns, the noisy voices and the swish of skates flashing by. After all these years — I still drive by there every time I get to Cleveland. The memories are there - they were good times. I'm glad I had the chance to grow up in Cleveland.

Other recollections include picking up hail stones the size of baseballs and putting them in the freezer after the tornadoes hit. We lost our garage roof but otherwise on Tudor Ave., off Triskett, we were out of the main devastation that hit the W. 130 St. area.

We had one of the many little side streets paved with red bricks. It is still paved with red bricks and during all these years, has taken less maintenance than most of Cleveland's streets. My daughter used to look forward to going to Grandma's on the brick road.

I also remember the air races. We'd pack a picnic lunch and take off with the family, my brother Herb, parents, and myself, and spend the day at the races at the airport. Loud speakers would keep us posted of who was in the lead, and also of the occasional crashes that happened. You'd sit on your car hoods or spread a blanket on the ground.

When we moved to Cleveland, the airport was very small. You could go up almost to the runway, only one then. A chain link fence separated you from the planes. A favorite pastime was to park at the end of the runway off Brookpark Road and watch the planes take off and land. Yes — this actually began as a family outing later to be considered a neat place to park with your girl friend or boy friend and watch the submarines come in!

Laren Branch Blackburn (1/57)

When the tornado struck we lived on St. James. My brother (Dave '64) and I had just gone to bed. All of a sudden, I heard what sounded like someone had run their hands across a dresser and knocked everything to the floor with a crash! I wondered what on earth my brother could have done! Typical sister! While we didn't have much damage, — only a few shingles missing and a garbage can lid gone —, the damage was great at the end of our block on West 130th. The scariest time was after the tornado when we realized how close we were to where it had hit! Dave and I attended Carl F. Shuler when it first opened. I still can remember how nice it was to have the school so close to us - only a block away! Everything was sparkling new! What a nice facility that was! Our favorite teacher there was Carol Hann in the music department.

The old neighborhood still holds many memories — fairly quiet, many long-time residents, and lots of activities which helped keep us kids occupied. We often rode our bikes to either the Puritas Avenue pool or the one on West 117th, enjoyed Puritas Springs Park, and roller-skated at the rink. It was a great place to grow up.

Carla Hoke Blinn (6/63)

Remember the knife sharpener who pushed his cart down the sidewalks every summer to sharpen knives and scissors or the paper/rags man who drove a horse wagon and shouted what sounded like papa raks! Remember the old streetcars that ran out Lorain St. from Downtown. The seats were caned, if you had to stand, you held on to handles as it rocked from side to side.

Remember the diner car on the corner of West 140th and Lorain or the French fry stand near the corner of Viola on West 140. Marshallites gave them lots of business. Remember the snow and ice on the streets and sidewalks-no road salt then-but some people spread ashes from their coal furnaces onto the walks and driveways for traction. One winter a horse and sleigh came down my street and I'd have loved to have had a ride in it.

Remember raking autumn leaves into huge piles along the curbs and then burning them, only after jumping and playing in them first. The blue pike fish frys at Herzogs on West 131st and Lorain-nothing tastes like them now.

Remember when parents sat on front porches and visited while kids played in the streets or ice skating at Halloran Park where it was frozen especially for the kids. Movies at the Variety or Riverside that were 10 cents, then 25 cents; cartoon day when you'd stay all afternoon, or the serials you'd go to see a chapter each week until it ended.

Remember roller skating at the Rollercade or Puritas Springs and all the fun rides at Puritas Springs, especially the roller coaster that went down into the valley on the first hill; going to the springs in the Metroparks to get fresh spring water from a faucet or going to Mastic Park and the bottom of the Puritas Hill for all day picnics and swinging on the swings, playing in the sand, wading in the pool, watching for fish and turtles in the river, skipping rocks, and hiking the trail to the trailside museum?

Remember the Spang Bakery truck and milk trucks that delivered door to door and left glass bottles of milk in the milk chute; or coal trucks coming and dumping coal down a chute into the coal bin?

Remember when pins were set by hand in bowling alleys? or Dairy Dells that had the long benches divided into little seats like desks and had what seemed like hundreds of flavors to pick from as well as shakes and malts? Yummy!

Joy Ehrhardt Brashwitz (6/54)

I remember the Thanksgiving blizzard of 1950. As a high school sophomore, we were thrilled to have no school. The entire city was immobilized. I lived off Warren Rd on Alger, three blocks from Winterhurst. All the kids who lived in that area on Fernway, Braemer Lakewood Heights Blvd., etc. took shovels up to Warren Rd and shoveled a path to Winterhurst. The ice rink opened for us so we could skate the whole week we were off school.

Jean Brock Bryson (6/53)

Since I have lived my whole life at the Kamm's Corner area or within two miles of there, I have many memories.

My Dad owned Landphair's Dry Goods and Men's Wear store from about 1913 until 1947, at Kamm's Corner. It was the only store of its kind for many miles around. He was a regular advertiser in the John Marshall Interpreter.

There were three girls in our family, and we all graduated from John Marshall. My Dad's store was a place for a girl

Figure C-1. Ad for Ladphairs

to go to get their sewing needs. Next to my Dad's store was Phillip's Drug Store, and I remember, the boys and girls in the upper grades going there and sitting at the Soda Fountain after school. Mr. Phillips daughter was a John Marshall Grad.

My favorite memories are of all the old locally owned Home Bakeries in the area: over time - Hermann's - Wilke's -Tregler's - Holmok's - Winkler's -Kaase's. Most of these families had children who attended and graduated from John Marshall. Also the many local families that owned Dairies - Blain's -

Figure C-2. Blaine's Dairy at 17439 Lorain Road on November 28, 1935. *Cleveland Public Library*

Walker's-Wilmerink-Dahm. The area was also known as the Greenhouse Capital. Memories of Saturday afternoon double features at the Riverside- ten cents. Another store I remember was Nisius at Lorain & Triskett. We bought our school supplies there - they had two sons who attended and graduated from John Marshall.

Lorain Ave hill down to the park was great sledding. In those days no traffic because there was no place to go after you got down the hill. Remember the old street cars and the Car Barns and turn around at Lorain Avenue near the Valley and Lorain Ave. Bridge.

My old big memory is the football playing field in back of George Washington School with stands and with the tennis courts at the school. In those days, there was a big rivalry with the Rocky River football team. The boys from River were supposed to be such BIG fellows because they were all farm boys. Rocky River was so far away. Anything past Kamm's Corners was far away - out in the country.

How many remember the old portables we had at old John Marshall? George Washington School had Kindergarten to 6th grade but for a couple years (or at lease while I was there). We stayed at Washington for 7th grade and classes were in the halls, and Home Room and classes were also in the Auditorium. In the 8th grade, we went to old John Marshall and had classes in the portables. When we got to 9th grade, most of the classes were inside the big building - Art -Music - Manual Training were still in the portables. As difficult as this was, there was no public uproar (like there would be now). This all changed when the new John Marshall was completed.

I was in the Orchestra and I have great memories of the City Wide Music Frolic - April 11, 1931. We won 1st place (tied with Lincoln for 1st place) (Lincoln was disqualified for the State contest because they had too many students to qualify for Class C School). The Trio won 2nd place in Ensemble City

298

Contest (I was part of that). The State Contest was held at New Severance Hall May 10, 1931. Just before we went on stage to perform, we were told that we were the first Cleveland Orchestra to play at Severance Hall. The Cleveland Orchestra had not yet had a concert there. I still have the program given us and the pin for admittance.

John Marshall did not have a Band; in fact, I can't remember any High School with a band. One game Mr. Matthews got some orchestra people together to play at a game. I was there and Mr. Matthews suggested I play the Cymbals. Monday morning I was called into the office and told it was not lady-like for a girl to play in a band.

Other memories from back then - our great wrestling teams. We had many individual City Champions.

June, 1932 - instead of a Prom they had a Dinner Dance in the Cafeteria with the 11th grade girls serving the supper. I played in a Trio that entertained during the dinner. No one today can even begin to realize how tight money was then, and we got along with as little expense as possible. I know the class of 1933 also had a Dinner Dance in the Cafeteria. We just did not have an extra 25 cents to spend on anything. Also, Graduation in the old days, we did not wear caps and gowns - the girls all wore white dresses.

I was telling my sister Ardis about writing you memories of John Marshall and she said right away - do you remember the Asplin Basket Factory next to old John Marshall - the SMELL - A certain time during the year they did some process at the factory that made the worst smell for several days. The smell came right into the class rooms. You could hardly stand it. This was the first thing that came into my sister's mind, I had forgotten. The Asplin's had two daughters that graduated from John Marshall.

My cousin Gladys Hyland Degner ('26) also mentioned about the football games with Rocky River. She said the River boys were so big and that the John Marshall boys were skinny.

This has been fun, thinking of old times and talking them over with other relatives. This is the first typing I have done in many years, not good, but at least it is more readable than my handwriting. - Unbelievable - I have two sons and they both graduated from Rocky River High.

LaVerne Landphair Buch (6/33)

In 1930, my parents built a home on Fernway Ave., in that NW pocket of West Park bordering on Lakewood. Isolated, we were the fifth house surrounded by a wooded area and open fields of elderberry bushes and goldenrod. The iceman from City Ice and Fuel, the "paper rex" man, and "Frankie" the fruit and vegetable man found their way to our door, however.

Belonged to a Four H handcraft club sponsored by Mrs. Far, meeting in her home on Fernway near Warren Road. The McDermott twins, Hinkle boys, Carl Alexander, Elaine Farr, and my sister, Arlene completed the group. My 1935 Blue Ribbon won a second place in the 1998 Cuyahoga Fair "memorabilia category.

I attended the "portable" Riverside School on the bend of Alger Road for the early elementary grades (Miss Thelma Jones was a favorite teacher), and then took the Warren Road bus to George Washington for the 5th and 6th grades. When I attended JMH for Jr. and Sr. High, the Lorain streetcar was added to the transportation schedule. The School Board reimbursed my parents for the weekly school pass at the end of each semester when we turned them in to the office.

I also belonged to a Camp Fire Group during my Jr. Hi days that met at the West Park Congregational Church with classmates Evelyn Baum and Phyllis Courter. County and State Fair activities were highlights.

My favorite West Park site was the Library! The summer reading programs were fun and the librarians would hand stamp each book with its return date. Reading to this day is a delight although I've graduated to some large print (or is it returned to?).

The after school dances at Marshall had live music provided by the WPA musicians, and it was always fun to attend the HiY dances at the "old JMH".

Phyllis Boner Bullock (6/42)

I was a roller skater and went to the rink at Puritas Springs very often. Ken Dombey played the organ at the rink and also had a radio show from there. I met my husband on a "robbers circle waltz". I did all the "skate dances" but my Ray was one of the best "flea hoppers." Our dating was interrupted by Pearl Harbor, and my Ray was drafted and went to Europe. We were married in '47 - but Puritas Springs was the start of it all.

Ray and I had one daughter, Tracey ('72) and we bought a house on Terminal Ave. when she was little over a year old. Shuler was built while we watched. Our house was always filled with young people, and one of the humorous things that they heard was that I went to John Marshall for 6 years! (at first, the reaction was that I failed often.) But they realized that we didn't have the middle schools.

I was born on West 128th and attended McKinley Elementary and John Marshall - I walked to school every day (no buses) but if weather was real bad in winter I could take the streetcar from West 127th and Lorain to West 140th for all of a dime a week. I think one thing the young generation needs to know is that my generation was denied a normal teen time because of the war. I was recruited by Ohio Bell Telephone Company and worked as an operator after school and on week-ends. The only extra curricular things I could do was choir because we met before the school day started in the morning. I became a "Government operator" handling "Priority One" calls. Cleveland was very important to the war effort. We had the steel mills, bomber plant-tank plant and many plants making war materials. My Prom night was spent at the switch board, but my Ray was in Europe doing his part too!. It seems to me that I was a roller-skating teen one day and the next day was an adult doing her bit. The war robbed me of a teenage time, but I was not alone. Many teens worked for the war effort. Born and raised on West 128, married and raised a daughter on Terminal - I guess you could call me a true native of West Park!

I think my next memory is unique! Miss Poniatowski was my PE teacher when I attended Marshall. She was a very great part of the teaching staff at Marshall. But that isn't unique - what is - is that Poni was assistant Principal at Shuler when my daughter attended there!!!. Poni and I talked many times of the rare case of a student/teacher relationship changing to a parent/student/teacher one. When she left to become Principal of Westropp, it was a great loss.

Memories-so many. But at my age, it's a joy to share them. And they also let our generation help the young ones of today.

Dona Bynak Casper (6/44)

When our marching band marched in the Fairview Park Memorial day parade. We did this several years

Norma Dunson Cole (1/49)

Puritas Springs Park was one of my favorite haunts. I clearly remember the roller coaster which went down the first steep hill along side the road going down into the valley. The Bug was another favorite ride of mine. Then there was the roller rink in the back where, on Thursday night, which was ladies night, you could get in for ten cents and the bus ride there and back only cost a nickel each way. May father was in business for himself, and I used to do his bookkeeping each month for a whopping $3.00, which would see me through a month of entertainment (three dollars certainly doesn't take you far today.).

Another one of my favorite places was the frozen custard stand that was on 140th between Marshall and Garfield. My girlfriend, Rita Bets, and I would go there every evening and get a chocolate malt and split it. I sure couldn't do that today without gaining 50 pounds.

It sure is fun to reminisce about the good old days when cars had character, and people were unique. When I graduated from school (Independence, I moved in my senior year), I got a job and bought my first car, a gray 1957 Ford convertible with red and white interior. Boy, wouldn't I give my eye teeth to have that car now.

Carol Grabowsky Csornok (6/56)

The first John Marshall High School was a beautiful, ivy covered building on Lorain Avenue near West 150th Street in Cleveland. It had served the community well for years but as the population increased, it became too small. About 1930 property was purchased on West 140th Street south of Lorain Avenue for the new high school. Construction began almost immediately. An access road was cut from Courtland Avenue to the rear of the school property so supplies, equipment, and workers could access the construction site.

My Aunt Rosie and Uncle Joe Thomas lived on Courtland Avenue, adjacent to this access road. They watched with fascination as the school began to take shape while many men of various trades labored on it. They knew that someday their children Lillian and Paul would be attending this high school.

Often the workers forgot their lunches, and since there were no stores or restaurants in that area, they had to go hungry. When Aunt Rosie noticed this, she offered to make sandwiches. The word got around, and soon she was making many sandwiches and lots of coffee. She was "in business." During the good weather, the men lounged on her grass but when it turned cold or rained, Uncle Joe opened his garage and built a few benches for them. He even cut a small window in the side of his garage to make serving easier for his wife. She soon added hot soup to warm the men and then added cookies, pies and cakes to her list.

With her quick wit and Irish sense of humor, it became a popular lunch place. For her, the extra income was a blessing during those Depression years. Young Lillian and Paul didn't let this opportunity slip by either. They sold homegrown radishes and onions to the men and were so thrilled to earn a few pennies.

My brother, William L. Thomas, was in one of the first graduating classes in 1935 and I followed in his footsteps, graduating in 1939, along with my future husband, Gordon Ehrhardt. As you can see, John Marshall High School holds many memories for our family.

Dorothy Thomas Ehrhardt 1939

I was 14 years old in August of 1927 when Col. Lindbergh came to town. We lived just north of Kamm's Corners off Rocky River Drive, and I had a great place to watch the triumphant parade as it came into view on its way to the airport - on the southeast corner. My Brownie 2A, loaded with film, was clutched in my hands. And I'd have gotten a great picture of Lindbergh, seated in the open car with Ambassador Myron T. Herrick, had I not turned to stone at that moment. Luckily, a many standing next to me grabbed the camera and got a good picture for me. I hope I came out of my trance long enough to thank him.

In September, I entered JMHS which at the time included eighth grade. Our class (June of '32) was the first to leave the old building in our last semester. We were the first to graduate from the new school on West 140th Street. Our parents had agitated for years to get a new high school. We never had a chance to think of the new building as our school.

At the old school I will never forget the old trees outside the Latin Room, the biology room and its four or five microscopes, and the cage of white mice. I even remember fondly the concave wooden steps leading to the second floor, and the "teachers lounge" tucked somewhere in the attic space, reached by a few steps.

I remember the portables, that prime talking point for a new school, hot in the warm months and slightly heated in winter by small coal stoves.

We had gym, but used the athletic field in back of Washington Elementary School, near Kamm's Corners. Last time I saw the old school on Lorain Ave; it was a furniture store. I wonder if it is still there.

Marion Tort Evans (6/32)

When I was 16, I worked at the Dairy Dell at Kamm's Corner. The policeman who patrolled the Riverside Theater came in for his daily coffee. The Monks garbed in brown robes and sandals (winter or summer) came in occasionally for a treat.

I lived on Highlandview in the West 130th area when the tornado struck. I was with my boyfriend, later to be my husband, and my parents called his mother and told her to keep me overnight. The next day we drove home, and the police let us through. Damage all around, but my family was spared.

Maryann Klimcyk Fabbri (1/52)

Lived on 18600 Brookpark Rd across from the airport - 1927 watched Lindbergh land at the airport after his Atlantic crossing. Watched many air races and many of the pilots and their mechanics stayed at our house during the races. Tony Levere raced from California to Cleveland in 1940. His mechanic stayed with us and took my Aunt Beatrice and me for a short plane ride to "try out a new Piper Cub that Tony would be using". What a thrill.

Jim Hogan's Grocery Store was at the corner of Rocky River Drive and Brookpark - later the Sky Way was erected in that spot right across from the La Conga Club where I worked as a lunch time waitress for a few years.

Remember when there was a "Whoopie Ride" on Brookpark Road that was lots of fun, and horse farms along Rocky River Drive?

Beatrice Lavelle Fischer (6/34)

I remember standing out in front of Our Lady of Angels School on Rocky River Drive in 1948 and waving to President Eisenhower as he passed by. Everyone in the early fifties has to remember going to Bearden's Drive-In after the Riverside show on Friday Nights. You saw everybody up there.

I remember roller skating, with Ken Dombey playing the organ, and riding the Cyclone at night as the cars roared through the valley trees at Puritas Springs. Also, being chased by the farmer when we picked his apples as we walked from the park to Rocky River Drive.

Sledding down the old Lorain Road Hill in the forties was great fun until my sled hit a tree and sent my friend Monica Celebreeze ('53) to the hospital, my feet became frost bitten waiting for the ambulance.

Joan McArthur Folmer (1953)

There was a very bad snow storm around Thanksgiving 1950. It was so bad that army tanks were driving on Lorain Avenue

Allen Fousek (1/49)

"Pops" delicatessen at the end of Tuttle and Granton, eating popsicles on hot August days while sitting under his store windows in the shade - I was 8-10 and at the time and it seemed like "Pops" was 80, at least!.

Denny Geduldig (6/60)

My special memory of Puritas Springs Park, of course, would be the roller rink, skating on that wonderful wood floor to the even more wonderful organ music of Ken Dombey. The memory of doing the "flea-hop" (with all the kids lined up) to "Elmer's Tune" just gives me goose pimples.

Elinor Gill (6/48)

Whenever we needed ice for the ice box, my dad would drive to City Ice and Fuel at Warren Rd. and Lakewood Heights Blvd. They'd put the ice on the car's bumper. My sister and I always wanted to go along to feel the cold spray from the water cascading down the huge coils. It was also noisy. If dad didn't go get it, you'd have to buy ice from the ice man who came around the streets. He'd always give kids small hunks of ice to suck on.

Betsy Taylor Havens (6/48)

Events and Landmarks I remember:

1. Puritas Springs Park being torn down. My mother was one of the first tenants in the River Park Apartments built on the Puritas Springs Park grounds.
2. The Rock Island Lumber Company, where the Harley-Davidson dealer is.
3. When the Forest City Lumber Yard and Mill burned down.
4. When the West Park Rapid Station was built. I could watch the men building it from my house across the street.
5. When Newton D. Baker Jr. High, where I attended 9th grade, and Carl F. Schuler Jr. High were built.
6. Bearden's Restaurant on Rocky River Drive. I lived in the first house on Sedalia Avenue on the Southwest corner of Rocky River Drive.
7. Reliable Drug Store (W. 134th & Lorain Ave) I used to work there.
8. Zickes Drug Store (West 135th Street & Lorain Avenue).
9. Gray drug Store (W. 137th and Lorain Avenue).
10. The building of Kamm's Plaza.
11. The building of the Collonade Apartments on Lorain Ave. I lived in one of the three houses on that site which were torn down.
12. The streetcars and tracks on Lorain Ave.

At the age of four, my parents and I moved into the little one bedroom house at the top of the west corner of West 143rd Street and Lorain Avenue which used to be an office for the James C. Heintz Company, where my father worked. I also lived in the 2nd and 3rd houses on West 143rd

As a child, I loved watching the trains stop to get water as well as hearing and watching the steam engines going by.

I also loved sledding down the hill into Lorain Ave, jumping into the snowdrifts in front of my house and literally being buried in the snow, and riding my 2 wheeler down the hill into West 143rd and literally giving my parents a heart attack. The day my family and I stood and watched the houses I grew up in being torn down is one of my special memories.

On Halloween, after spending about three hours trick-or-treating, my father would take my sister and me to several of the stores on Lorain Ave., and end up at Corrigan Funeral Home, because my father and the Corrigan Brothers grew up together.

Barbara Harwedel (6/63)

Figure C-3.We are looking to the northwest from West 143rd Street just south of Lorain Avenue. The 1955 photograph shows Barb Harwedel and over her left shoulder is the water tower on the north side of Lorain used by the railroad to refill the thirsty steam engines. *Barb Harwedel Collection*

My mom, Thelma Peepers Hafner, is 91 years old. When she was very young, she remembers living on Claire Avenue off Riverside Dr., opposite a convent. She walked through deep snow, through fields to school at the old John Marshall on Lorain. During WW I, when she was about 10, everyone wore a bag of something around his or her neck to ward off the flu.

Mom went to the Congregational Church at Kamm's. Tony's was a grocery store. A race track was where Baker and Washington schools are, and mom remembers watching the races through the fence.

The Minute Saloon, owned by Mr. Minute, was on the NE corner of Kamm's, a place my grandfather visited often.

Dorothy Sixt went to school with my mom. Her parents owned the building at Triskett and Lorain, the present Masonic Temple.

Probably around 1940, my two brothers and I ice skated on the river behind the hospital and also went sledding down the road leading to the park. The road would be closed for sledding, but I remember someone didn't make a curve, hit a tree and was killed. That ended the sledding down that road.

Mom also said they walked to Munn Road for their milk. Must have been a farm there.

Thelma Herrick (6/50)

When I was a young boy, we used to sneak into the air races. We had to climb two high fences, then wait for the playing of the National Anthem. While the National Guard stood at attention, we would run into the grand stand crowd and watch the entire show.

I was working part time at the airport when the tornado hit west Cleveland. I raced to CEI's Brooklyn Garage where I worked as a lineman. Ours was the first crew out of the garage, and our first stop was wires down at West 150th and Puritas which was 2 blocks from our house on West 148. Our house was spared, but many in the area were damaged.

Dick Hodona (1/44)

Tornado 1953. My late husband Dale ('49) was a load planner for United Airlines and he watched the funnel skip across the airport.

I went to the Riverside Theater a lot as a date or with a group of girls. We had a lot of fun there. I lived off Munn Rd. and spent a lot of time at Kamm's Corner. We had the tree shaped sherbet cones at Dairy Dell and burgers from Royal Castle. We ate at Benders which was later Tony's. Faith Baker died when we were in 7th or 8th grade in Miss Bickimer's home room, and we really were shocked that one of our age could pass away.

I had chocolate phosphates and chocolate cokes at Standard Drug and dated a couple of "Soda Jerks" there. We had Nutri Colas at Marshall's drug. A new sensation! We watched the air races on the cliff way at the back of St. Joseph's Academy. The pilots did their tricks over the valley.

Did some sledding on the Lorain Road entrance to the Valley. Girls were allowed to wear wool slacks to school under our skirts, but only to and from school. We never could have looked like kids look today. We were "neat nuts."

We used to walk to the West Park Library many nights, and it was the meeting place during the week. Sometimes we even studied.

I remember with fondness the Friday night community center. We square danced in the boys' gym. Had volleyball and basketball in the girls' gym. The guys ran the underground track, and we loved it. We were off the streets and out of trouble. Charlotte Barber and I rode the Warren Road bus, and she'd pick up a loaf of fresh bread for her mom at Lakewood or Kaase's Bakery. We'd sit in the back of the bus and eat half the loaf before we got off.

I went to Girl Scout meetings at West Park United Church of Christ. I am still working with scouts, and, in 1999, I'll receive my 35 year pin.

Alice Brisky Humphrey (1/50)

I grew up in the area of West 191st and Puritas. For most of my childhood, it was an undeveloped area. Hansen's Greenhouse was at the top of my street until Clara Westropp School was built in the late 60's. For the longest time my street was the last on the north side of Puritas until you reached Puritas Hill That area included Puritas Springs Park and what we called "the pit". "The pit" was a dugout area of land where we played all day long. The neighborhood kids cleared an area for a ball diamond and built tree forts. We also rode our bikes over mounds of dirt and went tadpole hunting.

Before "the pit" was developed into housing, we used to walk through the brush to get to the roller rink at Puritas Springs. Many a Saturday afternoon was spent roller skating there. I also remember sitting on our front stoop and watching the 4th of July fireworks from Puritas Springs Park.

Figure C-4. The "Pit" at 19210 Puritas in 1953. *Cleveland Public Library*

Norma Sauer Hydock (1/69)

As part of the class of 1950, I was very involved with the episodes of the class. We had a few interesting clubs. I was in the Hi-Y and Key Club. The Hi-Y met at the YMCA, which was behind the old John Marshall on Lorain. We met about every other week and had dances at the Y for high school people. Dances were usually juke box music, but occasionally we had a band. The Hi-Y group of young men planned other events both for the community and ourselves. Dances were on Friday nights.

One other thing I remember doing for the Key Club was showing movies at Crile Hospital for the injured soldiers and Air Force Men. All we had to do was set up the screens and run the projectors. They supplied the movies.

As a kid, I remember sledding down the hill behind the Fairview Hospital (which wasn't there at that time) with my grandfather who remembered president Lincoln. We also used to fish off the "old" bridge at the bottom of the hill by the Little Met Golf Course and also ice skate there during the winters.

Robert Hyland (6/50)

My special memory of Puritas Springs Park was working at the Cotton Candy stand when I was perhaps 13 or 14 years of age. What fun! Because we were at Marshall during WWII, and I lived on Pearldale (off Rocky River Drive - south of Lorain), we took the streetcar to West 140th and Lorain and walked south to the school—rain, snow, sleet. Guess it didn't hurt us "cause we're still here!!. Sometimes we would walk, cutting up West 159th to Chatfield, across the railroad tracks and through fields until we came to the football field. What a trip that was!!

Betty Whitty Keeler (6/45)

Puritas Springs Park: I remember saving Pepsi Bottle caps to gain free admission to the park. Remember the Rocket Ships?

Allen Krupar (6/69)

These are some of the memories I have while living in the West Park area. Although, the venues are not necessarily in the West Park area:

Ice-skating after school at Winterhurst. I especially remember skating to Glenn Miller's "String of Pearls" quite often. (In my Junior year I dislocated my elbow after being knocked down by a boisterous male skater); dancing at the Columbia Ballroom and Chippewa Lake Ballroom; Hamburgers at Bearden's Drive-In; Michaud's Restaurant with Phil McLean broadcasting live from the diner; seeing General Eisenhower in a parade in Lakewood after World War II; the air races, I remember the pylons were scattered throughout the area in Berea, Strongsville, and Brunswick. We used to watch them from my father's employer's farm in Brunswick while having a picnic. I remember the women fliers having a "Powder Puff Derby;" watching the Fourth of July Fireworks on the shores of Lake Erie in Lakewood.

Later in life, as a newly-wed, my husband (Gordon Cochrane '52) and I were expecting our first child. We lived in an apartment across the street from the Fairview Park Hospital that was being built on Lorain Road. I was registered in the prenatal program for Lakewood Hospital, had taken the courses & toured the hospital. But, at 2:00am on May 22, 1955, our son decided he was in a hurry to be born. My husband flagged down a police car in the apartment parking lot & the patrolman drove me across the street to the newly-opened hospital. My son was among the first babies born in the hospital. I think the hospital had just opened the week before. The admitting clerk was very upset that I didn't have a reservation—but, the young patrolman wanted nothing to do with possibly having to deliver a baby in his patrol car. He was more nervous than I was!

After living in California for 31 years, I remember how cold it was walking to school in the snow—and, I also remember the blizzards that would immobilize traffic for several days. We would take sleds to the stores to get bread & milk for the neighbors.

I remember getting ice-cream cones at a small stand near JMH. I also remember the little family-owned shops. In particular, I remember Wagenknecht's Grocery Store & Wilke's Bakery (Diane Wagenknecht & Linda Wilke were in my class of 6/53).

Every Spring taking the wildflower trail through Rocky River Park to see the violets, jack-in-the-pulpits, lilies of valley, etc.— the first signs of Spring.

I have not been back to Ohio since 1967—so, I am really surprised at how much I am remembering. It's difficult for me to visualize places after so long, and I am sure I would no longer recognize the area as it is today. Thanks for giving me the opportunity for a little nostalgia!

Shirley Diekmann Lamb (6/53)

Nino's Pizza, Happy Hour Tavern for Friday night fish fry-the old military base at West 130th and Brookpark-ice skating at Halloran Park or the basement of the old abandoned Linndale Train Station-collecting golf balls in the woods and returning them for money at Bellaire Beverage and Driving Range-Bowling at Bellaire Lanes where I won my first trophy for bowling a 117 game at age 7-singing Christmas Carol's at the Bellaire Nursing Home-riding our bikes along the creek which is now I-71, then riding on I-71 before it opened- going trick or treating up and down West 130th and Bellaire area and over to West 140th without worrying about anything-playing baseball and football in the street until we broke the front window of our house. Then we cut down the trees and plowed the fields to build our own ball diamonds in the woods-sledding down Memphis Hill-being able to camp out in your backyard with the only thing to be afraid of was what my dad was going to do to try to scare us such as dress up in costumes, throw things at the tent, pull out tent pegs, bang on tent, reach in and grab us.

Andy Mathews (1/70)

A group of guys and gals used to hold the record for most rides in one day on the Puritas Springs roller coaster, record was eight. Group consisted of Nancy and Nadine Claspy, Donna Gedeon, Joan Elicker, Bob Joslyn, Dick Holland, Neil Roper and Jim McArthur. Roper, Howard Ferguson and myself would ice skate on Rocky River and at Winterhurst.

James McArthur (1/55)

Remembered wonderful times at Puritas Springs Parks. The best roller coaster anywhere. Routed out over the valley, really scary. Roller skating at the rink there.

306

Kamm's Corner - Riverside show every Friday night followed by pizza at Luigis. Shopping at Lerners and getting hamburgers at Royal Castle. Stopping for chocolate cokes at Marshall's Drug Store.

Working in dietary at Fairview Hospital and using our breaks to go down into the valley to explore.

Dancing to the music of the big bands every holiday night, Thanksgiving, Christmas, Easter, etc. at Columbia Ballroom. They always ended with "Good Night Sweet Heart". What a great way to extend the magic of the holiday. Wish my own children had had that much fun.

Margaret Fischer Meacham (6/59)

Christmas when I was little. Mom was always very creative, making something beautiful out of little nothings. During my elementary school years, we lived in a house on Lorain Avenue that had a large double door, closing off the "parlor", which today we call the living room. Mom, my sister, and I made colorful paper chins. We decorated the windows with snowflakes which we cut out of white paper. We marked the days off the calendar while enjoying the overpowering fragrances of the Slovak filled cookies. Mom made soooo many of them. We thought we'd never eat them all.

But we had no Christmas tree during those preparation days. On Christmas Eve, after our supper of oyster stew and sausages, my sister and I willingly submitted to baths and bedtime. We knew the schedule. Even before we were sound asleep, we'd hear scuffling and low laughter. The pine tree was brought in and put in the parlor. Behind those closed doors, a magical transformation took place. The ordinary room became the anteroom to paradise! Mom always artistically and meticulously decorated the tree and the mantle.

The next morning we scrambled our of our bed, fussing and coaxing. Mom and Dad had to open the double doors. then "Oh....Ah...Oh...Ah" The tree lights twinkled. Our eyes did too. Christmas was real!

Lois Pankuch Miller (6/46)

My freshman year was spent at the original John Marshall in 1931. Remember dashing from the main building to a portable in rain and winter cold. Visited there 20 years later-it was Leopold Furniture where my husband and I purchased a bedroom set.

Thought the new school was beautiful. My three years there were some of the most memorable of my life.

I also recall visit to Cleveland of President Roosevelt in mid thirties. I stood on the curb at Kamm's Corners as his motorcade to the airport came by. He was in an open convertible and passed a few feet from me. This was all very exciting. At 21, the voting age at that time, he was the candidate, I first voted for President.

After seeing many movies at thc Tivoli and Lyric on West 117th Street which were small, no lobby and not very pretty, the Variety seemed very elegant and spacious.

Loved going to Puritas Springs Park since it was not as far to travel as Euclid Beach. The roller coaster there was a thrill going down into the valley. At the time, it was known as one of the longest plunges.

The National Y were a big thing for the Cleveland area. Recall the traffic jams on Rocky River Drive and Kamm's Corners. Was it the only way to the airport at the time?

Teresa Gunner Molash (1/35)

After a date a burger at Bearden's, rode the Cyclone at Puritas Springs for $.25 at least twice. I ice skated and played hockey on Rocky River by the Cow Path behind the Tyler Estate. We rode our bicycles to Brookpark Road at the airport, climbed into trees to watch Roscoe Turner win the air race (circa 1947).

Leo Morozko (1952)

I remember going up to Kamm' Corner's every Sunday to the Riverside show. Also, remember going to Dairy Dell for a sherbet cone. There were two dime stores at Kamm's. One was Scott's and the other was Woolworth's. There were several Drug Stores, one in particular I remember was Marshalls right on the corner across from Tony's Restaurant. On the other corner, where the Shell Station is, was a fruit stand.

I remember the old YMCA. It was on West 152nd off Lorain Avenue behind Leopold's Furniture. We used to go there for canteen. I went to George Washington Grade school, then went on to John Marshall 7th to 12th grade. I remember the football games at John Marshall. I remember the Puritas Springs fire. We lived on Puritas and could see it from our house.

Janet Osborn (1/49)

We had been watching "I Love Lucy" on TV, and the tornado arrived like a train roaring past. Daddy pushed me and my sister into the tiny space between the side of the refrigerator and the wall. My mother ran to my brother's room and shielded him with herself. All of the windows on the side of our house were shattered. We lived on a corner and all of the garage roofs from one street hit our house. A painter lived two doors down and his paint cans decorated our house, inside and out.

The tornado came by about 9:30 PM, and another tornado was forecast for midnight. Our family spent the night in the basement ready to dive under makeshift shelters. The midnight tornado did not occur, but we were hit by another tornado two years later while living in the same house on Bellaire Boulevard.

My friend, Joan (McNab 1/56), and I had our first jobs working at the dimestore at Kamm's Corners earning a whopping 50 cents an hour. The first Saturday we treated ourselves to lunch at the corner restaurant. When the bill arrived, we were shocked to see that we had spent more than we earned that day.

Faye Kunsch Reinhardt (1/55)

I attended every one of the National Air Races from about 1927 until shortly after WW2 when a terrible accident occurred during the running of the Thompson Trophy Race. One of the racers crashed into a home in Berea.

When we were nine or ten years old, we would walk or hitch-hike (it was safe then) out to the Airport, climb a tree along Brookpark Road on the north side of the field and perch there all day watching the races, the marvelous skills of the stunt pilots and the flying by the then Army pilots, the Navy Air pilots and the Marine pilots in the multi-plane formations. This together with the closed course racing by Jimmy Doolittle and Lou Bayles in their GB Specials, Roco Turner, the Howard racers, and Wendel Williams-they all became our special idols.

As we grew into our teens, we became a little smarter and found out that we could get into the Grandstand area if we sold newspapers. We got jobs selling the Plain Dealer, a morning paper which left us free in the afternoons to roam the grand-

Figure C-5. Looking on at the 1947 air show. *Cleveland Press Collection, Cleveland State University*

stands. Another perk was when it rained in the morning, we sold our papers as "rain covers" at a considerable profit.

All this exposure to "Those Daring Young Men And Their Flying Machines" created dreams that some day I would be up there with them. My dreams came true on June 23, 1943 when I received my "Navy Wings of Gold."

Albert Rolland (6/38)

I like to reminisce, but I think it can have a tendency to lead me into forgetting my blessings. However, remembering is also a blessing. Thank God. I remember: the "scrub" football games we had at Firewood Park (Lorain & 138th); climbing into a catalpa tree at that same park, to watch my brother catch for the U. M. Church team; riding my bike down to Rocky River to go fishin' and to look for stray golf balls' "belly-slamming" and grabbing rear bumpers for "a pull" on the West 138th Street hill; tennis in the street; hardball games with usually the same guys behind JMH; softball, behind Garfield; walking to the Riverside Theater, or the Variety, Lyric, or even the Almira; picking beans for a farmer in the morning, then crossing the street to Puritas Springs Park to spend my earnings, in the afternoon.

Bernard Rosier (6/43)

I remember being able to see the 4th of July fireworks at Puritas Springs Park from the second floor back porch on our house on Laverne Avenue. They were the first fireworks I experienced. I also remember the roller skating rink. I think that stayed open after other parts of the park closed. After finally getting my own skates for Christmas, I stopped going. There were always rumors in the neighborhood that the roller coaster cars fell into the woods below, but I don't recall ever seeing any. Some of us in the summer would swim in Rocky River at the foot of Puritas Road Hill. That was always cold water.

My favorite restaurant in the West Park Area was the Bearden's at the corner of Sedalia and Rocky River Drive. We often went there for a special burger after games on the weekends. Some years ago, while visiting the Cleveland area, I went to the Bearden's in Rocky River to reminisce and ran into a JMH classmate whom I had not seen in years. I had my first Peanut Burger at Bearden's. Bearden's hamburgers were always the best, even topped with peanut butter.

Gunning Playground was right behind our house. Before the sewers were installed, the rain water would pour off the playground and flood our basements. There used to be a small ice skating pond that was flooded next to Puritas Road every winter. When they were making the Gunning baseball diamonds, the whole playground became flooded one winter. When it was frozen over, it was like a big lake for ice skating all over. I remember when the swimming pool was built that it was too small from the start. In the hot summer afternoons, it was too crowded. I went swimming when others went home for dinner. Before the baseball diamonds, we played softball in the street. I remember the Show Wagons that came to Gunning Playground.

I remember seeing "Ike" at Rocky River Drive and Valley View. And I remember going to the old wooden Valley View Elementary School at West 168th and Valley View after WWII. I started at Puritas Elementary but it got too crowded due to the new temporary housing project after the war. In the middle of the first grade, I was transferred to Valley View with a few others. That Valley View was small and very special as a result. Who else remembers the first grade teacher, Mrs. Cunningham?

I remember sampling records in those little listening booths at Gilchrest's Record Shop. One of my jobs during high school was at the West Park Pharmacy. Yes, I made sodas, but preferred being referred to as a "soda clerk."

I remember going to the gym at the YMCA which had been the gym for the old JMH. I remember lining up there to get physical exams before going to summer Y camp.

Who can forget those street cars going from Puritas Loop to Public Square? It was fun going underground to go over the lower level of the High Level Bridge after leaving West 25th. In the summers, we rode the street cars to the Milk Man's Picnics at Euclid Beach Park by changing to the Euclid Avenue Streetcar at Public Square. Boy, was that a long, but cheap, ride. After the streetcars, we got the trackless trolley. They were great. They were very quiet and no more ruts in the street. I don't know anyone who preferred the smelly, noisy buses that came after. When I went to college in Pittsburgh in 1957, they still had their "big red" street cars. When I visited Seattle in 1993, we rode on trackless trolleys there; they're still better than the buses!

I recall the major snow storm on Saturday, November 25, 1950 and so does my sister, Nancy. That was to be her wedding day. Nothing was moving that morning. The wedding had to be put off until Wednesday.

Edward (Ted) Rummel (1/57)

I grew up on Triskett Road. I remember Poshke's Restaurant at Triskett and Lorain and their great food. My first date was in the 8th grade; I rode my bike to her house just off of Munn Rd. We walked to the Riverside Theater. Went to Dairy Dell across the street after the movies and then walked all the way home.

I remember skating at the roller rink at Puritas Springs and also riding the Roller Coaster. I coasted many times down the Lorain Rd hill. We used to go to the Riverside Drive-in movie after stopping at Fanny Farmer for their great candy.

During the air races, I spent the entire week at the airport. Got to know most of the pilots. Had my picture taken with Rosco Turner and Tony Lavier.

Cliff Steinbrick Jr. (6/46)

It's difficult to try to write about one West Park memory. Same for memories at JMH. But here are some: Manner's Big Boy; Gray Drug's; Fazio's' Reese's Market at Warren Village Shopping Center; listening to Johnny Holiday on WHK while doing my homework; "Bucky Joe", the ice-cream man in a light green truck; Eisenhower coming down Triskett Rd in a motorcade; Halloween Trick-or-Treating; crafts and bicycle brigades at Tuckahoe Avenue playground; walking to the West Park Rapid Station; singing solos and singing in the choir at West Park Congregational Church; the outbreak of German Measles at JMH; singing in the "Marshmellos" and All-City Chorus; being in our class play "Auntie Mame" as well as "Carousel", remembering the band playing "The Pink Panther" and "The Stripper" during rehearsal breaks; the tuba babies band; the skits we neighborhood kids put on and the clubhouse my father built; the center stairway to the band room at JMH; White Castle hamburgers and birch beer; our Girl Scout Troop #1238 and learning Hamlet and Macbeth with Ms. Lucas.

Mary Ann Stratton (1/65)

During the tornado that hit West 130 etc. my hubby Bud and I were at the Memphis Drive in They told everyone to leave. We couldn't - our 1950 Olds wouldn't start. The storm picked up our car - set it down hard. After the storm ended, it finally started and we headed for home. They wouldn't let us through to West 126 where I lived. It was scary but all turned out well.

Lois Bassett Summerlin (6/57)

I lived on Nichols Avenue off Rocky River Drive (It's Chatfield now). I watched the Lindberg parade as it went by Kamm's. I attended John Marshall on Lorain, and we were the first class to graduate from the new Marshall.

I attended Puritas School for first grade and when Washington was finished, attended second grade there. I also attended the theatre at Kamm's when it was a tent. I think the show was "The Bat," but I have no idea who the actors were. Before my time, Mother and Dad, lived above Albers Grocery Store. Ladphairs Dry Goods was nearby and Dillon's was on the corner where the Interurban Cars turned south- the motorman and conductor stopped for coffee.

Genevra Short Thorn (1/33)

Some of the parts of Puritas Springs Park that I recall was the skating rink, and I used to skate a lot there to the music of Ken Dombey. We used to go to the Tianon on the east side to dance or also the Southern Tavern on Carnegie and also Herman Perchner's Alpine Village for the prom. At one time, I worked at the Variety Theater as usher, Chief of Staff and Doorman.

I used to go to the playground between 132nd and 133rd on Lorain and play ball there and at times whistle at all the pretty girls passing. Today that would be an offensive tactic. When the tornado hit the West Side, I remembered it well as I lived on West 127th street. I went over to look at the devastation, and it made quit an impression. I remember seeing Ike Eisenhower in Cleveland - also served under him in the ETO. I also remember when we used to sled down the "hunchback" in Metropolitan Park. One of the things I remember was ice skating to church on a Sunday morning, and I bet no one has ever accomplished that since those days. How many remember Racers which was the store close by the school where some of the students went for lunch period?

Hal Treat (6/40)

Was a "flat" in fall of 1948 from Riverside Elementary School-Babe Ruth had just died and one famous teacher at JMH- one who had most students return to visit - Louis James Nairy -collapsed after testifying at a trial over his stepson.

Remember Euclid Beach Park Nickel Days? Friday nights at the Fairview Theater? Pitching Duels between Bob Feller and Hal Newhouser of Detroit with Jim Hegan catching. Bob Feller and Lou Boudreau and the pick off play. Otto Graham, Paul Brown, Max Speedie, Dante Lavelli and Lou the Toe Groza.

JMH Rat pack of the 50's was Herbert Rath, Eugene Gibbons and William Tomko.

Donald Lee Uhrine (6/54)

Rather than choose one of may specific memories, I would rather remember JMH and those days by gentle, general impressions: the song "Love is Blue" playing during Mr. Thrall's print shop class, the musty smell of the underground track, the crunch of gravel underneath the car tires while finding a good spot at the Memphis Drive-In, flipping through the booth juke box at Perkins in Kamm's Plaza after a football game, working for Kessler's Clothing located next to Murphy's, riding my bike up to Hobby Castle to check out the latest models, playing ball up at Gunning, watching the construction workers building the new rapid station at 150th, getting a birch beer at Royal Castle and listening to "I Can't Get No Satisfaction" on WIXY, picking up our families' fish dinners at the Orange Hut, playing miniature golf at Kiddie-Park, seeing if my buddies at the Red Barn on 117th could get me any free food (thanks for nothing Doug!), going to Sears, Kresgee's, and Giant Tigers at Lorain and 110th - especially at Christmas, buying suits at Robert Halls, football rivalry with the West Tech Warriors, getting a hair cut at Rocco's, being called to the office to see Mr. Burke, singing with the Marsh-Mellows, going to the only department store in North Olmsted - The May Co. to buy look-a-like tee shirts for Prom weekend at Cedar Point, being in the play, "My Fair Lady", parking at Hopkins to "watch planes" (this was one of my favorites!), walking down my street on a warm summer's night listening to the sprinklers and smelling freshly cut grass, wondering what Vietnam was all about, surfer crosses, black regals, madras, paisley, wide belts, elephant bells, cashmere overcoats with white silk scarf's and hot pants!

unknown

Hanging out at Bearden's, sledding in the Metroparks, Birch Beer at Royal Castle, Riverside Theater, ball at Gunning Field.

Richard Van Bergen (6/60)

The second floor of the West Park City Hall (later the first district Police Station) was used for dances. Playing handball with friends on the courts that were behind the fire station. Watching sulky races at the "Rockport Racetrack." Once skated from Lorain all the way to the lake on Rocky River. Working on construction of the Riverside Theatre in 1934 or 35, also worked there as a ticket taker. Riverside had "Bank Nights" when cash prizes would be given away.

Worked parking cars at the air races, first airplane ride was at the races, paid $3 to ride in a little open cockpit plane for a few minutes. The Asplin Basket store on the southwest corner of West 150th Street and Lorain and the factory located behind it. A dairy on the SW corner of West 152nd and Lorain.

A blacksmith shop on the south side of Lorain not far from West Park Avenue

Robert Walter (6/33)
as told to his daughter Gail Walter (1/63)

311

I recall Puritas Springs Park and going up there when still in grade school in the 40's. I enjoyed the roller coaster, the roller skating rink and the cool clean water that ran from the spring. Sometimes we

guys would ride our bikes up from Kamm's Corners and hang out for an afternoon.

In the 50's on a Friday or Saturday night we teens would often end up with our dates at Bearden's Drive Inn on Rocky River Drive. I recall that they had good burgers, but I suppose it was more of a case of both being seen and seeing who was there.

While still in grade school at Our Lady of the Angels, we guys started hitting the Riverside Theater just about every Saturday and Sunday matinee we could afford. On Saturday, we got a cartoon, news of the world, and a serial such as "Don Winslow of the Coast Guard." Exciting stuff! My first date, when I was about 14 in the 40's was to take her to the Riverside Theater for a Sunday matinee. Afterwards we had a soda across the street at a pharmacy in what was then the Cleveland Trust Bank Building.

Throughout my grade school and high school years, we loved to sled down the Lorain Road Hill. In later years, the city started to plow the hill in winter, but as kids, we loved going down when it was blocked off after a new snowfall. Once a buddy climbed on my back and we went down tandem. About two thirds of the way down there was a right turn, almost 90 degrees. We hit ice and the sled would not turn, I remember yelling, "bail out," and he rolled off, I rolled off, and he and I, with the sled side by side, going like the Devil, just fit under the guard rail, and we all ended up in a shallow ravine on the other side of the guard rail. Scary. After we would go down the Lorain Road hill, we usually went over to the Hogs Back and went down a few sled runs there. The Hogs Back was surrounded by a nine hole golf course (Little Met). It was fun, but we knew that we always had that long slippery climb back up the hill to our homes around Kamm's Corners.

When we had a real cold snap in the winter, parts of the river would freeze over. We looked forward to that as most of my buddies and I had ice skates and we would set up impromptu hockey games, although we raced each other and sometimes tried figure skating; usually with a quick spill, and then it was back to hockey. A favorite place was just north of the Lorain Street Bridge, perhaps a quarter of a mile as there was still water there. Sometimes we would build a little fire on the river bank for warming.

Prior to WW2, my folks would take me out to a friend's farm close to the airport. I have no recollection of this, but I was told in later years that I would hide in the car and scream when the racers passed overhead. I always hoped to pass this on to Jimmy Doolittle, but never got the chance. It is ironic that I spent many years as an Air Force pilot!

After WW2 we guys would ride our bikes out to the airport and hang around in the days leading up to the races and would eavesdrop and take pictures of the pilots and aircraft. During the weekend of the races, we would go out and sit along the fence or in a tree and watch all the action.

The houses in our four street area (Allien Ave) were built in the 1920's, 30's and early 40's. Prior to the shopping center being built it was an undeveloped piece of land with both woods and open space. We kids built a ball diamond there during WW2 and used it for years. We had lots of open space for play. Of course, we were only a short hike from Rocky River and there was lots of hiking, bike riding, fishing, and swimming down there. We were lucky.

Daniel R. Weber (6/50)

The better part of my youth was spent in a home on the corner of Sedalia and Rocky River Drive. This put me across the street from Bearden's Drive Inn and that was a huge part of our growing up. I always knew who was dating whom by just sitting on my front porch and watching the action across the street. Bob Cousins (1/61) was 6'8" tall and had an original VW Beetle. I can see him now, with all the doors of the little car open, seats pushed forward, crawling around, looking for a lost contact lens.

We grew up at Puritas Springs Park but mostly in the Roller Skating Rink. My memories are the strongest at the Riverside theater, especially in Jr. High. We all went every Fri. night, Sat. Matinee and

Sunday Matinee. The side "boxes" were only used by "the older kids" and I do remember sitting in the balcony a lot. When we were little, our Mom took us to the Riverside, and I remember the "give-aways" between movies. Once, I went up to draw a name, and I drew my mother's name.

I have great memories of Newton D. Baker Jr. High because my class was the first class to go all the way through it when it was brand new! I even had my picture on the cover of Press Sat. Magazine with Carol Hummel and Marilyn Wagner in the wonderful skirts we made in 7th grade sewing class at this wonderful new school. Mike Massa was our social studies teacher in the 8th grade. It was a really great place.   When I think of Kamm's Corners, I think of the Gilchrest Record Shop and Mr. Gilchrest who was always nice to us kids. These were the days when you went into the little booth and listened to the 45 record hit of the week. I pestered that man for weeks for a record by a new guy and by the time it came in, "Wonderful, Wonderful" by Johnny Mathis was number one.

At the end of Sedalia Avenue, you could walk/climb carefully down into THE VALLEY. I spent a lot of time in the valley as a child. Mayor Celebreeze lived at the end of the streets (Valley View and Sedalia) and we always had our street plowed because for some reason, his driver would come out onto the Drive from Sedalia (not at the light at Valley View). His son Tony was our paper boy, and his Mom had a group of Camp Fire Girls. I remember what nice people they all were.

On the corner of Valley View and Rocky River Drive was a drug store with a soda fountain. We all went there for "cherry cokes." I miss soda fountains!

Carol Lausch Wenk (1/61)

Washing private airplanes at Cleveland Airport for airplane Rides!. It peaked my interest in "aviation" as my career field. I became an Army then a USAF pilot. Retired after a 32 year Air Force career.

Frank Willard (6/40)

Figure C-6. *Author collection*

313

Index